S0-AWR-529

DIGITAL MUSIC MAKING FOR TEENS

Andrew Hagerman

THOMSON

COURSE TECHNOLOGY

Professional ■ Trade ■ Reference

DIGITAL MUSIC MAKING
FOR TEENS

SVP, Thomson Course Technology PTR: Andy Shafran

Publisher: Stacy L. Hiquet

Senior Marketing Manager: Sarah O'Donnell

Marketing Manager: Heather Hurley

Manager of Editorial Services: Heather Talbot

Senior Acquisitions Editor: Todd Jensen

Senior Editor: Mark Garvey

Associate Marketing Manager: Kristin Eisenzopf

Marketing Coordinator: Jordan Casey

Project and Copy Editor: Marta Justak

Technical Reviewer: Brian Smithers

Teen Reviewer: Drew Wright

PTR Editorial Services Coordinator: Elizabeth Furbish

Interior Layout Tech: Sue Honeywell

Cover Designer: Steve Deschene

Indexer: Katherine Stimson

Proofreader: Gene Redding

CD Producer: Andrew Hagerman

©2005 by Thomson Course Technology PTR. All rights reserved. No part of this book may be reproduced or transmitted in any form or by any means, electronic or mechanical, including photocopying, recording, or by any information storage or retrieval system without written permission from Thomson Course Technology PTR, except for the inclusion of brief quotations in a review.

The Thomson Course Technology PTR logo and related trade dress are trademarks of Thomson Course Technology PTR and may not be used without written permission.

Cakewalk is a registered trademark of Twelve Tone Systems, Inc. Cakewalk Home Studio 2 and the Cakewalk logo are trademarks of Twelve Tone Systems, Inc. Quartz AudioMaster and Quartz AudioMaster Freeware are registered trademarks of Digital Sound Planet, S.A. Virtual Sound Canvas is a registered trademark of Roland Corporation. All other trademarks are the property of their respective owners.

Important: Thomson Course Technology PTR cannot provide software support. Please contact the appropriate software manufacturer's technical support line or Web site for assistance.

Thomson Course Technology PTR and the author have attempted throughout this book to distinguish proprietary trademarks from descriptive terms by following the capitalization style used by the manufacturer.

Information contained in this book has been obtained by Thomson Course Technology PTR from sources believed to be reliable. However, because of the possibility of human or mechanical error by our sources, Thomson Course Technology PTR, or others, the Publisher does not guarantee the accuracy, adequacy, or completeness of any information and is not responsible for any errors or omissions or the results obtained from use of such information. Readers should be particularly aware of the fact that the Internet is an ever-changing entity. Some facts may have changed since this book went to press.

Educational facilities, companies, and organizations interested in multiple copies or licensing of this book should contact the publisher for quantity discount information. Training manuals, CD-ROMs, and portions of this book are also available individually or can be tailored for specific needs.

ISBN: 1-59200-508-X
Library of Congress Catalog Card Number: 2004107744
Printed in the United States of America
04 05 06 07 08 BH 10 9 8 7 6 5 4 3 2 1

THOMSON

COURSE TECHNOLOGY

Professional ■ Trade ■ Reference

Thomson Course Technology PTR, a division of Thomson Course Technology
25 Thomson Place
Boston, MA 02210

http://www.courseptr.com

Dedication

This year has been filled with blessings, and I'm overjoyed to dedicate this book to two very special women. As always, my gratitude and my heart go to my wife, Junko. Her love and support (and, of course, the late-night snacks) have made this book possible. This work is also dedicated to Sachiko Elizabeth Hagerman, who will be born a couple months after this book is published. It's a wonderful world, my darling daughter—welcome!

Acknowledgments

There are so many people to thank that it's hard to know where to begin.

Thanks first to the great team at Thomson Course Technology. You guys have made it a real pleasure to create this book. To Todd Jensen and Jenny Davidson, who managed the project, thanks for coordinating everything. Marta Justak, your superb editing really brought out the best in this book. Brian Smithers, a great friend and a great inspiration, your tech editing chops kept me right on track! And last, but certainly not least, thanks go to Stacy Hiquet, the publisher, and Drew Wright for helping as a teen reviewer.

Without great companies supplying the music community with powerful creative tools, we'd be nowhere, and my hat goes off to three great companies that have helped make this book possible. First, to Twelve Tone Systems, for a proud tradition of solid software design, including Cakewalk Home Studio 2, thanks for making such an intuitive product. To the Roland Corporation, developers of the Virtual Sound Canvas, your products continue to deliver high quality at any price range. To Digital Sound Planet, makers of Quartz AudioMaster Freeware, thanks for helping so many get into the world of music creation.

When I'm not writing, I'm working with some really fantastic folks and their energy is a constant source of inspiration. First, to my brothers at Singularity Arts, thanks for all of your support—it's a rare pleasure to work with folks who are as dedicated to excellence as Dave and Kevin Oxenreider. Also, to the faculty, staff, and students at Full Sail Real World Education in Winter Park, Florida, thanks for all the faith and for allowing me to be a part of such a special place. In particular, I'd like to thank Julius Hocott, Jason McClesky, Mike Orlowski (m.p.s.e.), Marc Pinsky, and Brian Young for your contributions to this title.

Lastly, thanks to Charley, Frances, and Jeanne. Your visits this past summer made writing this book a truly memorable experience.

About the Author

Andrew Hagerman has performed in and composed for numerous ensembles worldwide, including Disneyland, Walt Disney World, and Tokyo Disney Sea. Hagerman has been very active in the creation of planetarium and science center soundtracks, and his work has been seen and heard from the American Museum of Natural History in New York City to Sunshine Planetarium in Japan. Hagerman is currently an associate course director and lecturer for the "Advanced Workstations" course at Full Sail Real World Education in Winter Park, Florida. There, he helps guide and coordinate one of the largest digital audio workstation labs in the world. He also remains an active composer and producer with Singularity Arts, serving the worldwide planetarium community.

Contents

TABLE OF

Introduction

I want to thank you for taking the time to read this book, even if you're just browsing through it on a bookstore shelf. Nice to meet you, and welcome to the world of digital-age music creation. Before we get down to business, let me tell you a little about what *Digital Music Making for Teens* is all about and what we're setting out to accomplish together.

About This Book

So, who are you? Is this the right book for you? What will you learn between its covers? Read on, and you'll see what we'll learn together.

What This Book Is

There's an old saying—"A journey of a thousand miles begins with a single step." There's a lot of truth in that phrase, I believe, which relates to the mission of this book.

On its face, this adage has a simple meaning, which is simply that any great endeavor must begin with a single small "step" if it's ever to be completed. Sounds like basic common sense, right? Sometimes, however, it seems that the more complex and involved the goal is, the harder it is to work up the nerve to begin the process of reaching that goal. Certainly, the goal of musical expression can be daunting, and so complex and involved that many people find it hard to know where to begin. That's where this book comes in—to help you take that important "first step."

If you really want to reach your goal, this critical first step must be headed in the right direction, and you should be well equipped for the journey. When considering the field of music, heading in the right direction with all the necessary tools means that you'll need *information*. All the cool software and hardware toys out there don't mean much without the knowledge to use them well. Too many potential musicians don't take the time to establish a solid fundamental understanding of today's music production tools, and they simply feel their way around the software, clicking this and trying that. Occasionally, they'll stumble onto something cool, but more often than not, they'll get frustrated and give up. When that happens, all of that great (and sometimes *expensive*) equipment winds up sitting in the corner collecting dust.

Don't get disheartened. With a little information and a clear picture of how to use that information, you can get up and running fairly quickly. Better than that, as you grow in your artistic experience, you'll have the fundamental knowledge to comprehend more advanced applications. That's the follow-up mission of this book—not only to help you take the first step, but also to make sure that it's a well-informed step in the right direction. That way, you'll be in it for the long run, making the most of any gear you use.

What This Book Isn't

If you're looking for the best way to rip tracks from CDs and make copies, or how to download songs from MP3.com, keep looking—this book isn't for you. Although we will talk about tracks on CDs and what happens to audio in MP3s, this book goes beyond those issues to the topic of music *creation*, not simply music copying. Not that there's any problem with burning a tune to a CD, but it'd be better if it were *your* tune, wouldn't it?

As you shop for the right book, you'll find that there are more than a few books out there that bill themselves as "Hits in a box." They suggest that in a ridiculously short time, you'll make the transition from absolute beginner to hit-making powerhouse. Geez, that sounds great—gimme that book, and my Grammy will be in the mail, right? Obviously, it doesn't work that way, and anyone who tells you otherwise is selling something (in their case, a book).

Now, I won't say that it's *impossible* to break into the music business at a young age, but such events are exceptions and not the rule, and even the fortunate few who make the break into stardom at a young age have done so as a result of hard work and perseverance. My position is that products that propose to be a shortcut to artistry perpetuate a dangerously misleading deception, usually leading to frustration and disappointment. This book isn't a get rich (and famous) quick scheme—rather, it *is* designed to give serious students the means to discover their own creativity in their own time.

This Book Is for You If...

Digital Music Making for Teens is going to help you if you're a beginner. So, if you own a computer and would like to create some music on it, but don't know where to begin, then that's where this book will come in. We'll make no assumptions here, and even though we'll go a long way down the road of musical exploration, we'll define our terms along the way. We'll begin with the most simple concepts of computer music—like hardware and software setup, for example—and move step-by-step to more and more advanced topics. By the time you get to the back cover, you'll be amazed at what you've learned.

Are you ready to start creating music? We'll work on that, too. At the heart of digital music is the same music that humans have been creating throughout history. You'll learn the basics of the language of music, which will help you bring the music in your head to life. We'll talk about basic concepts of rhythm, pitch, and even a little notation—the building blocks of all music. Of course, no single book is going to make you the next Mozart or Stravinsky, but a solid basic understanding of musical concepts will give you an appreciation of music's rich heritage and the cognitive tools you'll need to understand the software of the future. Do you know something about music, but not digital music in particular? That's great because this book can fill in the gaps, so you can start using the computer as the powerful creative tool it is.

Here's the bottom line. If you're ready to stop listening to music and start creating it, this book is going to help you get started. If you're serious about getting started on the right foot, *Digital Music Making for Teens* will give you the tools you need to create music now and for years to come.

How to Use This Book
So, how is this book organized and how can you use it as both a learning tool and a reference as well? Here's how everything's laid out.

Building Skills
Music, by its nature, is a building process. The most complex symphonies begin with a single note. It's the same with learning the craft (and art) of music production—a building process from the most basic elements to the full realization of musical ideas. This book is organized to begin with the basic elements, which are system setup, synthesis, and basic MIDI. You'll proceed to the next level by learning how to use digital audio to its fullest advantage in editing and mixing. Finally, you'll bring it all together with an exploration of mastering techniques and how to use your music in a number of settings.

Each of the concepts in this book will build upon the concepts in previous chapters. The good news about this constructive approach is that if you get lost in a concept or stuck in an exercise, all you need to do is look back to an earlier chapter, get clear on what's going on, and move on from there. The table of contents and index will help in tracking down information.

Chapters and Exercises

This book won't be just a dry lecture on digital music concepts. Coupled with our discussions, there will be a series of exercises, also moving from simple concepts to more advanced ones, to give you hands-on experience as you learn. Each exercise will include extensive graphics to guide you through the task at hand. It gets better—the accompanying CD will give you all the tools that you need to get the job done—from software tools right down to audio files and MIDI data to get you up and running quickly.

After you've gone through all the chapters and exercises, *Digital Music Making for Teens* will serve as a valuable reference. At the end of the book, as well as on the Web site (www.courseptr.com/downloads), are some appendices on a number of topics, and important terms in this book will be indexed for easy access. In addition, all the procedures that are discussed will be shown in the exercises. If you forget how to do something, just refer back to the exercise, and you'll be back on your feet in no time.

The exercises shown in this book will be using PC computers with the Windows XP operating system. Though it certainly isn't the only kind of computer out there, the popularity of this platform makes it the obvious choice for the broadest compatibility. Better still, you won't even need a super-fast PC to run the applications we're using.

Conventions

In addition to the conventional text and exercises in this book, you'll find informational boxes from time to time:

NOTE

Note boxes provide additional information about the topic at hand, providing a deeper understanding of a particular concept or procedure. Look here for additional cool facts.

TIP

When working with computers, there are often multiple ways to get things done, some of which can save you time. Look here for information on doing it better, faster, or easier.

 CAUTION

Watch out! Caution boxes warn you of potential pitfalls and how to avoid them.

A Message to Parents

Okay, if you're a parent shopping for a book for your child, this section is for you.

First, congratulations on having a child with an interest in music. If you're leafing through this book, then you're interested in cultivating your son's or daughter's passion for this important art form—good for you. I don't need to tell you about the obvious benefits of musical study, such as enjoyment and building discipline, but studies have shown even more advantages associated with musical study that you might *not* have heard of, such as the following:

- ❄ Better verbal memory.
- ❄ Improved spatial-temporal reasoning—skills necessary for mastering math and science.
- ❄ Improved abstract reasoning.
- ❄ Better reading and communication skills, which can even aid students in learning foreign languages.
- ❄ Healthier self-esteem/self-image.

So, the benefits to musical study are far more than skin deep. (In fact, magnetic resonance imaging of the brains of musicians shows a more highly developed auditory cortex where sounds are processed.) Studies have shown that musical study has a positive effect on academic achievement, psychological well-being, and even social skills, even if students decide not to make music their life's work. If it sounds like I'm laying it on thick, you're right, but I honestly believe in the findings of these studies. I'm living proof of the healthful effects of music study.

Now, in *our* day (and I'm specifically speaking to you parents out there), we were often limited to studying in a traditional school setting. (I played tuba in my school band.) Digital music making hadn't really made it to the masses yet. However, in today's society with the power of computers, new opportunities for musical study and growth have opened to students who otherwise might never have had a chance at this powerful form of artistic expression. In truth, the democratization of computer-based music production may be the only option open to some parents, who desire to nurture their child's musical interest in the face of ever-dwindling school music programs. Bottom line—kudos to you for nurturing your child's pursuit of his or her musical vision, and if this book can help in some small way, that makes me happy.

Let's Go!

If you're still hanging around in the bookstore, I hope you'll see this book as a valuable aid to your musical quest and pick it up. If you've already bought the book and are conscientiously reading the introduction, thanks for buying it, and let's get to work!

NOTE

Additional appendices can be found on the Course PTR Web site at www.courseptr.com/downloads.

1 Sound and Music in the Digital Age

There are a lot of folks who say that the introduction of the personal computer to our society changed everything. Personally, I think that's right and wrong at the same time. True, the computer revolution changed the *way* we do things, making us generally more efficient at the work we do and the manner with which we connect to the world outside our studios. There's no getting around the fact that the power of the microprocessor has opened new doors to us and brought much of the power of multimillion dollar facilities within the grasp of the desktop musician.

Still, there's much that hasn't changed about music, despite the great influence of the computer revolution. We still make music for the same reasons, and we still are essentially crafters of sound. Sound hasn't changed either, and even though computers give us greater control over sound waves, those waves still operate as they have for ages. That's the thrust of this chapter's discussion. In this chapter, you'll learn:

※ How to approach the study of music and audio.

※ How sound works.

※ What the differences are between analog and digital audio.

※ What the connection is between audio and music.

The First Day of Class

Hi! Andrew Hagerman here (you can call me Andy). I'm the author of this book that you're holding, and I gratefully accept the responsibility of guiding you through the basics of digital music creation. Fortunately, I've got some experience teaching this subject, so you're in good hands.

My Name Is Andy

Through the years, I've found that when beginning any kind of class, it helps immensely to tell a little bit about myself. That way, you have some idea of just who is talking to you here. First, though, let me put a face to the name—here I am (see Figure 1.1).

Figure 1.1

This is what I look like (on my better days).

Well, obviously, I'm *not* a teenager, but I do bring a unique perspective to the table. You see, the fact that I'm 39 years old means that I was just graduating from high school and going to college in 1983 when the music world changed. This was the year that Musical Instrument Digital Interface, or MIDI, came onto the scene. MIDI allowed me to play a synthesizer keyboard *slowly*, record MIDI data into a MIDI recorder, then speed up the tempo on that MIDI recorder and play back exactly what I had played earlier, but *faster*. For me, this was a way that I could overcome my awful keyboard skills and be a more effective composer. No lie, it was the coolest thing I'd ever seen, and from that moment on I was hooked! I immediately set to work to learn as much about this new MIDI phenomenon as I could.

After the emergence of MIDI, life for musicians changed quickly. With this new technology, creative people not only could speed up slowly played parts, but also create complex music with many different parts and edit the music entirely within a computer. Hot on the heels of MIDI came digital audio in the form of compact discs (CDs), which replaced boxes and boxes of vinyl records with clean digital sound. After that, multitrack digital recorders, invaluable to digital music production, became accessible to the average musician. These advancements eventually led to hard-disk recording, which allowed multiple tracks of digital audio to be recorded directly into the computer. The modern digital audio workstation (DAW) is the fusion of all these technologies—MIDI and digital audio, computer and hardware, all together in one integrated package. Whew!

I've seen these technologies arrive and evolve, and I've made it my business to learn how to use this new power creatively. In the process, each of these advancements has made its mark on my effectiveness as a musician and composer. In addition to using MIDI to compensate for my lagging piano chops, I've come to appreciate the advantages of digital audio, recording my MIDI-controlled synthesizers as digital audio files to my hard drive. The massive power of today's DAWs lets me shape the sound of these files, mix them together, and create fully finished projects. Quite a far cry from my humble beginnings as a keyboard-challenged tuba player, and I owe much to my understanding of today's tools of the trade.

That's right, in addition to being a certified technophile, I'm also a musician. I grew up playing the tuba and later picked up the electric bass, mostly because playing tuba in a rock band just looks stupid. I attended Northwestern University after high school, where my interest in composition was born. (Thank goodness MIDI was there to help out!) After graduating from college, I became a musician at Walt Disney World and played in a number of the bands there, and in a wide variety of styles. After Disney, I set my sights on production, and these days I'm composing and producing for my own company and teaching about DAWs at a school in Florida called *Full Sail*, a college that specializes in topics related to media production.

Over the years, I've learned some fundamental truths about music technology: First, technology will continue to advance, and the cool gear we work with today will pale in comparison to the creative tools of tomorrow. Second, given the fact that technology will continue to march onward, the real trick for the artist is to *learn how to learn* and thereby keep pace with technological advances. To do that, the artist must have a solid understanding of the basic building blocks of today's computer-based music production and the concepts behind them. That's my goal with this book: to give you such a solid understanding of how digital music works that you can be creative not only now, but for years to come as new technologies reveal themselves.

Some Thoughts on the Study of Music

Being a musician myself, I've noticed that more than a few of my musician friends are a little worried about the impact of today's music technology. Being classically trained instrumentalists, vocalists, and composers, they're afraid that the power of the computer will replace their hard-earned musical skills. I guess it's an understandable apprehension—the evolution of computer science has been used to replace human workers in other industries. In the music industry, technology has proved to be powerful tool, and it has made many production-related tasks *much* easier. In some cases, "sampled" sounds have indeed been used to replace live musicians. What if the trend continues, and musicians are completely replaced by computer-generated programs that compose, record, edit, and mix hit songs all by themselves? Yikes!

The truth is that my nervous musician friends don't have a great deal of cause to worry when it comes to the music tech revolution, but they have much to gain. There is no magic button in some software that is named "create hit song," which does all the work while the musicians fall by the wayside. The truth is that computers are pretty incredible when it comes to performing complex mathematical tasks, but they're not tremendously creative on their own. Bottom line: Computers and other digital music technology are great *tools* for musician, but not musicians themselves. Certainly, any truly creative artist has little to fear (and much to gain) from this march of progress.

The trick is not to fear the power of computers, but rather to learn to use them as tools, much like a musician uses an instrument. To tell the truth, the study of computer-based music production is like learning to play an instrument. To begin with, one must learn the basic operations—how it works, how to make sound, and how to control it on a basic level. From that point, you refine those basics, broaden your range, and learn a few tricks along the way. By the time you reach a point of mastery, the "craft" of the instrument becomes second nature, freeing you, the artist, to concern yourself with creating *art*.

What does that mean to you, as a newcomer to the world of computer-based music production? It means that you too must approach the computer with as much intensity and respect as any musicians have for their instruments. You'll need to learn the basics of MIDI and digital audio, understand the nature of the technology, and learn how to make a sound. Continuing, you'll build knowledge upon this solid foundation and learn how to make music more efficiently and powerfully. Like any true artist, the goal is to use the computer intuitively and move on to the greater task of bringing your creative vision to others—the essence of all art.

Pretty heavy stuff, no? Does it sound like I'm proposing that you approach this study like a musician? Yep. Isn't the goal of digital music production to be a musician in your own right? You betcha. Don't worry, you can do it, and wield this technology with the best of `em. Of course, true artistry doesn't happen overnight, but you'll be amazed at the cool stuff you can create right out of the gate with the computer's help.

So what does it mean to be a student of the fine art of music? More than anything else, it takes willpower. Willpower will give you the patience to learn the craft of computer music. Willpower will give you the discipline to create a meaningful musical work from simple building blocks. Willpower will give you the drive to take those assembled pieces and tweak and polish your music to a high shine, so that you'll be proud to show off your work! Finally, willpower will drive you to improve your skills and strive to constantly improve and create better and better work. If it sounds like hard work, you're right, it is, but it's also some of the most fun hard work you'll ever do. You'll have a ball!

The Physics of Music

Okay, school's in session. Hope you like science a little bit, because we're going to get into some physics for the next section of this chapter. If you *don't* like science too much, I completely understand, but bear with me for just a while—understanding how sound works will help you to control it.

What we call *sound* is actually waves of compressed and uncompressed air that radiate from vibrating objects around us. When an object vibrates, it moves back and forth, actually knocking into the air molecules around it, causing areas of higher air pressure (called *compression*) and lower air pressure (called *rarefaction*). These waves emanate from the sound-making object much like ripples move outward from a disturbance on an otherwise calm pond. Our ears pick up these waves and perceive them as sound. If we take a sideways look at a sound wave, it might look something like Figure 1.2.

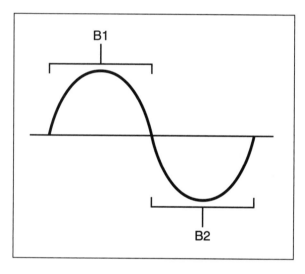

Figure 1.2

A common audio wave, showing areas of compression and rarefaction.

❋ Compression (higher air pressure)

❋ Rarefaction (lower air pressure)

Volume (Amplitude)

So what makes a sound louder or softer? Let's go back to the pond image. If I drop a heavy object into my calm pond, it will fall with more energy and therefore create bigger ripples. Sound works much the same way. An object that vibrates with more intensity will create greater disturbances in the air around it, and the wave will have greater pressure differences between compression and rarefaction. This will be perceived as a louder sound (see Figure 1.3).

Figure 1.3

A waveform with a greater difference between compression and rarefaction is heard as a louder sound.

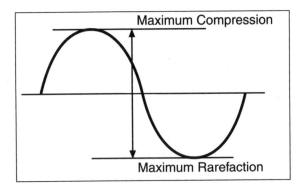

An object that vibrates with less intensity will result in a lower energy wave, with only a small difference between compression and rarefaction, and be heard as a softer sound, like Figure 1.4.

Figure 1.4

Less difference between compression and rarefaction equals a quieter sound.

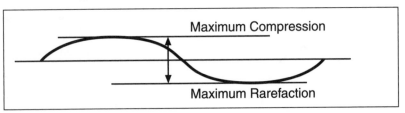

The loudness or softness of a sound is often referred to as its *volume*, and in technical terms, its *amplitude*. Amplitude of a given sound is measured in decibels of sound pressure level (dB SPL). The human volume range is from 0 dB SPL, which is silence, to about 130 dB SPL, which is the human threshold of pain).

Pitch (Frequency)

If the amplitude of a sound wave determines the volume of that sound, what determines the pitch? Pitch is determined not by the intensity of a vibration, but by its *speed*. An object that moves back and forth more quickly will create more compressions and rarefactions in a given time and will be heard as a higher pitched sound. Given that fact, an object that moves slower will be perceived as a lower pitched sound (see Figure 1.5).

Figure 1.5

Two waves: same volume, different pitch.

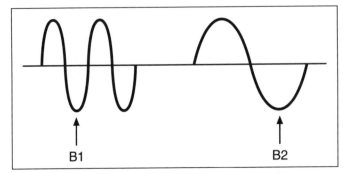

❈ Higher frequency = higher pitch

❈ Lower frequency = lower pitch

As you can see, the speed of these compressions and rarefactions determines the pitch, or *frequency*, of the sound. Each compression and rarefaction is called a *cycle* or *Hertz (Hz)*, and this is the way to measure a sound's frequency. The human ear can perceive between 20 and 20,000 cycles per second, which when measured in Hertz works out to a human frequency range of 20 Hz to 20 kHz (kilohertz), with lower frequencies being recognized as lower pitches and higher frequencies heard as higher pitches.

This kind of sound is commonly called *analog* audio. Whenever an object (like a speaker for instance) moves the air around it, sound is transmitted to a listener. This means that *everything* you hear is analog, even if you're playing a digital CD! Okay, so if every sound ever heard is analog, what the heck is digital audio? Read on....

Analog to Digital

So when is audio analog and when is it digital? Well, all *heard* audio is analog, but we can *store* audio in either an analog or a digital state.

When audio information is stored onto a magnetic media (like tape) or onto a record album, we consider that to be an analog method of storage. In this manner, a constantly changing magnetic field or groove in a record is used to represent the original audio information. This method of storage can yield very high quality audio and is still a preferred method used by many audiophiles. But there is a drawback—this method suffers quality loss as copies are made, and even original master tapes can degrade over time.

On the other hand, there's digital audio. When we say that audio is digital, basically that means that the original analog audio has been translated from its original analog form to a series of *digits*, or numbers. Before audio can be used in a computer-based environment, analog audio must be converted in such a way (the process is called *digitization*) so that it can be stored, played, or manipulated by audio software. The process of digitization is called the *analog-to-digital* (A/D) conversion, and the playback of digitally stored audio is called the *digital-to-analog* (D/A) conversion.

There are some real advantages to storing audio digitally. For one, digital audio is far more resistant to the ravages of time than analog—the digital numbers that represent an audio wave will tend *not* to change, whereas the magnetic field that stores audio signal on tape will naturally weaken and change over time. Second, digital copies of digital audio, if done right, can preserve all the sonic quality of the original, even when copied from a copy. Last, because digital audio is essentially binary computer numbers, we can apply the massive raw processing power to the computer to manipulate audio in ways never before possible.

We'll talk about the nuts and bolts of digital audio later. For now, let's talk briefly about how all this figures into the art of music.

The Art of Music

Everybody knows what music is—at least on a basic level. For example, you all can recognize a song when it starts playing on the radio. (Now, whether it's *good* music or not is another matter!) But recognizing music when you hear it is a good deal different than creating music from nothing. Let's take a deeper look at how a musician thinks about music.

Music as an Expressive Form

The *Encyclopedia Britannica* defines music as "Art concerned with combining vocal or instrumental sounds for beauty of form or emotional expression, usually according to cultural standards of rhythm, melody, and harmony." For the musician, the key words in this definition are "emotional expression"—that's what we all strive for when we create music. Above all, this is a conscious effort to communicate some idea or emotion through a skillful arrangement of sounds.

Sometimes, we take pleasure from the sounds of nature. You hear the chirp of the birds in the trees, or the gentle rush of a breeze, or the rhythmic pulse of the ocean on the shore—is it music? We may carelessly call it music ("listen to the beautiful music of the birds' songs!"), but that would give these natural phenomena the credit of having sentient thought. Certainly, we can't think of the sea as being a musician. No, nature cannot communicate an emotional message, although these sounds can inspire us to create.

So, it takes a human mind to actually make music. More than that, it takes a special kind of person to create music—an *artist*. True artists are people armed with a number of skills: senses to take inspiration from the sounds around them, the mind to translate that inspiration into a new artistic creation, and finally the intellectual skills to create those sounds through some sort of instrument (including a computer).

Elements of Music

Music can be broken down into two elements: sound and time. Let's take a quick look at these two fundamental building blocks of music.

First, the most basic element is sound. Obviously, there has to be some sort of vibrating object disturbing the air around it like we discussed in the earlier section of this chapter, but music goes way beyond the basics of amplitude and frequency. When we deal with musical sounds, we don't talk about frequencies as much as *pitch*. Pitches are described through letters (for example, the open strings of a guitar are E,A,D,G,B,and E) and arranged in *scales*, which are linear arrangements of pitches (a "C" major scale is C, D, E, F, G, A, B, and C). Don't worry about this too much at this point, we'll illustrate these concepts further in Chapter 3, when we explore the musical power of MIDI.

The distance between any two specific notes is referred to as an *interval*. When two notes are played together, an interval can be either *consonant* or *dissonant*. A consonant interval is one that results in a general pleasing harmony. Dissonance occurs when two notes "clash," resulting in a lack of pleasing harmony and often a sense of tension. These are obviously subjective terms, and what might be dissonant to one person might be perfectly consonant to another. Even so, dissonance sounds like a bad thing, doesn't it? In truth, both consonance and dissonance have important roles in music, and you'll use both in your compositions.

Music is a time-based art, unlike some other art forms (like paintings or sculpture). To fully experience a three-minute song, for example, listeners must invest three minutes of their time. Of course, this is an obvious aspect of music, but composers can take advantage of this time element by introducing musical elements as the song progresses, leading the listener through a unique artistic experience.

At the heart of music is the *tempo*, or the speed of the song (a ballad, for example can be said to have a slow tempo). The tempo is divided into beats. We usually measure music by *beats per minute* (120 beats per minute, for example, is common moderate tempo).

Beats are organized into groupings called *measures*. Listen to your favorite dance song and count along with it "1-2-3-4-1-2-3-4. . . ." What you're actually counting are *beats* (each individual number) and *measures* (in this case, each group of four numbers). It gets better: The number of beats in each measure determines its *meter*. For example, a waltz (counted "1-2-3-1-2-3. . . . ") has a different meter than your four-beats-per-measure dance track. These time-based elements will also be explored further in Chapter 3.

How does a composer use these ingredients of sound and time to their greatest advantage? There are many different ways and as many different compositional approaches as there are composers. You will develop your own creative style as you gain experience. Here is some food for thought: Consider the power of repetition and variety in music. Repetitive elements, like a looping drum groove, can play a powerful role in music and provide a solid foundation for your other elements. A well-constructed repetitive musical framework can give a frame of reference for other musical elements in your song. Beyond that, repeating figures can often put listeners into the "groove," penetrating their minds on a fundamental level, and even inducing a feeling of "dynamic calm." Listen again to a favorite dance track. The groove alone, constant and repeating, can really make the mood, no? But if you *only* repeated musical figures over and over with no change at all, the tune would get boring *very* quickly.

That's where a little variety comes in handy. New musical elements make an immediate impression, as they stand out from the surrounding repetition and grab your attention. Songs that build in complexity and texture not only get the listener's attention, but keep it as well. But beware — the relationship of repetition and contrast must be carefully crafted. Just as too much repetition can become monotonous, too much variety can easily result in chaos! Bottom line: Both contrast *and* repetition need to cooperate to get your musical message across.

※ **TIP**

The interplay of sound and time, repetition and variety, makes music the interesting art form that it is. Listen critically to one of your favorite songs. Can you pick out consonance and dissonance? When does the artist use both types of intervals in the music? How about the tempo—is it fast or slow? Does the tempo stay the same or does it change during the course of the song?

As you learn more about the different aspects of music, you'll become a better critical listener. Over the years, as your critical listening continues to improve, you'll even be able to analyze other artists' work and draw inspiration!

Taking Back the Creativity (or the Difference Between Making Music and Copying Music)

If you're a teenager, you probably don't really remember a world without the power of the personal computer. To say that it's changed everyday life—radically—is no understatement! For example, before computers, I would have written this book on a *typewriter*. That means with every misspelling, I'd have to physically pull out a sheet of paper and use white-out. And forget cutting and pasting chapters. And spell-check—without a computer, you can forget about that as well.

Just for a little perspective, let me tell you a little about the dark days before PCs, and how musicians produced music. Musicians, who spent their time perfecting their craft, wrote music on paper. Then other musicians would have to be assembled to further refine the music. Of course, all this takes time and effort in copying the music, scheduling the musicians, getting the rehearsal space—you get the picture. If you're extremely talented and lucky, you could save up your money to get into a local studio for a recording session, then another editing session, and so on until you had your record in your hands. Sounds like a lot of work? You bet. And more than that, it was so *expensive*! Often, creative musicians were denied the pleasure of creating and recording their work because it was so prohibitively costly. Of course, the computer has changed all that. Now a computer musician, armed with knowledge of what MIDI is and how to use it, can use the computer to create and edit musical notes in previously impossible ways. Want to change the key? Fix a wrong note? Copy or move a section of music? No problem, and if you don't like the changes you've made, then you can always undo them. You can fully tweak your music on your own, so you're completely prepared *before* your band comes in to rehearse. When you're ready to record audio, you can record directly to your computer's hard drive and process that audio in ways were only available previously in costly recording studios. Think of your computer as a musical "word processor"—manipulating musical data with the same power that word processor applications manipulate letters and words.

And it gets better. After you've created your masterpiece, you can take it to the world in a number of different ways. In the days before digital audio, you had to send your master tape (representing perhaps thousands of dollars of expense) to a record pressing facility (yet more expense). These days, there are certainly quicker and thriftier ways to go. Want to make an audio CD? No problem, as long as you've got a CD burner. Beyond that you can make other files, such as MP3 files, which are more suited to distribution on the Internet. Surround sound mixes? DVDs? CD-ROMS? All of these are within the reach of the computer musician, at a fraction of the price it would cost in the old analog-only days.

Yes, the computer revolution has brought power to the people, but the news is not entirely rosy. The same technology that makes music creation easier also makes copying music easier. The power of computers and the Internet has made it all too easy for music to be taken from any number of sources, from copying CDs to downloading MP3 files from the Internet. Of course, there are legal considerations often involved with music copying, currently a hot topic in the music industry, but we won't debate that issue here. What is certain, though, is that music copying isn't music creation, and those who simply copy music without creativity are certainly not being the artists that we are striving to be in our study of digital music making.

So that's the moral to the story: We've been given great power, but with great power comes great responsibility. (I got that pearl of wisdom from a comic book!) First, let's earn the basics of the language of music and the skills of digital audio editing to use our powerful digital audio workstation (DAW) well. You can do it! Let's get started.

2

For Fun *and* Profit:
The Business of Music

Anywhere you go these days, you hear music, so much so that you might take things for granted. Of course, there are the songs you hear on the radio, but that's not the only work out there for a creative-minded computer musician—not by a long shot! Radio, television, film, even the Internet and games, all hold opportunities for us. Let's take a look at just a few of the many careers out there (though there are almost as many variations to these traditional roles as there are professionals in the industry). In this chapter, you'll learn about these areas of interest:

* Music Composition

* Audio Production

* Audio for Games

* Audio for Film and Video

The Challenge: Doing Good Work on a Budget

There's a popular misconception in the industry these days that to do good musical work with a computer you have to lay out a *lot* of money. I'm talking thousands, sometimes tens of thousands of dollars! Okay, it's true that there are very cool software and hardware toys that we play with in the industry, and I admit freely that the features and specs that they carry make high-end production faster and easier, but to say that you've *got* to have all the latest bells and whistles to make music is just wrong. Think about it—great digital music has been composed over the past 20 years with far simpler tools than we have today. In fact, some of the cheapest applications today boast more features by far than high-end applications of the 1980s.

This book will demonstrate to you that you *can* make music on a tight budget. Specifically for this demonstration, I've set up a computer-based system in my studio that is specifically designed to be *minimal*. I'm starting with a modest computer, the kind you might get as a hand-me-down from someone else in your family. Here's a rundown of my system:

* Pentium III 600 MHz processor
* 128 megabytes of RAM
* 20 gigabyte hard drive
* Microsoft Windows XP Home Edition (operating system)
* Creative Labs Sound Blaster PCI512 sound card
* Roland PC-160 MIDI Keyboard Controller

Added to this basic system, I'll use only the most inexpensive software. The software I'm using will be either freeware, shareware, or very budget-conscious indeed. Along with this book, you'll find a CD-ROM disk. On the CD-ROM will be tutorial materials to use with these applications:

* **Quartz AudioMaster Freeware 4.6** (Freeware—You can download it from www.digitalsoundplanet.com/SoftwareHouse/Products/Audio_Master/Freeware/freeware.phtml). A basic MIDI and audio production tool, with a few proprietary plug-in effects.
* **Edirol Virtual Sound Canvas** ($40—Learn more about it at www.edirol.com/products/info/vscmp1.html). This is a non-shareware/freeware synth, but it is such a useful and versatile instrument and will provide the useful and accessible sounds for your exercises (and will also introduce the concept of General MIDI). If you purchase Cakewalk Home Studio, a version of the Virtual Sound Canvas is included.
* **GoldWave** (Shareware (about $45)—Find download links at www.goldwave.com/release.php). Another great audio editor.
* **Cakewalk Home Studio 2** ($149 list price—Learn more about it at www.cakewalk.com/Products/HomeStudio/default.asp). The only non-shareware/freeware production tool on the list, this product will bring concepts into a more real-world focus. Though very thrifty when compared to other DAW programs on the market, this product boasts some very useful professional applications.

> **NOTE**
> Some of these applications, like Quartz AudioMaster freeware, for example, don't specifically mention that they're compatible with Windows XP. Don't worry—I've tested them successfully on my system.

TIP

When it comes to shopping around, there's the *list price*, which is determined by the manufacturer, and then there's the *retail price*, which is what you'll actually pay from any retail vendor. This retail price is usually significantly lower than the manufacturer's list price. Take Cakewalk, for example, which lists for $149 on Cakewalk's Web site, but is much less. I've had no problem finding it for about $100 (at the time of this printing) when purchased from a retailer (your neighborhood music store or an online music retailer like Sweetwater.com). Happy hunting!

You'll note that these applications are decidedly entry-level, and you may ask "why bother learning on these kinds of applications only to have to learn other applications later?" You might also recognize that some of these applications seem to do similar things, so why learn two applications when one might do just fine? Good questions, and here's the answer: Entry level equipment, in addition to being thrifty, is often the best for teaching important concepts. Sure, you'll have to do things the hard way, but while you're doing that, you'll be learning *how* this technology works! As far as learning multiple tools that seem to do the same thing, learning to get around these basic software products will help you understand how more professional applications are laid out, and getting the job done in more than one way, with more than one program, will help you attack similar situations more logically with professional-level software.

With luck and time, you will probably work with more advanced hardware and software in the years to come. The concepts you'll learn in these first steps will help you figure out those products of tomorrow. In short, you'll learn how to *learn*, which in the ever-evolving world of digital music just might be the most valuable skill an artist can have.

With that knowledge, there are lots of avenues you can pursue, either as a professional in the field or as an enthusiastic hobbyist—read on.

Composition

Music composition, or music writing, has been around as long as there's been music. I mean, there'd be no songs if there weren't composers out there to write them, right? Take a look around—every song on the radio, every movie score, every background song for a TV commercial, all needed a composer to start the ball rolling. Even before the days of modern media, composers have been at the center of the musical community, even back to the days of Mozart and Bach (they were commissioned by the royalty and church of the day for ceremonial music, and so on). As long as there is music, there will be a need for the skills of a composer.

Although all the phases of musical creation are critical to the final product, the final musical product starts with the inspiration of the composer. The particular job of a composer is to draw upon the sounds around him, his experiences and history, and his observations of the human condition as a whole to create sounds that are interesting and moving to the listener. This is a special kind of creativity—the ability to create something out of nothing. As professional composers, we are usually directed by some motivation (for example, writing a soundtrack for a monster truck show would naturally lead us in different musical directions than the romantic scene in a movie) and often other concrete limitations as well (like a specific time limitation—for example, a 30-second radio spot will demand a different approach then a three-minute song). Although these guidelines might seem to be a limitation at first, many composers (myself included) find that having some boundaries to work within gives us much-needed focus and structure for working.

What defines today's composers are the same abilities that have defined composers for hundreds of years. Creativity is a must, of course, but there are other technical skills that go hand in hand with that creativity. Absolutely critical to composers' abilities is their understanding of the instruments and styles they're writing for. (For example, what role do drums play? What notes can a guitarist play? What is the range of an alto saxophone?) Understanding the written language of music—beats, measures, notes—although not *absolutely* necessary for all composers, can really aid in communicating ideas to the musicians performing a composer's work.

The power of the computer has only added to a composer's speed and efficiency, but it's important to keep in mind that none of the composer's basic skills have been replaced. As a music writer, you'll still need to know the workings of the instruments you're using, only now you'll have to add the computer itself to that list. With the computer, you'll be able to use MIDI to control a wide variety of synthesizers (both hardware and software) and to create complete musical works in the computer. If synthesized sound isn't what you want and you want to use live musicians, you can even use the computer to print out sheet music for your players.

Indeed, the composer is at the beginning of musical creation, but the job isn't done by a long shot.

Digital Audio Production

Once music has been written, it must be recorded before it can be distributed to the masses. Recording, however, is just a part of the job of production. Generally speaking, digital audio production includes the tasks of *recording*, *editing*, *mixing*, and *mastering*. Sometimes, these tasks are all performed by one person, but often a team of skilled professionals cooperate to get the job done.

In the recording (also known as *tracking*) phase, audio is captured to some sort of storage medium. In the studio, this medium can be either analog or digital (though for the purposes of this book, we'll concentrate on digital storage). The primary job of the tracking engineer is to record the best performance of the studio musicians, and to do this, the engineer needs to understand which microphones (*mics*) to use for different instruments and where to place those mics to accurately capture the character of those instruments. After recording actually begins, the recording engineer will store each instrument (in its raw form) on its own individual track (hence the name "tracking"). This multi-track recording is perfect for the remaining stages of production.

After the audio has been recorded, it can be manipulated in a variety of ways. The editing phase of production can include a number of different activities. For example, an editing engineer might create a single vocal track from a number of vocal takes (this is called *compositing* or *comping* for short). Armed with a powerful DAW (digital audio workstation), an editor can also fix timing problems, cut out wrong notes, and even fix pitches! Last, but not least, an editor often assembles musical sections into complete songs by arranging musical segments. For example, do you need to remove a verse? How about looping a measure of drums? Easy for a skilled editor armed with a DAW.

Next comes mixing. After the music has been recorded and edited, all the individual tracks must be skillfully combined to a usable form. For example, a mixing engineer might take 100 tracks and render them down to a two-track stereo that might eventually be played on somebody's CD player. Of course, the art of mixing is much more involved. The mixing engineer must be able to coordinate a number of tracks in such a way that they don't interfere with each other, and each instrument can be heard distinctly. Beyond that, effects such as reverb, compression, and equalization (see Chapter 11) give the mix an extra shine and sense of space. Also, the mixer must be intimately familiar with the style of music being worked on, as different styles of music demand different mixing approaches. Truly, the mixing engineer is an artist in his or her own right!

In many cases, mastering is the final step in the production process. Once the mixing engineer has finished his "final" mix, the mixed-down tracks are sent to the mastering engineer for final tweaks. The mastering engineer is a rare breed indeed—part scientist, part artist. Armed with an encyclopedic knowledge of physics, acoustics, psychoacoustics (human perception of sound), and music, the mastering engineer further crafts the audio until it is ready for duplication and distribution. This stage is typically reserved for professional level work, and a good mastering engineer is a vital link in the professional production process.

Becoming a composer or engineer (though certainly tried and true career paths) isn't the only option open to you. The next two fields, game audio production and audio production for picture (video and film), are growing fast these days, so fast that I've gotten some professionals in those fields to give us their latest thoughts.

Audio for Games

Games are a growing business these days. In fact, game production has outgrossed film production for years. Because audio is an integral part of the gaming experience and certainly deserves a special mention here, I've talked to some game producers of note, so they can give us their take on the state of game audio and a peek into the future.

First is **Julius Hocott**, who at the tender age of 27 has already accumulated some impressive titles with EA Sports, including "John Madden Football 2003," "NCAA Football 2003," and "Nascar Thunder 2003." Next, we've got **Jason McClesky**, who has worked extensively on PC games, including titles such as "Ascension," "Dark Armada," "Guardians of Neverwood," and "Alloy 51."Last, we have **Marc Pinsky**, a lecturer on the subject at Full Sail and audio producer for "Mary Kate & Ashley's Crush Course."

Q: What exactly *is* game audio? Are we talking about musical soundtracks, sound effects, or what?

Julius: The term *game audio* basically is *everything* that you hear in a video game. Nowadays, it's not just music in the background or an explosion sound when you blow something up, but also a lot of other elements that oftentimes go practically unnoticed. For example, the "click or beep" sounds that are heard when you are selecting your characters or entering in your name or the commentary from the announcers during a sports game.

Jason: Yep, it's everything pertaining to musical soundtracks, sound effects, and dialogue.

Marc: And it's more—game audio is a magical elixir of sound. It's *more* than music or sound effects. It's about *how* the music and sound effects involve you as a player, making you feel like you are living inside the game.

Q: Game audio production is a bit off the beaten path. I'm betting that you've got an interesting story of how you broke into this kind of work. Care to share it?

Jason: I started with an internship, and due to tons of hard work and perfect timing, it turned into what it is now (and it keeps getting bigger).

Marc: Oddly enough, for me it was a case of speaking up at the right time. I was working in music retail at the time and learned that one of my customers was the vice president and co-owner of a video game company. I took it upon myself to ask him if we could meet up to discuss what we had to offer one another.

Julius: For me, it was quite an accident really, and at the time I had never even thought of doing game audio before. I was working around town as a recording engineer and had gotten a bit of a reputation for being able to get the job done, no matter what the gear or situation. One day, I got a call to do a session with a band that was entirely Spanish-speaking except for one member who spoke a little bit of English. Even though I didn't speak any Spanish at all, I was able to get the session done and was asked to do the rest of their album. To make a long story short, the studio owner was the current sound designer at EA Sports Tiburon, and when it came time for them to take on another person to work on the games they were developing at that time, they asked me.

Q: How long does it usually take to get a game done, from concept to completion? How much of that time is devoted to audio production?

Julius: Every company is different. Some games I've heard of were under development for years and some less than a year. I suppose the determining factors are how many people are working on it and also how complex the game is. In the case of the three titles that I worked on, they were released every year; so from start to finish, it was one year. At EA there were several different departments, one of which was audio, and each department had a year to complete its portion of the project.

Jason: There are many variables to consider, such as the amount of money in the budget, the size of the team, the quality of the team members' work, and the dynamic relationship between team members. As far as time devoted to production, it usually takes the audio team up to a third of the time that it takes the programming team. Music takes the most time!

Marc: Yes, it really varies depending on the type of game. Generally speaking, it takes approx 2–3 years for a game to be made. Sadly, audio is one of the last elements to be added. The audio crew sometimes isn't called into duty until the last 9 months of production. On other games, they can be involved from the very beginning.

Q: At first glance, there seems to be a lot of similarity between traditional video (like TV or films) and video games. What is the same about the two media?

Marc: I'll be honest, when I first got involved with video games, I thought it would be a launching point for sound design for film. I couldn't have been more wrong. Games and film share the same three elements of audio: dialogue, music, and sound effects, but beyond that, they've been very different kinds of work for me.

Julius: For me, sometimes doing audio for games is done exactly as it would be in a film or TV. In fact, there were even some bonus "behind the scene" video segments in some games that are actual video clips. For the most part, to accurately represent a scene using audio, anything that happens during game play that would make a noise should have a sound to go along with it, also the ambience or background noises must be put in to add realism. For example, if there is an explosion but no sound for it, or if you're standing next to a river but hear no water sounds, it would just feel like something's not right. Any dialogue or speaking parts are done very similarly as well. In both media types, vocals are recorded in a studio and read according to a script.

Jason: Traditional video and video games are very much alike in the sense that they both tell a story and follow similar patterns of character development and story progression (intro, climax, conclusion, and everything in between).

Q: Along those same lines, what's different?

Jason: The way the sounds are implemented and the format in which the sounds are compressed and finalized are different. Also, video games are more interactive. You get to be a character, thus becoming part of the story instead of simply watching it unfold!

Marc: Jason's right. Movies are linear—meaning that the story is the same every time you watch it. All of the events are planned out well ahead of time, so as a sound designer, you know what happens next since you are able to watch the movie. Video games, on the other hand, are different in that they are much more dynamic. Every time you play the game, it is different. You move to different places, interact with different characters, spend different amounts of time in different places, etc. So, as a sound designer, you are forced to think of every single possibility that can occur in the game.

Julius: The biggest difference, I think, is that with games there is one major limitation. All the same elements still have to be there for the audio to be realistic, but with games there is a size limitation that is unbelievably small that determines how many sounds can play out of the console at a time. This size cap is due to the memory resources available within each gaming console. After all the graphics and other game elements are accounted for, audio ends up with about 2 to 3 megabytes of memory that can be available for triggering sounds at one time. The bottom line is that some sounds have to be left out or lowered in quality.

Q: Films have teams of audio professionals who work together, each specializing on a certain aspect of production. Given the apparent similarities between film and games, I'm guessing that there are teams that work together on games as well. What are the different types of specialties in game audio, what do they do, and what jobs have you personally done?

Julius: Starting from the top level, there is the manager, who oversees the audio team and assigns projects and deadlines to them. Next is the audio programmer, who takes all of the sound elements and implements them into the game (this is called *coding*). Then there's the sound designer, whose job it is to create the way the sound effects will change as you move through the game. Helping the sound designer is an assistant sound designer, who goes out and records and edits sound effects and dialogue, as well as any other miscellaneous audio stuff. Of course, there's a composer, creating the music of the game. Last, but absolutely not least, are testers, who play the game and search for any bugs or mistakes!

Of course, every company is different, and these positions are not set in stone at all. My responsibilities were almost entirely to work with the dialogue of the commentators, since this was such a huge part of the game.

I had to take hours and hours of recorded dialogue, chop it up into thousands of little phrases, make it all sound tonally the same, and then I had to make sure that it all sounded smooth when the different phrases were played back in the order that the game called for.

Marc: From what I've seen, game audio departments tend to be much smaller than their film counterparts. Most game companies are actually quite small. As a result, they don't have a huge staff. Some companies may only have two or three audio engineers. Each one of them is able to create sound effects as well as compose music. Other larger companies are able to hire dedicated sound designers and dedicated composers. However, you can write the best music and create the most amazing sound effects in the world and *still* have them sound like junk if they are not implemented or placed in the game correctly. Implementation requires a knowledge of coding. Generally speaking, musicians and audio engineers typically don't have that particular skill set, so the company has a dedicated programmer responsible for the audio. There are tools that have been designed to allow sound designers to implement the sound in the game without coding or programming, though.

Jason: Sometimes, the audio team depends upon the game budget. Audio is often one of the last priorities, so we are at the end of the money and decision chain and have to be multitalented and do more than one of the jobs Julius mentioned! On the other hand, sometimes there may be different teams for music, field recording, sound design, studio recording, and voice talent. Most projects require that the team consists of two or three people that can do all of these things. I, personally, have done all and many times have been the only person on the project. This gives me much more creative freedom, but is very labor intensive!

Q: How do you approach a game project? What are the things that you have to really keep an eye on to make a professional project?

Marc: Oddly enough, I approach games as interactive movies. I try to imagine what it would be like to live in the world of the game. I'll sometimes write descriptions of locations in the game and try to think of any existing *real* locations like them. If there are, I'll take a trip to them, sit on a park bench, and just listen. I'll sit with my eyes closed and try to hear all of the different sounds around me. Then I'll go back to the studio and try to re-create what I just heard.

Jason: I approach every game project the same way. I read the design document, which is a very long and in-depth breakdown of everything that has to do with the game (the story, the mission statement, the asset lists, and many more pages of useful information). Then I talk to the programming team and creators (or whoever is in charge) and look at the idea of the game from their point of view. From this point, we start throwing ideas on the table. I do this knowing that every game should be different in some way, and the programmers usually want to push the boundaries and come up with something new and improved and maybe something never done before! This seems to get the creative juices flowing.

The game audio specialist should always try to see the game the way the creators and the programmers see it. The music has to be good enough to be marketable to the general public (in a soundtrack for instance). The sound effects have to be consistent (the levels should be similar, if it's a very realistic game, the sound effects should probably be more realistic and visa-versa). And always make more sound effects and record more dialogue than asked for and make them very diverse (this gives the decision-makers a choice of what to use, and it also gives the audio specialist more creative freedom). Remember that the rest of the team is depending on you to be creative with all the audio and come up with ideas of your own for the project—that's why they hired you!

Julius: Attention to detail is an important quality for a game professional. There are thousands of files to keep track of, and some of the work is quite tedious. Everyone on your team must realize that the game's sound will only be as good as you make it. In some cases, that may make your team want to work extra hard just so they will be personally proud of the end result.

Q: There are a lot of different skills related to digital audio. Of course, for different types of work, different skills are more important. In your opinion, what are the most important skills and knowledge that an aspiring game audio producer should work to acquire?

Jason: Bottom line—the more you know or are able to do, the more marketable you are, and the more money you can charge. Be good and fast at sound design and be able to communicate well with others. Good personal communication skills are a *must*. It's not a digital audio skill exactly, but people generally want to be around people they get along with or can communicate with! Field recording is very helpful, and studio recording is a necessity also, and once again, you have to deal with voice talent, so personal communication skills are involved. Last, but not least, be able to create all styles of music (especially orchestral). The reason music is last is because sometimes the music is licensed or someone outside the team is hired to do the music, but once again, the more you know, the more marketable you are!

Marc: Of course, engineering skills are needed. Being able to read music, while not essential, is definitely a bonus. I personally feel that one of the most important skills to have is the ability to listen. Not just to instructions, but to the world around you. Your job is to make a fictional environment come alive. Without the sound, it is lifeless. I've played too many games where I felt like a spectator. I want to be *in* the action. Listen to real-world sounds and locations, and make the fictitious ones come to life.

Julius: Knowledge and skills on digital audio programs and concepts are absolutely essential. The faster you are at these programs, the more valuable you are. Also, studying synthesis helped me to understand the possibilities of what can be done with sound, and in my opinion, the way that the game console triggers sounds is much like a sampler, so being familiar with samplers can't hurt.

Q: The game industry is growing so fast, even outpacing feature films. What kinds of changes do you see in the future of gaming? How will that impact the audio industry?

Marc: More jobs! As games get better and better, they are going to require more audio designers to think outside the box. It's sad to say, but I just haven't been that impressed with the CDs that have come out in the past few years. Nothing is really innovative or interesting. It's rehashing stuff that's been done before. Video games are just beginning to grow up. People are just beginning to recognize how important the role of audio is to a game, so they are making games in which audio has a greater role. You're going to need more talented audio individuals to create a better world for gamers.

Julius: One thing that I can foresee is that as gaming consoles get bigger and more powerful, the type of realism that can be achieved with audio will be truly amazing. Audio will be a necessary part of the game play, and hearing which direction the enemy is coming toward you will be just as important as seeing him coming. With this improved realism, in the future maybe even people with visual disabilities can play video games based just on their sense of hearing.

Jason: I feel it's only going to grow, and the audio industry will only benefit from it! The quality of the games keeps getting better, as well as the game consoles, computers, and programs. Also, the limit of what can be done in all aspects of video games (3D art, animation, 2D art, audio, and programming) keeps being reinvented by all the creative and talented people making the games today! Very soon it will be industry standard for all games to utilize surround sound (many already do)!

Q: Any parting words of wisdom to the game audio producer-to-be?

Julius: My motto: If you start now and don't stop no matter what, you will reach your goal—eventually!

Jason: Be creative, never stop learning (never think you know everything or even know enough), be open minded (learn to always think outside the box), and most importantly, *have fun* at what you do. If you don't enjoy the work, then why do it in the first place?

Marc: Love what you do! What it comes right down to it, do it because you love doing it—not because of a paycheck. There are sadly too many people working in jobs because of money. To them, it's just a job, and as a result, they are miserable. But if you truly love what you do, you'll perform better than you thought possible. It won't seem like a job because you'll be getting paid to play!

Sound for Picture

Let's keep the ball rolling with another roundtable discussion, this time about audio production for picture, commonly referred to as *postproduction*. First is **Brian Young**, who in addition to film credits like *The Bug, Florida City,* and *Mantrap,* heads up the Audio Post Production course at Full Sail, a college for media technology in Winter Park, Florida. Joining him is **Michael Orlowski, M.P.S.E. (Motion Picture Sound Editors, a professional society)**, who in addition to also being a lecturer at Full Sail, has worked on such films as *Soul Survivors, Crime and Punishment in Suburbia,* and *The Mummy Returns.*

Q: OK, what *is* postproduction? Certainly, it is a term commonly associated with sound for film, but what makes it *post*production?

Brian: The term *post*production stems from the fact that the work we do does not begin until *after* the film has been shot, and at the very least, roughly edited.

Mike: Postproduction is the art of storytelling. We take a story that we heard from someone else, and we embellish it. At least that's the theory, but sometimes in practice, postproduction turns out more like the emergency room for solving all of the life-threatening problems of the project that could have been prevented if addressed earlier!

Q: How much time is usually given to the audio portion of a feature film? How much of the film's budget?

Brian: This question is very open-ended because every production is a little different. A good rule of thumb for a modest feature is a bare minimum of four weeks of editorial and a bare minimum of one week to mix. From there, the amount of time budgeted only grows.

Mike: Brian's right, but in my experience, typically a crew of six or more can tackle a feature film in four weeks. That's about three weeks of preparation and editing and a solid week of mixing. We'd all love to have more time, but the trend is to have shorter timelines.

Q: How about engineering sound for TV? How does that workflow differ from feature films? How is it the same?

Mike: If you wanted a visual representation of how the sound quality differs from film to television, think of a wedding cake versus a cup cake. There is so little time to work on television, so the detail is just not there. Also when working on TV, there is such a chain of [signal] processors compressing and expanding the audio that the fidelity is just shot. We cram in as much as time permits and hope it's enough.

Brian: One of the biggest differences is the mix to pix concept. Mix to pix is a term used to describe simply throwing the source material up onto a console and going straight to the final mix without actually predubbing. When I say "predubbing," I'm talking about the process of blending source audio elements from the editing phase of production into more manageable "sub" mixes. Due to the large number of source elements in a feature film, this is necessary to make the best use of all the faders at a mixer's disposal. However, due to the very quick turnaround for a TV show, there is not time to predub. Also, not nearly the same amount of time and effort goes into creating brand-spanking new effects. Beyond that, the workflow is very similar.

Q: If I'm reading my movie credits correctly, there seem to be a lot of different types of jobs associated with making a film. What are the main specialties in making a feature film?

Brian: Dialogue editors specialize in, you guessed it, dialogue. Hard effects editors work on the simple effects. Background editors cut the ambiences (environmental sounds), and designed effects editors or "sound designers" will cut the fun stuff. The gaffer and the sound effects rerecording engineer mix the film, and the supervising sound editor is responsible for all of the sound elements in the film.

Mike: At the top of the list for me personally would be the supervising sound editors. They run the show creatively in editorial. Their skill set has to be as much creative as administrative. The team of editors is skilled in their craft of editing. Someone might be the guy to go to for cutting (editing) cars, while others might be perfect for sword fights. The editors tend to get pigeonholed into the type of sounds they are good at editing. For me it was the background ambiences. We all work in a small crew environment with each person knowing his duties. If all goes well, it's a well-oiled machine.

Q: Assuming you haven't already, could you talk a little about what ADR is? Roughly how much of a typical film is ADRd?

Brian: ADR is Automated Dialogue Replacement. This is replacing lines of dialogue that do not work for whatever reason. In an action film, it is possible to have as much as 100% replacement; in a "date" film (such as *When Harry Met Sally*), you may have as little as 40% replacement.

Mike: Oh, ADR... The original purpose for ADR was to re-record lines of production audio that were unusable. We bring the actors back into a controlled environment getting a pristine version of the line. Of course, when the directors became aware of the possibilities of ADR, the process changed dramatically. Now we use ADR for all sorts of things. We replace or re-voice actors because the original actor didn't have the right voice. A lot of directors use ADR to fix weak plot points or to add extra lines for humor. The other saving grace we receive from ADR is TV-safe lines. We constantly bring actors in to replace foul language.

All in all, I'd say that ADR is a tool that can tend to be overused. The difference between a good film and a great film is when we do not notice the work ADR has done to enhance the performance.

Q: When you work on a film, how do you approach the job? Are there any specific things you look out for to give you direction?

Brian: First, I sit down with the director, sound supervisor, or even the picture editor and find out what the story is and what they expect out of the sound. Then I look at the budget, both time and financial, and start to prioritize and schedule accordingly. In my opinion, the best thing to give direction is asking yourself what you can do to use sound to push the story, as well as what can be done to enhance the symbiotic relationship of image and sound.

Mike: Because I'm primarily an editor, typically I am asked by a supervising sound editor to start work on a film and am more or less assigned to a project. As a staff editor, this is normally the way you are hired to work. On independent films, I can work more with the director. As far as direction on a project, hopefully the director will know how to convey how he or she wants the film to sound.

New directors have trouble expressing this, and that's why you want to read the script. Many times you will find some great ideas if you read the script before you watch a rough version of the video. The most important thing is to let your imagination go wild and try not to discount any ideas you may have.

Q: There are a lot of different skills related to digital audio. Of course, for different types of work, different skills are more important. In your opinion, what are the most important skills and knowledge that an aspiring audio post-production engineer should work to acquire?

Brian: Timecode and Sync are a great place to start. Beyond that, the *most important thing is to develop your ears!*

Mike: Absolutely—listen to sounds as much as you can. Then listen to them again. Our listening skills are the most important asset we have. Record sounds around you; then try to use them in your projects. When you build a library of sound effects, you will start recognizing good sounds. Organization is also very important. Get organized. Know your workstation. I don't care if you use Pro Tools, Logic, or Cakewalk. Understand the tools you have, and think of new ways to use them. When you see a shortcut, force yourself to memorize it. Time yourself on how long it takes to do a task and then try to cut that time in half. Speed is really important in our business.

Q: Where do you see the industry going in the future? How do you think advances in digital audio will impact the way you work?

Mike: Personally, I feel that in the near future you will be able to mix and edit on an iPod. Apple and other major companies are equipping the average consumer with some truly amazing programs. I don't see a need for the modern filmmaker to use a multimillion dollar facility. This both opens the door to the new talent of the future but also requires us to have a strong business sense. The days of working for a large studio are dying fast, and you need to market yourself if you want to stand a chance of making it.

Brian: The advancements in digital technology are a double-edged sword. They can make workflow easier and faster but frankly, more mechanical. What this detracts from, however, is the artistic side. As more pressure is put on to work fast, you can find yourself without the time to experiment or think things through.

Q: Any parting words of wisdom to the post audio producer-to-be?

Mike: Never ask if it will be hard to work in this business. Once you open that door of doubt, it will be so hard to change your mind.

Brian: And listen!

3 MIDI Basics

MIDI, for all its usefulness and power, is often a misused and misunderstood member of our creation arsenal. To really use MIDI well, you've got to get to the root of what MIDI is (and what it isn't). In this chapter you'll learn:

- The history and evolution of the MIDI standard.
- The difference between MIDI and audio and how to get the two to play together.
- Basics of written music and how that pertains to MIDI.

What *Is* MIDI, Anyway?

Before you can start using MIDI, it's helpful to know what exactly MIDI *is*, what it does, and where it comes from.

A Tale of Two Keyboards (and Beyond)

Fair warning—I'm going to tell you one of those "when I was your age" stories. Don't worry, though, I won't go on about how I had to walk uphill to school in the snow (even though I did!). Instead, I'm going to tell you of the dark days before MIDI. I recall the first baby steps down the road of music technology—the birth of synthesizers—and how the world changed. Wow, we could buy a MIDI keyboard that was *way* smaller than a piano and play sounds that ***nobody had ever heard before***!

You'd think that would be enough to be happy about, wouldn't you? But no, there was a price to be paid. If you wanted more sounds, it meant buying more synthesizers, and that meant that not only did you have to lay out more money, but also before you knew it, you'd have a truckload of keyboards to lug around to every gig (back then we called live performances "gigs"). Worse than that, the stage would be crowded beyond belief with row upon row of keyboards. It gets better, because of all those synthesizers, only two could be played at a time (assuming that the keyboardist wasn't playing with his feet as well as his hands). Overall, quite a waste, but hey, that's what we had to work with.

Then, in 1979, a really interesting change started popping up. Some of these synthesizers began including computer-style plugs in the back of them, allowing them to be connected to other synthesizers that had the same plug and basically networking the two devices. Take, for example, the Oberheim OBX, which had a plug that would connect it to another OBX. In this way, a single keyboardist could play the first OBX, and not only the first OBX would sound, but the second one as well! This was a really cool way to get fat, layered sounds.

Of course, Oberheim wasn't the only brand to implement this idea (others joined the bandwagon), but there was one serious limitation. You see, only devices of the same brand (and usually the same model) could be connected in such a way. So a problem still remained because different brands had different kinds of sounds—one brand might be great for horns, but another was good for strings, and still another would give strong keyboard-type sounds. So, as long as this sort of connectivity was proprietary to each brand, this was only a partial solution to this mounting problem.

That's when MIDI came on the scene. It started as a group of synthesizer manufacturers, all members of NAMM (the National Association of Music Merchandisers), who met and discussed the idea of a cross-manufacturer, universally standard language by which data might be shared between devices of different makes and models. It was such a good idea that it received international support. Companies worked cooperatively on creating and developing this standard language, including many Japanese companies (most notably Roland) and U.S. companies (led by Sequential Circuits, who is generally credited with getting the ball rolling in the first place). Finally, in 1983, the first synthesizers with MIDI arrived. That's when things started getting really interesting.

The first effects of MIDI's introduction were obvious. Now, with MIDI, musicians could have one keyboard in front of them, and from that single keyboard, control a host of other synthesizers. Imagine the thrill of playing your Yamaha keyboard with its strong keyboard sounds, and at the same time triggering the rich horns of an Oberheim, *and* also playing the smooth strings of a Roland synth. You think linking two of the same keyboards gave you thick sounds, you ain't seen nothing yet! Better still, we got all this richness without having tons of keyboards on the stage. I remember reading in the magazines how the technically minded bands of the day had extravagant MIDI setups *under* the stage, while they had only one or two MIDI keyboards on the stage. How cool!

But technology marched on even further. Manufacturers started seeing other ways to use MIDI. For starters, they took a look at the types of setups that seemed to be evolving. People were generally setting up a couple of keyboards to play, specifically the ones that felt good, and set other synthesizers aside to be controlled and triggered via MIDI. With that kind of a setup in this MIDI controller/MIDI slave kind of relationship, why did the keyboards that weren't being directly played have to have a keyboard at all? Enter the synthesizer module, which was essentially a keyboard synthesizer without the keyboard. This kind of device had the benefit of being cheaper, since the consumer didn't have to pay for a keyboard that he didn't want to use anyway. On top of that, they were smaller and lighter. Now, a MIDI controller could trigger an armada of synth modules that wouldn't break your back to lug around and could sit on the stage right next to the keyboard player and occupy a space on stage no larger than a mini-fridge.

This controller/slave relationship didn't only change the construction of the slave devices, but also the controller devices. Dedicated keyboard MIDI controllers came onto the scene with a full range of keys that looked and felt like a real piano or organ—a truly professional instrument for the discriminating keyboardist. Many of these controllers were actually built *without* built-in sounds. If you think about it, why bother? The idea was to buy a high-quality keyboard and then use the synth modules to deliver the sounds. That way, musicians didn't have to buy new keyboards whenever they wanted new sound modules, and vice versa.

The advancements didn't stop there, though—not by a long shot. You see, MIDI is a digital language. Digital data can be recorded, stored, and recalled. That's what the first MIDI sequencers did—they were hardware devices specifically designed to be connected to a MIDI controller, capture the MIDI data as the MIDI musician plays, and then "play" that data back at the touch of a button. But that was only the beginning of the power of sequencers. Even early sequencers allowed MIDI data to be recorded at one speed and played back at another. This fact meant that a less than virtuoso keyboardist (like yours truly) could play a musical part *very* slowly, and then the tempo could be sped up upon playback.

Other features came with the birth of MIDI, like transposition (changing pitches) and individual note editing. About this time, the PC revolution was beginning to pick up speed, and computers seemed to be a perfect match for MIDI. After all, what would be better for the digital language of MIDI than the digital processing power of a PC's CPU? So, although there are still hardware MIDI sequencers to this day, a host of software MIDI sequencers are available now. Computer-based sequencers take advantage of not only the considerable resources of your computer but also the relatively large screen that you've got as well (many hardware sequencers have smaller editing windows, which can make your work go a bit slower).

Nowadays, MIDI sequencers and multitrack audio programs have combined to become the modern DAW, an integrated environment where MIDI meets digital audio. Cakewalk Home Studio, which you'll use in the next chapter, is an excellent low-cost example of such an application. Now that you understand the history of MIDI, what do you say we start learning how to use it?

The Essence of MIDI

Electricity can be sent over a number of different kinds of wires to do a wide variety of tasks. Audio going from an amplifier to a speaker is electrical, similar in many ways to data that comes through an Ethernet line to your computer's cable modem. For example, in both cases energy (specifically electricity) is traveling along the line from a source to a destination at roughly the speed of light. There are differences as well. For example, the power going from an amp to speakers is used to create analog audio and uses a specific kind of cable designed for that specific purpose. On the other hand, the electricity sent to your modem sends binary computer data along a completely different cable. Because of these differences, each type of signal is designed to work with its own specific hardware and would be virtually useless if used in any other way.

MIDI data is also a very specific kind of data, and it demands specific cabling and hardware. It is binary in nature, which means that the MIDI data stream is, at its most basic level, a string of 1s and 0s. The arrangement of these 1s and 0s determines exactly what kind of MIDI message is being sent. (There are lots of different types of MIDI messages, which we'll discuss in Chapter 5.) Sending a given MIDI message from one MIDI device to another will cause the device on the receiving end to respond in some specific way, depending on the message being sent.

MIDI data is sent as serial digital data. Serial simply means that events are happening one after the other, instead of a number of events happening together. In the case of serial binary data, that means that the 1s and 0s are sent one after the other in a stream something like this:

10011011011101001001001001001

Since data is being sent one digit at a time, all you need for data transfer is a single cable. That single cable is appropriately named a MIDI cable and is comprised of five separate connectors (see Figure 3.1).

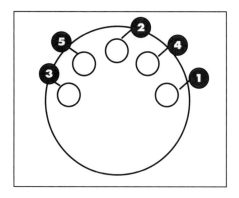

Figure 3.1

Anatomy of a MIDI cable.

1. **Pin #1:** Believe it or not, this pin isn't being used! In fact, with many MIDI cables, this pin isn't even connected to a wire. It was once thought that this pin might be used for some future improvement of the MIDI spec, but in the two decades that MIDI has been around, this hasn't happened.

2. **Pin #2:** This pin is used for shielding the MIDI cable. Basically, this shielding prevents electromagnetic interference from disrupting the MIDI data.

3. **Pin #3:** This plug is also not being used.

4. **Pin #4:** This pin provides the grounding needed by the system.

5. **Pin #5:** Finally, the pin that actually carries the DATA! Remember, because MIDI is *serial* data, all you need is one pin connected to a wire to get the job done.

❊ **NOTE**

Notice that the numbering of the pins in a MIDI cable doesn't go from left to right (or right to left for that matter), but actually skips around. This is intentional and part of the MIDI specification.

Now, given that each MIDI cable only has one cable dedicated to data transmission, it stands to reason that a single MIDI cable can only transmit data *from* one device *to* another. That's why the vast majority of MIDI gear has at least two, and sometimes three, separate MIDI ports (see Figure 3.2).

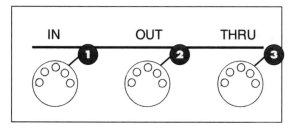

Figure 3.2

Three different kinds of MIDI ports.

1. **MIDI In:** This is the port used for bringing data into the MIDI device. This cable carries MIDI data from a MIDI controller or MIDI sequencer to the device and allows this device to be controlled from that remote device.

2. **MIDI Out:** This is the port that allows the MIDI device to *be* a controller. From the MIDI Out port, MIDI control data is sent from the MIDI device to another MIDI device or to a MIDI sequencer.

3. **MIDI Thru:** This port sends a copy of the data received at the MIDI In port to another MIDI device in a MIDI chain.

> ❄ **TIP**
>
> To see diagrams of typical MIDI configurations, see Appendix A, "Setting Up Your Studio."

> ❄ **NOTE**
>
> Important safety tip—the MIDI Thru port only sends a copy of the data received at the MIDI In port and does not transmit any of the data that is being created by the playing of the MIDI device. The performance of any given MIDI device only goes out of the MIDI Out port, not the MIDI Thru.
>
> There are exceptions to this rule that you might run into. Some manufacturers (Roland, for example) will merge the MIDI Out and Thru ports into a single plug. In these cases, the single Out/Thru port will transmit data that's being created locally on the device *and* pass on data coming in on the MIDI In port.

MIDI versus Audio

There's something that must be understood about MIDI—*MIDI ain't audio*. I know, I know, when you play a MIDI controller keyboard, you can make sounds through your MIDI modules, so it's really easy to just go ahead and assume that MIDI is some sort of audio, but that couldn't be farther from the truth. So, if MIDI isn't some sort of audio, then what *is it*?

Here's a mental picture for you that might describe what MIDI is and what it isn't. Back in the old days, there was such a thing as a player piano. You might have seen one—there are still a few around. The cool thing about these pianos was that built into the piano was a mechanism that was connected to each of the keys. This mechanism was designed to read control data that was written on a roll of paper, in the form of a sequence of punched-out holes. You would load the paper roll into this mechanism, and as the holes were read by the player piano's machinery, it pressed down the piano's keys and caused the piano to play. For its time, it was a pretty cool idea!

When thinking about a player piano, it's important to make a distinction between what is doing what. What is making the sound? Obviously, the piano is where the actual tone comes from. Where is the song? Well, that would be encoded in the holes of the piano roll. What would happen if you took a piano roll out of one piano and put it into another piano? The same song would play, but the different tone of a different piano would be heard. Bottom line: The piano role *controls* the instrument, it is *not* the instrument or the sound itself.

MIDI takes the concept of the player piano to a *way* different level. Instead of big cumbersome pianos, which can only sound like, well, pianos, we now have powerful MIDI synth modules that might have hundreds of different kinds of tones, from drums to horns to strings to sound effects. Instead of a roll of paper with holes in it, we have MIDI's digital language, which is not only more portable but more flexible.

Indeed, MIDI messages go far beyond simple musical commands to very complex and powerful operations. Great power indeed, but again—with great power comes great responsibility, in this case an understanding of MIDI messages and how they relate to music making.

Before MIDI: A Music Notation Primer

To truly understand what MIDI messages can do, you'll have to understand a little about written music. MIDI is a different way of expressing the same kinds of things that written music communicates to a live musician as he plays a piece. The only real difference between a sheet of music, a player piano roll, and a MIDI file is the kinds of instruments they control and the complexity of their instructions.

At its most basic level, MIDI does the same kind of job as a sheet of music sitting in front of a musician. In fact, it's reasonable to say that MIDI has evolved from written music. So, a basic understanding of how written music works will help you harness the power of MIDI. Don't worry—you won't have to become sight-reading fiends or be able to understand a huge orchestral score in one sitting (in fact, one big advantage of MIDI is that you *don't* have to have these skills to get the job done), but you will have to understand the most fundamental aspects of written music. With this in mind, let's take a brief journey into the fundamentals of music reading.

The first step to understanding how written music works is to understand how it deals with time.

Tempo

How fast is a song? How slow? Does the song speed up or slow down as it progresses? These are all issues of *tempo*. Tempo is how fast we count, how fast we dance, or how fast our drummer counts off a song. We measure tempo in *beats per minute*, and in a written piece of music, it looks something like this (see Figure 3.3):

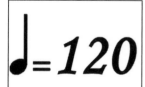

Figure 3.3
Tempo markings.

This figure shows a tempo where a quarter note, or a beat, is 120 beats per minute, which works out to two beats per second (given that there are 60 seconds in a minute), or one beat every half second. So what *is* a quarter note, or a beat for that matter?

Measures and Time Signatures

Written music is arranged in groups of beats called *measures* (or *bars*). A measure looks like this (see Figure 3.4).

Figure 3.4

A measure.

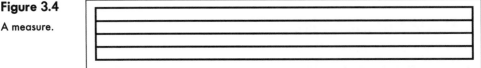

Measures are partly a convenience for the musician reading the music, but they are also a reflection of how we as humans perceive music. For example, with a typical house mix, we naturally count 1-2-3-4-1-2-3-4 and so on, and this would be said to have four beats per measure. That's where the time signature (also referred to as *meter*) comes into play. You can find the time signature at the far left-hand side of a staff of music. A time signature tells us how many beats are in a measure and what kind of note gets a beat. An average time signature might look like this (see Figure 3.5).

Figure 3.5

Time signature.

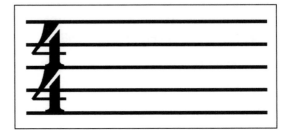

* The top number of a time signature tells the musician the number of beats per measure. In this case, there are four beats per measure.

* The bottom number tells the musician the kind of note that represents one beat. In this case, a quarter note would be played as a beat.

* To fill a 4/4 measure like the one here, you could have four quarter notes, and the bar would be completely filled (don't worry, we'll talk more about what quarter notes are in the next section).

Here's another example of a time signature that you might find in music. This one would be a good representation of a waltz time signature, and based upon what you just learned about time signatures, you should be starting to understand their meaning (see Figure 3.6).

Figure 3.6

Time signature.

1. In this case, each measure would get three beats, so if you were counting along with the music, you would count 1-2-3-1-2-3... and so on.

2. Instead of a quarter note representing a beat, an eighth note gets a beat. For example, a bar of 3/8 time could be filled with three eighth notes. You'll learn more about eighth notes later in this chapter.

> ❄ **NOTE**
>
> You'll see 4/4 time more than any other time signature, so much that it's considered the default time signature for music. It's so common that it's also known as *common time* and can be represented by a "C" where the time signature would normally be.

Notes and Pitches

After knowing the tempo and time signature of a piece of music, then we start dealing with notes, and one of the first things we need to know about notes is the duration of the note (or how long to play a single note). Different durations are represented by different types of notes, as shown below (see Figure 3.7).

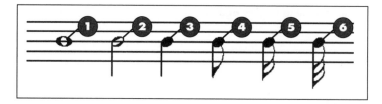

Figure 3.7

Notes of different durations.

1. **Whole Note:** A whole note must be played for four beats. So, in 4/4 time, a whole note fills an entire measure.

2. **Half Note:** Half of a whole note, a half note is held for two beats. In this time signature, two half notes can fill a measure.

3. **Quarter Note:** A quarter note gets one beat.

4. **Eighth Note:** An eighth note is played for half of one beat.

5. **Sixteenth Note:** Continuing to get briefer in duration, a sixteenth note gets a quarter of one beat.

6. **Thirty-Second Note:** At almost any tempo, even a slow one, a thirty-second note is a brief note, being held for only a eighth of one beat.

The math is pretty simple. Each note you see in the Figure 3.7 is half the duration of the note before. There are two ways to write down a note that would be held for three beats (see Figure 3.8).

Figure 3.8

Two ways to make a three-beat note.

1. A **tie** is a symbol that links the duration of more than one note. Any combination of notes can be tied. In this case, a half note (two beats) is tied to a quarter note (one beat) to make a duration of three beats.

2. A **dot** after a note adds half of that note's value. For example a dotted half note gets three beats. Any note can be dotted (for example, a dotted eighth note would get three quarters of a beat).

You can't be playing notes all through a piece of music, or it would be way too busy. Rests are symbols that tell the musician not to play for a given time, and they follow the same logic as notes (see Figure 3.9).

Figure 3.9

Rests of different durations.

1. **Whole Rest:** Do not play for four beats. Take it from me, orchestral tuba players see a *lot* of these! Get enough of these symbols in a row, and you can have a sandwich while you're waiting to play again!

2. **Half Rest:** Don't play for two beats.

3. **Quarter Rest:** A quarter rest gets one beat.

4. **Eighth Rest:** Don't play for half of one beat.

5. **Sixteenth Rest:** Don't play for a quarter of one beat.

6. **Thirty-Second Rest:** Don't play for an eighth of one beat.

Just as notes can fill up a measure, so can rests. For example, four quarter rests will fill up a measure of 4/4 time. Additionally, rests, like notes, can be dotted. For example, a dotted half rest would mean that you're not supposed to play for three beats.

But notes aren't just about duration, but pitch as well. That's where the staff comes in. A staff is a group of five horizontal lines. The position of any note on the lines or spaces of a staff determines its pitch, with notes that are positioned higher representing higher pitches. Of course, there are many more pitches than a single five-line staff can provide, so additional symbols, called *clefs*, were created. At the far left end of any staff is a clef symbol, usually either a treble clef or a bass clef. A treble clef staff can represent the higher range of notes, whereas the bass clef represents the lower pitches. The two staffs (actually the plural of staff is *staves*) can be paired together in a grand staff, which is most commonly used in piano music. Here are some illustrations of ascending series of notes on different staves (see Figures 3.10 a-c):

Figure 3.10a

Notes on a treble clef staff.

Figure 3.10b

Notes on a bass clef staff.

Figure 3.10c

Notes on a grand staff.

So far so good? There's just a bit more to talk about regarding pitch. The relationship between pitches is measured in terms of "whole steps" and "half steps." Imagine a piano's keyboard, with white keys and black keys. If you played a middle "C" (a white key) and then played the next white key to the right (a "D"), you would have moved one whole step up in pitch. Take a closer look, and you'll notice that there's a black key between the "C" and "D" keys. That key is one half step higher than "C" and one half step lower than "D," and it can be called either "C-sharp" or "D-flat." To notate a sharp note or a flat note, you'll need specific symbols, as shown in Figure 3.11.

Figure 3.11

B-flat, B-sharp, and B-natural.

1. A **flat** symbol before a note *lowers* that note by one half of a step.

2. A **sharp** symbol in front of a note *raises* that note by one half of a step.

3. A **natural** symbol specifies that the note be played *without* a flat or a sharp, as shown here.

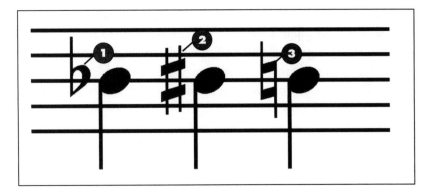

Often, in a given piece of music, a note is *always* (or almost always) going to be flatted or sharped throughout an entire piece. Instead of tons of flats and sharps cluttering up your music, here's another way to write it down, called a *key signature*. The key signature can be found at the left end of a staff, just after the clef, and just before the time signature. Here's how it looks (see Figure 3.12).

Figure 3.12

Key signature.

1. In this key signature, there's a flat symbol on the "B" line of the treble clef staff, which means that unless otherwise noted, all "Bs" will be flatted.

2. There's also a flat on the "E" space, which means that unless otherwise noted (with a natural or sharp symbol), all "Es" will be flatted.

More Expressive Notation

There are loads of other symbols that are used in music, from flowery Italian and German words for tempo changes and emotional attitudes to the strange symbols and shapes in experimental twentieth century orchestral music. Frankly, to study all of them would go beyond our purposes and take months of concentrated study. There are, however, a few more notational devices that are relevant to MIDI musicians.

Dynamic Markings

We've talked about how speed and pitches are represented in written music, but what about the loudness of the music? That's the job of dynamic markings, like the ones shown in Figure 3.13.

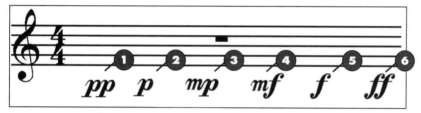

Figure 3.13

Dynamic markings.

1. **Pianissimo:** If you see this marking below a staff of music, play the music after the marking very softly.

2. **Piano:** Play softly.

3. **Mezzo** (pronounced "met-zoh") **Piano:** Play moderately softly (the softer side of medium).

4, **Mezzo Forte** (pronounced "for-tay"): Play moderately loudly (the louder side of medium).

5. **Forte:** Play loudly.

6. **Fortissimo:** Play very loudly.

As you've no doubt noticed, the piano-based dynamic markings are the softer of the dynamics, and the forte-based ones are for louder dynamics. In fact, you can make these dynamic markings even more extreme by adding more "Fs" or "Ps" (for example, three "Fs" stands for "fortississimo" or very *very* loudly). Do these distinctions seem a little open to interpretation? You bet, and that's part of the fun of reading a sheet of music. What might be soft to one musician might be medium loud to another.

Here are a few more dynamic-related symbols (see Figure 3.14).

Figure 3.14

Crescendo and decrescendo.

1. **Crescendo:** This symbol is used to show a gradual transition from a softer dynamic to a louder one (for example, from piano to forte).

2. **Decrescendo:** As the name and the shape would suggest, this does the opposite of a crescendo—a transition from a louder dynamic level to a softer one.

❄ **TIP**

There's another thing to keep in mind when talking about dynamic markings, and it involves going into the mindset of an instrumentalist, let's say a drummer. Let's say that you get a piece of music that starts off with a piano dynamic marking. No problem, you'll just play softly and quietly. Halfway through the piece, the dynamic marking changes to fortissimo. Wow, now you start playing loudly! What happens when you make this change? Well, for one thing you'll wind up using more force to strike the drum, which will raise the volume. There's a secondary effect, though, which is a change in the sound quality (or *timbre*) of the instrument.

So, in this example, the drum's volume will not only increase, but the tonal color of the instrument will be transformed as the instrument is played louder. Now, let's say that you record this drum piece, make a CD, and play it on your stereo. You play with the volume a bit to get a good comfortable level of sound (but not too loud—you need to protect your ears!). Now think about what volume is doing. If you simply change the volume during playback, does it affect the timbre of the instrument in the same way as a drummer playing louder or softer?

Truth is, raising or lowering the volume will have very little effect on the timbre of the music that was recorded. Crank up a drum played at pianissimo, and what you'll hear are the tonal qualities of a softly played drum, but at a higher volume. Conversely, if you record a drummer kicking out a fortissimo beat but then turn the volume way down, then you'll hear all the energy of a drum set really being banged on, but at a very low amplitude. Here's the bottom line: The velocity at which the musical instrument was struck is not exactly the same as the volume at which it was played.

More Articulation Markings

Here are a few more commonly found markings. These particular markings deal with how a note is articulated, or attacked. These markings determine how forcefully an individual note is to be played (see Figure 3.15).

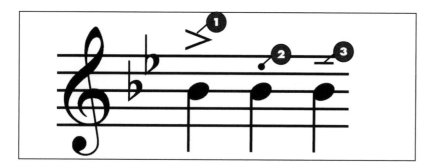

Figure 3.15

Accent, staccato, and legato notes.

1. **Accent:** Play this note with a more forceful attack than normal. In this example, the first note will be played more aggressively than the others.

2. **Staccato:** Play this note shorter than its written value. In this example, the value of the quarter notes will be slightly cheated, resulting in a small amount of space between the notes.

3. **Legato:** Play this note at full length and with a very soft attack.

Sometimes, a note is actually not articulated at all, as in these two cases (see Figure 3.16).

Figure 3.16

Slur and glissando.

1. **Slur:** A smooth transition from one pitch to another without reattacking the note.

2. **Glissando:** This cool little symbol tells the musician to smoothly bend the pitch from one note to another.

❋ **NOTE**

You might wonder why you need to understand written music if you're not going to be working on a computer. Consider this—there is often a staff window in many MIDI sequencers, and even a basic understanding of written music will help you use that window. Also, as you dig deeper, you'll see that much of the MIDI language is based upon the same ideas as written music, and understanding this written form will help you use this more virtual, electronic musical language.

Next, you'll learn the basic operations of a MIDI application, and you'll begin to see how these basic musical aspects have been implemented in the MIDI language.

4 Exercise 1: Getting Started with MIDI

Now comes the beginning of the payoff. You've taken the time to learn what MIDI is, what it does, and how it works. You've given yourself a solid understanding of the job that MIDI is designed to do, and later you'll get a comprehensive look at the MIDI language and the messages that it uses. Now you'll see MIDI in action. In this chapter, you'll learn:

* ❋ How to set up your MIDI software and hardware.
* ❋ How to set up and play a MIDI file.
* ❋ How to save your work.

Getting Started

The first thing you'll have to do with any MIDI application is set it up to be used with your system. After that's squared away, you can focus on the task of opening a song and playing it. Pretty straightforward stuff, but there are sometimes a few issues that need to be ironed out to make the song sound right.

❄ **NOTE**

Perhaps the most important goal of this course is to learn how different applications work and see the similarities between them. By comparing different applications side-by-side, you'll see how their organization and ways of dealing with data are similar and how they differ. For this exercise, we'll be using two applications. First, we'll use Cakewalk Home Studio 2 by Twelve Tone systems. This is a solid introductory package, loaded with useful features, but it won't break the bank. We'll also take a look at a very useful and budget-friendly application called Quartz AudioMaster Freeware 4.6 by Digital Sound Planet. This program is also very useful and has a couple of unique features.

Each task in this exercise will be broken down into two sections, each devoted to getting the job done in each application. For consistency's sake, I'll go through the procedures in the Home Studio software first and the Quartz AudioMaster second. This isn't to imply that the Quartz software is an afterthought at all, but because it is freeware, it sometimes has a few limitations that the Cakewalk software doesn't.

If you are only using one of these applications, that's no problem—just skip the sections that refer to the application you're not using. Also, if you want to go from start to finish with each of the applications, just go through the chapter following just one application and then start again with the other.

As for software synthesizers, we'll use the Virtual Sound Canvas 3.2 by Roland. This General MIDI–compatible soft synth has a powerful combination of solid sound quality and a General MIDI patch list. The sound quality of this application goes well beyond most sound cards. However, if your sound card supports General MIDI, getting this software synth is optional.

Before you continue with this exercise, you should consider installing these applications. The installation of all these applications is very straightforward. After you've finished loading the applications you choose (which should only take a few minutes each), you'll be all set to continue.

Setting Up Your Hardware

After you've installed your software, the next order of business is to set it up to work with your hardware. Luckily, Windows XP does much of the work for you, and as long as you've got the drivers for your sound card and MIDI interface installed, the process is pretty easy.

❄ **NOTE**

In order to get MIDI into and out of your system, you'll need a MIDI interface. Don't worry—they don't have to be expensive. Learn more about what MIDI interfaces do, what to look for in a MIDI interface, and how to connect them to your computer by referring to Appendix A, "Setting Up Your Studio."

Using Cakewalk Home Studio

The first thing is to choose your audio outputs, so you can hear your music (see Figure 4.1).

❋ **NOTE**

If this is the first time you've launched Cakewalk Home Studio, you'll notice that a number of driver and registration dialog windows appear. Just click "OK" or "Yes" to these dialogs, and you'll be on your way!

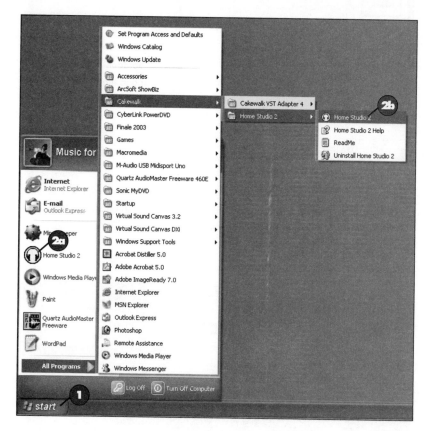

Figure 4.1

1. **Click** the **Start** button.

2a. **Click** the **Home Studio 2** icon to launch the application, or

2b. **Click** the **All Programs** arrow, **choose** the **Cakewalk** folder, then **choose** the **Home Studio 2** folder, and finally **click** the **Home Studio 2** icon.

Either way, the software will launch. You'll see a "tip of the day" window, which is always good for learning new ways to work. After that, you'll see "No MIDI Outputs Selected" and "No MIDI Inputs Selected" windows. Just choose the Continue button for each of these windows, and you'll see a blank project window, looking like Figure 4.2.

Figure 4.2

3. **Click** the **Close** button because you're not ready to work with a project yet (see Figure 4.3).

Figure 4.3

4. **Click** the **Options** drop-down menu.

5. **Click** the **Audio** menu option. The Audio Options window will appear (see Figure 4.4).

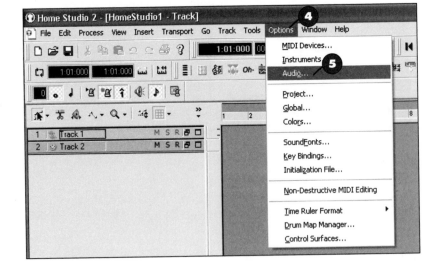

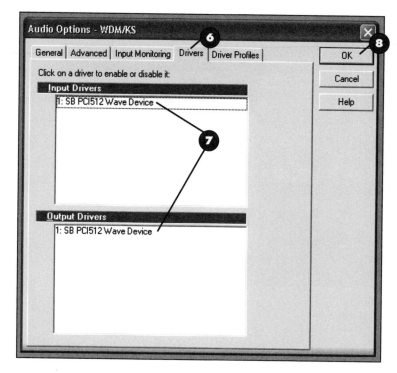

Figure 4.4

6. **Click** the **Drivers** tab. The Drivers page will be shown, as you see here.

   The list of drivers (both input and output) reflects the audio hardware you have installed in your system. If you have installed an audio interface, it will appear here, and if you have multiple audio input and output devices, they will form a list in their respective boxes.

7. If they're not already selected, **click** the **audio** devices that you want to use. In this case, clicking the "SB PCI512 Wave Device" (which in this case represents a SoundBlaster sound card) in each list will allow recording and playback using this device.

8. **Click OK.** A dialog box will appear, telling you that your changes won't take effect until you re-launch the program. You may do that now if you want or continue setting up your MIDI gear and restart after that.

❈ **NOTE**

Not sure whether you have an audio interface or not? Learn more about sound cards and audio interfaces by reading Appendix A, "Setting Up Your Studio."

❈ **NOTE**

Actually, setting up your audio hardware will have no real effect on the software's ability to control and record MIDI. It will, however, allow you to hear any digital audio that you might want to use later in your project. Since most DAW workstations support MIDI and audio, it's generally best to set everything up now in this beginning stage, so you don't have to worry about it later when you start working with audio.

Figure 4.5

1. **Click** the **Options** drop-down menu.

2. **Click** the **MIDI Devices** option. The MIDI Devices window will appear.

   The MIDI Devices window does much the same job as the Audio Options window, but this time you'll be deciding which MIDI devices you want to use. This window gives a bit of insight as to what's connected to your system (see Figure 4.6).

Figure 4.6

a. In the Inputs window, you'll see all the possible ways to get MIDI into this particular computer. The "in USB MIDI 1x1" is an M-Audio MIDI interface (connected to a MIDI keyboard), and the "SB PCI512 MIDI UART" refers to the MIDI input of a SoundBlaster sound card.

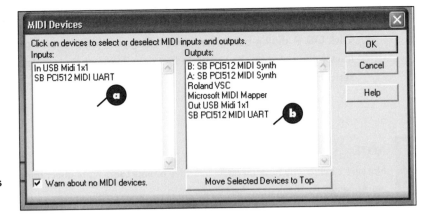

b. The Outputs window shows the possible places MIDI data could be sent in this particular system. To start, there are two SoundBlaster synth engines (named "SB PCI512 MIDI Synth") built into a sound card. Next, there's a Roland VSC (Virtual Sound Canvas) software synth. The Microsoft MIDI Mapper is built into Windows XP. An M-Audio MIDI interface appears as "Out USB MIDI 1x1," and last there's a MIDI output plug on a SoundBlaster card ("SB PCI512 MIDI UART"). See Figure 4.7.

> **NOTE**
>
> The devices listed in the MIDI and Audio Devices windows will vary, depending upon what hardware and software are in your individual system. In these figures, you're seeing the devices attached to my PC.

> **NOTE**
>
> While SoundBlaster sound cards have the ability to send and receive MIDI data, the cards themselves have no MIDI plugs. You can add MIDI In and Out plugs to your sound card by picking up a MIDI adapter (available at most music stores).

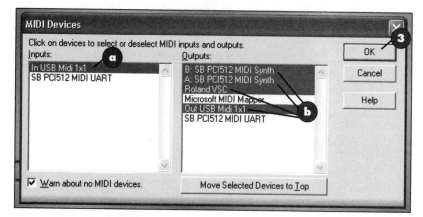

Figure 4.7

3. The task at this point is to choose the MIDI devices that you want to use in your system. All that needs to be done is to **click** on the **devices** you want to use (they will be shown highlighted). Then just **click** the OK button.

For this particular system, here are my choices and why:

a. For Inputs, I chose the M-Audio MIDI interface MIDI In port (which shows up in the list as "In USB MIDI 1x1"). This port will receive MIDI data from my controller keyboard. Since I don't have the adapter cable to give me a MIDI Out port from my SoundBlaster card, I didn't choose it.

b. As far as **Outputs** go, I chose the two SoundBlaster synths, as well as the Virtual Sound Canvas (I generally prefer the Sound Canvas sounds, but there's no real reason *not* to include the SoundBlaster synths). Just in case I decide to add an external MIDI device to my system, I'll also choose the M-Audio MIDI output ("Out USB MIDI 1x1"). Again, since I haven't got the SoundBlaster MIDI adapter to give the sound card a MIDI Out port, I didn't include it on the list.

There's a little more customization that you can do in Cakewalk Home Studio. You can give the Home Studio software specific details about individual MIDI devices in your system. For example, you can tell Cakewalk Home Studio that a synth is General MIDI compatible. Once the software knows this, notes, patches, and even controllers can be arranged to suit the instrument you're using. This is really only a convenience to you, but as far as conveniences go, it's a nice one. Here's an example—let's configure the Roland Virtual Sound Canvas as a General MIDI instrument (see Figure 4.8).

❅ **NOTE**

You'll learn more about what General MIDI is and how it can be used in Chapter 7.

❅ **CAUTION**

To make this sort of configuration work, you have to make sure that you know your MIDI instrument's setup. Setting up the Virtual Sound Canvas as a General MIDI instrument works only because the Virtual Sound Canvas *is* a General MIDI instrument. Configuring it as anything other than what it is only causes confusion down the line.

Figure 4.8

1. **Click** the **Options** drop-down menu.

2. **Click** the **Instruments** option. The Assign Instruments window will appear (see Figure 4.9).

Figure 4.9

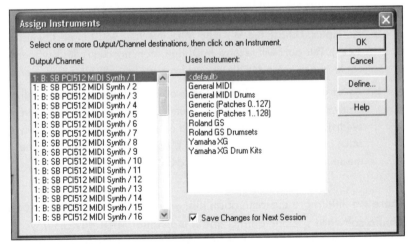

This window is an extension of the choices you made when you selected your MIDI devices. Each device shows up in the left-hand window, broken out to each of the 16 MIDI channels in the MIDI language (MIDI channels are a way of organizing MIDI messages, which you'll learn about in Chapter 7). On the right-hand side are the different ways of arranging instruments or sounds. You'll see many of the common ways of arranging these sounds. For your purposes, you'll continue to set up the Roland Virtual Sound Canvas as a General MIDI instrument (see Figure 4.10).

❋ **TIP**

In Chapter 5, you'll learn that some devices count their patches from 0 to 127, while other count from 1 to 128. Be sure to check your synth's documentation before you choose either of the generic patch numbers, or you could wind up choosing sounds that are always one patch off from the patch you really want.

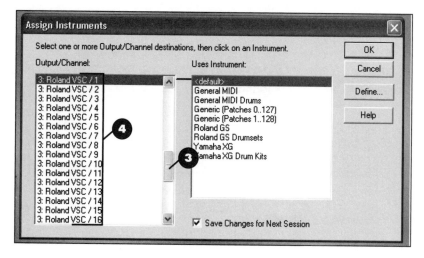

Figure 4.10

3. **Scroll** (using the scroll bar or arrow keys) to the **instrument** you want to set up. In this case, you're setting up the Virtual Sound Canvas.

4. **Click** on **Roland VSC/1**; then **hold down** the **Shift** key as you click on Roland VSC/16 to select all 16 VSC channels. When you're done, the screen should look like Figure 4.11.

Figure 4.11

5. To set the entire 16 MIDI channels of the Virtual Sound Canvas at one time, simply **click** the **General MIDI** option in the Uses Instrument area. Now the Virtual Sound Canvas is identified as a General MIDI synth.

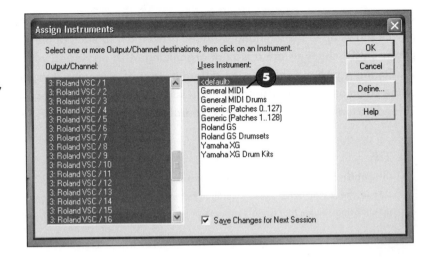

MIDI channel #10 is reserved for drums in the General MIDI spec, so change the Virtual Sound Canvas on MIDI channel #10 only (see Figure 4.12).

Figure 4.12

6. **Click** the **specific device** *and* **channel** you want to configure (in this case "3: Roland VSC/10"). The single item will be highlighted on the list.

7. **Select** the **instrument set** that you want to assign to this specific MIDI device and channel. In this case, you're telling Cakewalk that the Roland Virtual Sound Canvas is a General MIDI Drums device.

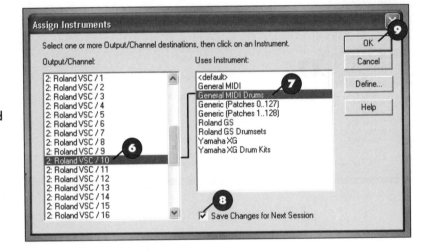

8. Make sure that you **check** the **Save Changes for Next Session** box, so that Cakewalk will remember these settings from session to session, and you don't have to redo these configurations every time.

9. When you're done, **click OK**.

❊ **TIP**

This is an example of how to set up a single MIDI device, but as your MIDI setup grows and you add more gear, you should consider setting up all of your devices. This little bit of preparation will make the process of production go much smoother over the long run.

Using Quartz AudioMaster Freeware

Setting up audio and MIDI in AudioMaster bears some striking similarities to Cakewalk Home Studio. The only real difference lies in the amount of power that you'll have with this freeware application (you'll get the same things as Home Studio, just less of it). Take a look at Figure 4.13.

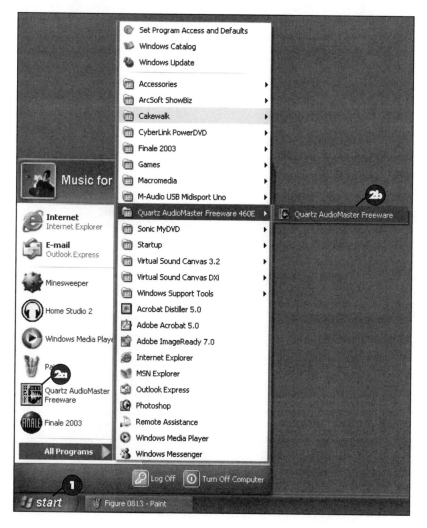

Figure 4.13

1. **Click** the **Start** button.

2a.**Click** the **Quartz AudioMaster Freeware** icon to launch the application, or...

2b.**Click** the **All Programs** arrow, **choose** the **Quartz AudioMaster Freeware 460E** folder, and then **click** the **Quartz AudioMaster Freeware** icon.

Either way, AudioMaster will be launched, and you'll see the application's window, as shown in Figure 4.14. Start out by setting up your audio devices.

Figure 4.14

3. If this window comes up, just **choose Continue**, which will let you set up your system (see Figure 4.15).

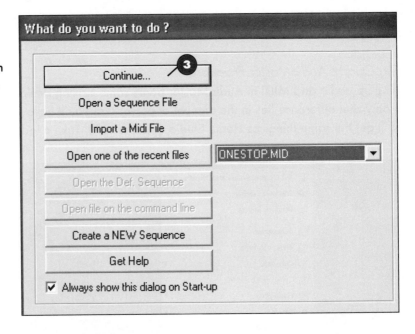

Figure 4.15

4. **Click** the **Options** drop-down menu (sound familiar?).

5. **Choose** the **Audio Devices** option. The Options (Audio Devices) window will appear (see Figure 4.16).

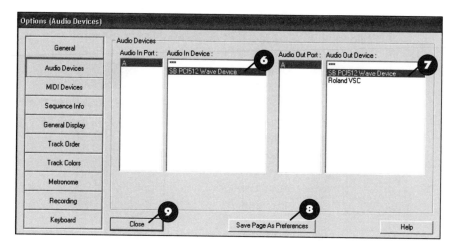

Figure 4.16

6. **Click** the **device** in the Audio In Device window that you want to use as your recording source. In this system, since I'll be recording through my sound card, I've chosen "SB PCI512 Wave Device" (the driver for my SoundBlaster sound card). The devices you see listed on your computer will reflect the audio hardware in your own system.

7. **Click** the **device** in the Audio Out Device window that you want to connect to your monitor speakers to hear your music. In this system, the sound card will be used for that as well, so the "SB PCI512 Wave Device" is chosen here.

8. To save your settings for future sessions, **click** the **Save Page As Preferences** button.

9. **Click** the **Close** button, and you're done.

❄ **NOTE**

The AudioMaster Freeware only supports one audio input device and one audio output device and a maximum of two channels. That means that if you have an audio interface *and* a sound card, you'll have to choose only one of them. Upgrading to the project version of the software will give you double the inputs and outputs, and the professional version will give you up to 32 channels of input and output. You can explore the different versions of AudioMaster on the manufacturer's Web site: www.digitalsoundplanet.com.

Now let's take a look at setting up your MIDI gear (see Figure 4.17).

Figure 4.17

1. **Click** the **Options** drop-down menu.

2. **Click** the **MIDI Devices** option. The Options (MIDI Devices) window will appear (see Figure 4.18).

Figure 4.18

3. Just as you did with Cakewalk Home Studio, **choose** your MIDI interface's **input port** to let the software know where MIDI data will be coming from. Just **click** the **device** you want to use. The selected device will be highlighted. Since

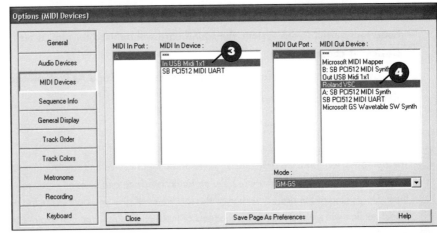

this figure shows my computer's hardware, I'm choosing the MIDI In port of my M-Audio USB MIDI interface.

4. **Click** the **device** you want to use to receive MIDI information. In this figure, I've chosen the Roland VSC (Virtual Sound Canvas).

❄ **NOTE**

Again, you'll encounter a limitation of the AudioMaster Freeware. You can only set up one MIDI input and output device at a time. Again, upgrading improves the situation. Until then, you can use one device at a time (if you want to change the synth you're using, all you need to do is go back to this window and change the MIDI output device).

After you've selected the MIDI out device, you can tell the AudioMaster software what kind of synth it is by selecting a mode (see Figure 4.19), just as you chose instruments in the Cakewalk software earlier.

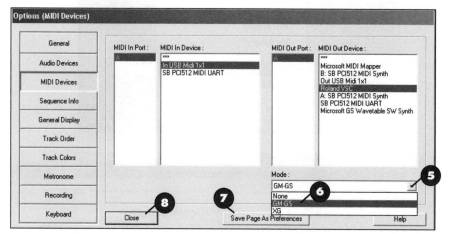

Figure 4.19

5. **Click** the **arrow button** to the right of the Mode window to reveal a drop-down list of the possible options.

6. **Click** the **mode** that best matches your instrument. Since the Sound Canvas operates as a General MIDI synth, choose the GM-GS option ("GM" standing for General MIDI).

7. After you're done, **click** the **Save Page as Preferences** button to save your setup for future work.

8. **Click** the **Close** button, and you're finished.

❄ **NOTE**

The Mode feature in AudioMaster does much the same job as the Instruments window did in Cakewalk Home Studio. By identifying the Sound Canvas as a GM synth, AudioMaster can now give more descriptive patch names.

Even though you've set a mode for your device, you can tweak it even further. Here's how you might set up the Sound Canvas to be seen as a General MIDI Drum device on channel #10 (see Figure 4.20).

Figure 4.20

1. **Click** the **Options** drop-down menu.

2. **Click** the **Sound Names** option. The Sound Names window will open (see Figure 4.21).

Figure 4.21

a. This drop-down list shows the possible configurations for each device and channel in your setup.

b. This drop-down list identifies the device and channel to be configured. Since this version of the software only supports one device, the list will only show A01 through A16 (16 MIDI channels). You'll be setting up A10 only (see Figure 4.22).

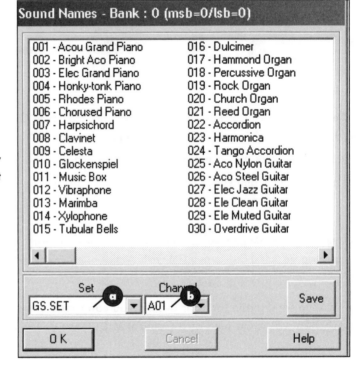

NOTE

Since you've already set up the Virtual Sound Canvas as a GM/GS device, all MIDI channels are set to the GS configuration.

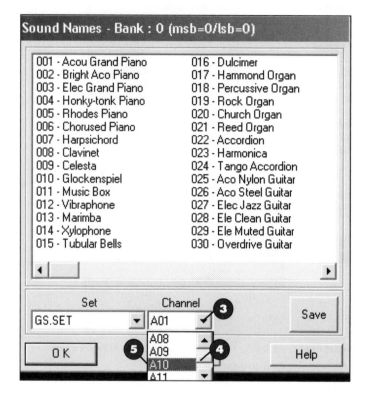

Figure 4.22

3. **Click** the **Channel** arrow button to reveal the Channel drop-down menu.

4. Using the scroll bar or arrow keys, **navigate** to the **desired MIDI channel** (in this case, it's MIDI channel #10).

5. **Click** the **MIDI channel** you want. The drop-down menu will close, and the channel will be selected (see Figure 4.23).

Figure 4.23

6. **Click** the **Set** arrow button to reveal the Set drop-down menu.

7. Using the scroll bar or arrow keys, **navigate** to the **desired patch set**. In this instance, it's "GMDRUM.SET"–General MIDI drums (which might already be selected, depending on your system).

8. **Click** the **desired set**. The drop-down menu will close, and the set will be selected.

9. **Click** the **OK** button to confirm your settings and close the window.

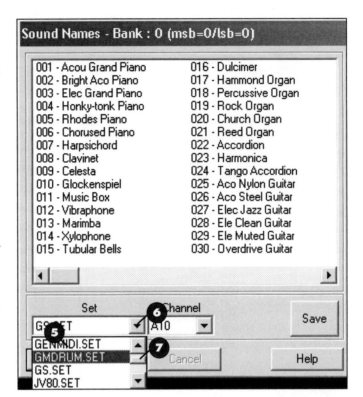

Sound Names - Bank : 0 (msb=0/lsb=0)

001 - Acou Grand Piano	016 - Dulcimer
002 - Bright Aco Piano	017 - Hammond Organ
003 - Elec Grand Piano	018 - Percussive Organ
004 - Honky-tonk Piano	019 - Rock Organ
005 - Rhodes Piano	020 - Church Organ
006 - Chorused Piano	021 - Reed Organ
007 - Harpsichord	022 - Accordion
008 - Clavinet	023 - Harmonica
009 - Celesta	024 - Tango Accordion
010 - Glockenspiel	025 - Aco Nylon Guitar
011 - Music Box	026 - Aco Steel Guitar
012 - Vibraphone	027 - Elec Jazz Guitar
013 - Marimba	028 - Ele Clean Guitar
014 - Xylophone	029 - Ele Muted Guitar
015 - Tubular Bells	030 - Overdrive Guitar

Set   Channel

GS.SET   A10   Save

GENMIDI.SET
GMDRUM.SET   Cancel
GS.SET
JV80.SET   Help

TIP

Take a second to explore the other options in the Set drop-down menu. You'll see a wide variety of synthesizers specifically supported by AudioMaster, beyond the most standard configurations.

There's a little more configuration to do with AudioMaster. You might have noticed that the program window opens a little small on your desktop (depending on your screen resolution), as shown in Figure 4.24. Making your production desktop user friendly will help you work more efficiently, and it's best to take care of such things before settling down to work, so let's do the job now.

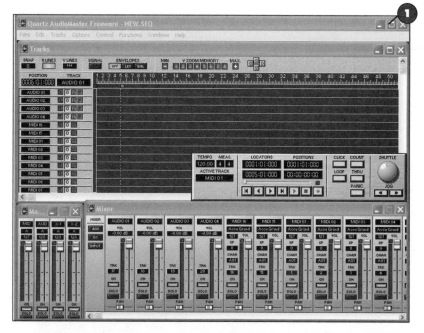

Figure 4.24

1. **Click** the **window maximize** button in the upper right-hand area of the window. Although the window expands to cover your entire desktop, the arrangement of windows in the application does not change.

2. **Click** and **drag** your **windows** to maximize the desk space available. There are no set rules for this, and it really comes down to personal preference, but here are some guidelines:

   ❄ You'll do most of your initial work in the Track view, so it's common to give the Track window the majority of real estate on your desktop.

   ❄ Seeing many tracks in your Mixer window will allow you to see more of your mix at one time and minimize the need for scrolling. So, making your mixer as wide as possible is generally a good idea, when possible.

   ❄ Other windows, like the piano roll, staff, or MIDI event list, may suit your individual writing style. You can arrange these now so that they become a default whenever the program is opened, or you can just open them whenever your project needs them.

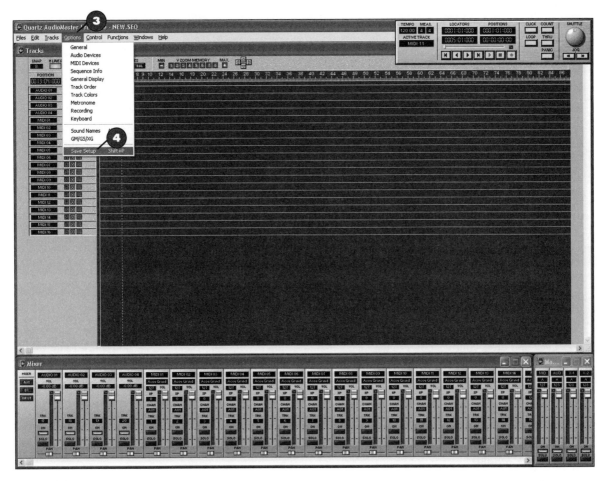

Figure 4.25

3. When your windows are arranged to suit your taste, it's time to save them for future sessions (you don't want to have to do *this* every time you open the software!). **Click** the **Options** drop-down menu.

4. **Click** the **Save Setup** option. The Save Setup window will open (see Figure 4.26).

When you're done, your desktop might look like Figure 4.25.

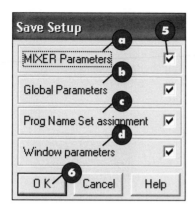

Figure 4.26

This window saves different aspects of your setup as program defaults:

a. **Mixer Parameters:** Saves pan, volume, and other mixer information.

b. **Global Parameters:** Saves your audio and MIDI device setup, as well as recording setups such as click track settings (see Chapter 10).

c. **Prog Name Set Assignment:** Makes the current settings in the Sound Names window (which you just set up) the default for the program.

d. **Window Parameters:** Saves your current desktop setup and maintains the window's position and sizing.

5. **Click** in the **appropriate check box** to enable the options you want to make program defaults (at this point, it doesn't hurt to have them all checked).

6. **Click OK.** Next time, AudioMaster will open up as you see it now.

❋ TIP

One of the cool things about working with a computer is that rarely is anything permanent. If any of these settings needs to be changed in the future, just make the changes, and go through the Save Setup procedure again. What could be easier?

Opening a File

Now that you've set up your system, the next step is to get to work. To get started a little quicker, I've included a standard MIDI file on the CD-ROM with this book. Imagine that we're working together on a project, and I've just handed off a musical idea for you to run with (actually, some of the tracks in this MIDI file *are* from some of my past projects, so this isn't too far from the truth!). I've gotta warn you, though. This file is far from complete, and there are some specific problems that I've built into it that must be solved before it sounds good, so you've got your work cut out for you! Let's start by just opening the file.

Using Cakewalk Home Studio

If Cakewalk Home Studio has not been launched, do the following:

1. **Launch** the **Cakewalk Home Studio application**. The application will be launched with the Quick Start window visible (see Figure 4.27).

Figure 4.27

2. **Click** the **Open a Project** button. The Open window will appear (see Figure 4.28).

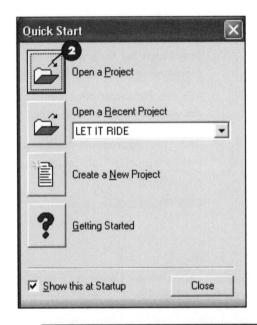

Figure 4.28

3. **Navigate** to your **CD-ROM drive**; then **open** the **Exercise** folder, and finally **open** the **Ex_01** folder.

4. **Click** the **file** named Ex_01 (this file may be listed as Ex_01.mid, depending on your computer's setup).

5. **Click** the **Open** button. The MIDI file will be opened by Cakewalk Home Studio.

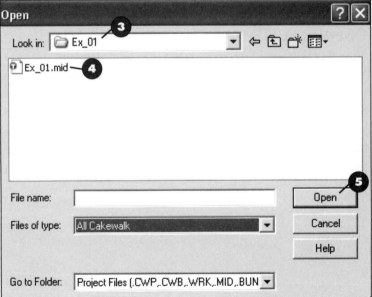

If Cakewalk Home Studio is already active, follow these steps:

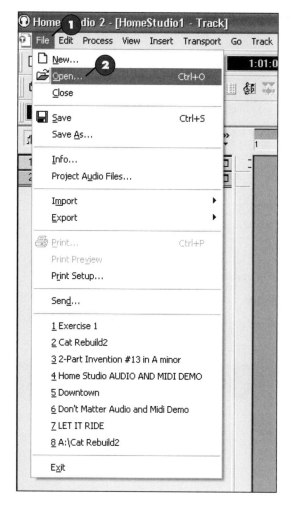

Figure 4.29

1. **Click** the **File** drop-down menu.

2. **Click** the **Open** menu item.

3. The Open window will appear. You can locate and open standard MIDI file Ex_01 according to Steps 3–5 of the preceding procedure.

Using Quartz AudioMaster Freeware

If AudioMaster has not been launched:

1. **Launch** the **AudioMaster application**. The application will be launched with the "What do you want to do?" window visible (see Figure 4.30).

Figure 4.30

2. **Click** the **Import a Midi File** button. The Import Midifile window will appear (see Figure 4.31).

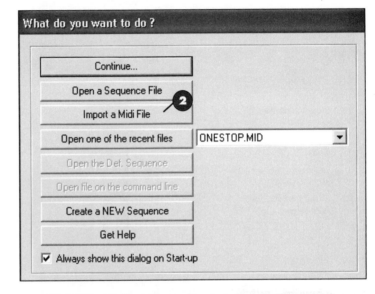

Figure 4.31

This window works like the Open window in Cakewalk Home Studio. In fact, virtually every Windows-based program uses a window like this (under different names, perhaps) to open files.

3. **Navigate** to your **CD-ROM drive**. **Open** the **Exercise** folder and then **open** the **Ex_01** folder.

4. **Click** the **file** named Ex_01 (or Ex_01.mid, depending on your computer's setup).

5. **Click** the **Open** button. The MIDI file will be opened by AudioMaster.

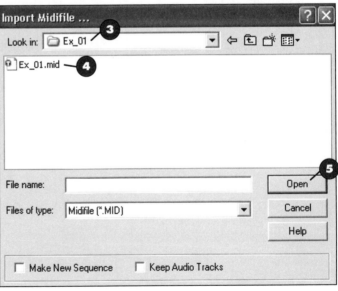

If AudioMaster is already active, follow these steps (see Figure 4.32):

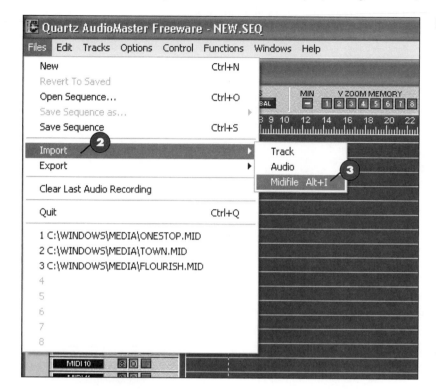

Figure 4.32

1. **Click** the **Files** drop-down menu.

2. **Click** the **Import** menu item. A secondary list will open to the right, showing the different types of files that can be imported.

3. **Click** the **Midifile** menu item. The Import Midifile window will open. You can locate and open the standard MIDI file Ex_01 according to Steps 3–5 of the preceding procedure.

Playing a MIDI File

After you've opened the file, playing the file is a pretty simple matter.

> **NOTE**
>
> You'll notice that this file doesn't sound quite right. For starters, all of the notes are being played by the same instrument, and there are timing and pitch problems. Don't worry because you'll fix all of this beginning with the second exercise. For now, just make sure that you hear something and can control playback.

Using Cakewalk Home Studio:

After you've opened the file, you'll see a screen that looks like Figure 4.33.

Figure 4.33

a. Each horizontal strip, called a *track*, represents a different musical part.

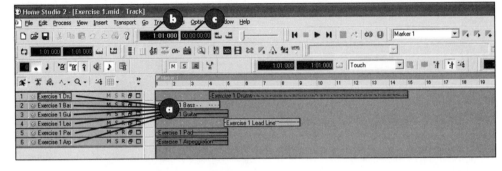

b. There are two windows that will tell you where you are in your music. This window measures time in Bars:Beats:Ticks.

c. This window measures time in Hours:Minutes:Seconds:Frames (subdivisions of a second).

> ※ **NOTE**
>
> Frames, the subdivisions of a second, are part of SMPTE (which stands for the Society of Motion Picture and Television Editors) time code. This form of time code is often used when aligning audio and video (or film). There are many different frame rates (different ways of dividing a second) for different kinds of applications. For now, you don't need to concern yourself with those frame rates, and you can use this SMPTE display to tell where you are in time.

There are a few different ways to hear your music (see Figure 4.34).

Figure 4.34

a. **Click** the **Play** button, or

b. **Click** the **Transport** drop-down menu and **click** the **Play** menu item, or

c. **Press** the **spacebar** on your computer keyboard.

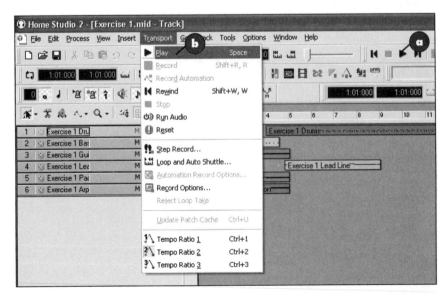

Here's what you'll see when playback starts (see Figure 4.35).

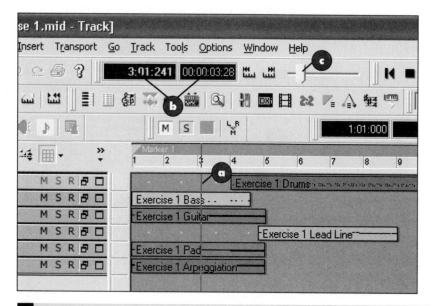

Figure 4.35

a. The play line will move from left to right as the session plays.

b. The counter windows will mark the times as it passes.

c. The location slider will move from left to right.

> ❋ **NOTE**
>
> Don't worry if the song doesn't sound right, you'll tackle that next!

Here are some other ways to navigate around your song (see Figure 4.36).

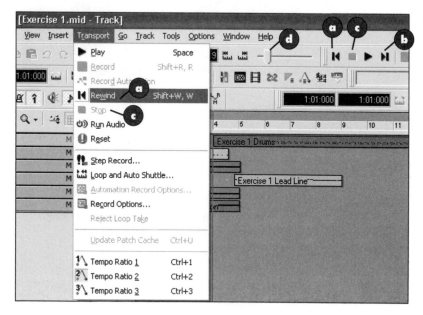

Figure 4.36

a. **Rewind** goes to the beginning of your song.

b. **Go to End** goes to the end of your song.

c. **Stop.** No, I'm not gonna tell you, you have to guess. . .

d. Dragging the location slider moves the play line proportionally.

Very often, you might want to play a section of your song over and over again, to work on it specifically. This sort of playback is called *loop playback*. Making loop playback work is a two-step process: First, you have to define *what* you want to loop; then you have to enable loop playback. Here's how to do it in Home Studio.

Figure 4.37

There are a number of ways to set your loop. Here's one way:

1. **Click** and **drag** with your cursor to select an area on the timeline.

2. **Click** the **Set Loop to Selection** button. Your selection will be captured.

3. The Loop On/Off button will be automatically engaged. You're ready to start loop playback.

Here's another way to go (see Figure 4.38).

Figure 4.38

1. **Position** your **play line** where you want to start your loop.

2. **Click** the **Set From = Now** button to capture the position of the From window to the right of the button.

3. **Position** your **play line** where you want your loop to end.

4. **Click** the **Set Thru = Now** button to capture the position to the **Thru** window to the left of the button.

   The two windows represent the beginning and end of your selection. As soon as you set the two points, the corresponding area on the timeline will be selected.

5. **Click** the **Set Loop to Selection** button. Your selection will be captured.

6. The Loop On/Off button will be automatically engaged.

❋ **TIP**

You can type locations directly into the location in the From and Thru windows. Remember to press the Enter key after you set your values to enter them.

And yet another way (see Figure 4.39).

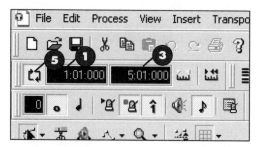

Figure 4.39

1. **Type** the **desired point** for the beginning of your loop into the Loop Start window.

2. **Press** the Enter key to confirm the value.

3. **Type** the **desired point** for the end of your loop into the **Loop End** window.

4. **Press** the Enter key to confirm the value.

5. After your start and end points are set, **click** on the **Loop On/Off** button to set yourself up for loop playback!

Once you've set yourself up for loop playback (using any one of these three methods), all that remains is to start playback. Just click the Play button (or press the spacebar) to start playing. You'll notice that the selection repeats over and over, giving you the opportunity to listen critically without having to start and stop every time you want to listen to the section.

Using Quartz AudioMaster Freeware

The good new is that all the features in Home Studio can be found in AudioMaster, but you've got to hunt them down a bit. The key is in the Control window (many software applications would call it the *Transport window*). Take a look at Figure 4.40.

Figure 4.40

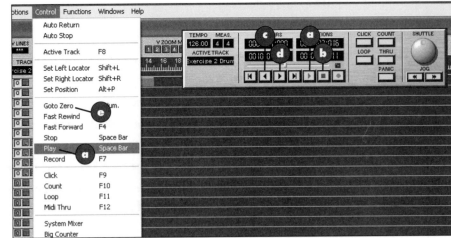

a. **Play** (pressing the spacebar also starts playback in this program).

b. **Stop** (pressing the spacebar will stop playback).

c. **Rewind** moves the play line quickly backward (no playback).

d. **Forward** moves the play line quickly forward (no playback).

e. **Goto Zero** moves the play line to the beginning of the song (this can also be done by pressing the zero key on the numeric keypad).

Figure 4.41

a. Moves the play line to the **Left Locator**.

b. Moves the play line to the **Right Locator**.

c. Displays the position of the **Left Locator**.

d. Displays the position of the **Right Locator**.

e. Displays the current play line location in **Bars:Beats:Ticks**.

f. Displays the current play line location in **Hours:Minutes:Seconds:Frames**.

So what's the significance of the left and right locators, and how can we change them? In addition to being quick go-to points, the left locator and right locator serve as the boundaries for the loop play-back feature (see Figure 4.42).

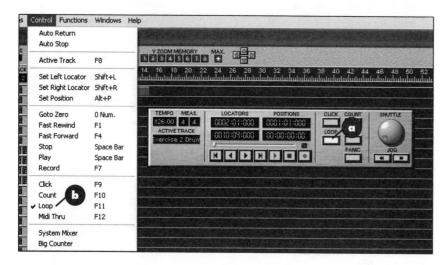

Figure 4.42

a. To enable loop play-back, **click** the **Loop** but-ton on the Control window, or

b. **Click** the **Loop** item on the Control drop-down menu (the shortcut key is F11).

After loop playback is enabled, starting playback will begin an infinite repetition between the left and right location points (until you hit stop, or until your parents go crazy). In this figure, looping will occur between 0002:01:000 (bar 2, beat 1, tick 0) and 0010:04:000 (bar 10, beat 4, tick 0). There are a few different ways to change these location times (see Figure 4.43).

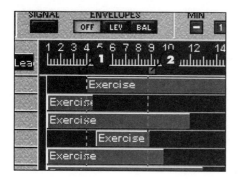

Figure 4.43

1. **Click** and **drag** the **blue marker** just below the timeline to change the left locater position (this will determine where your loop playback will start).

2. **Click** and **drag** the **red marker** to change the right locator posi-tion (which will set where your loop will end).

Here's another way to set your location points (see Figure 4.44).

Figure 4.44

1. **Click** in either the **left** or **right locator display** in the control window (depending on which location you want to set). A location window will appear.

2. **Type** the **desired time** (in bars, beats, and ticks) for the locator (left or right, depending on which display you clicked).

3. **Click OK**.

And yet another way to set location points (see Figure 4.45).

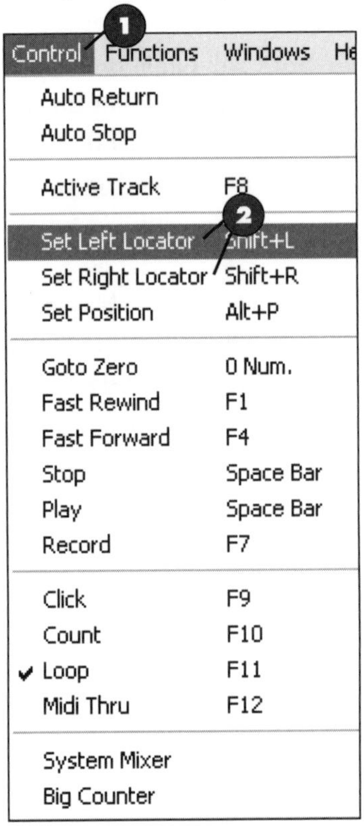

Figure 4.45

1. **Click** the **Control** drop-down menu.

2. **Click** either the **Set Left Locator** or **Set Right Locator** menu item, depending on which location you want to set. A familiar-looking window will appear (see Figure 4.46).

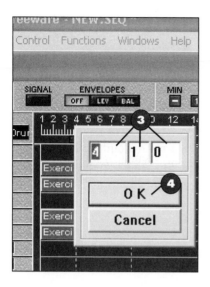

Figure 4.46

3. **Type** the **desired time** (in bars, beats, and ticks) for the locator (left or right, depending on which display you clicked).

4. **Click OK.**

Once that's done, you need to enable loop playback (either from the control window or the Control drop-down menu, as described earlier in this section). When you start playback, the time between the left and right locators will loop infinitely (until you stop playback). As you can see, the features of Home Studio and AudioMaster bear a great deal of similarity, although the means to get to those features differs just a little.

Let's take just one more look at AudioMaster's control window to see a couple navigational features that Cakewalk Home Studio *doesn't* have (see Figure 4.47).

Figure 4.47

a. The Shuttle wheel moves the play line forward or backward in time. Turning the wheel to the left of center moves the play line earlier in the song, and the farther you turn to the left, the faster the play line moves. The same is true when you turn the wheel to the right, except, of course, the play line will move to the right, or later in your song.

b. The Jog buttons will move the play line to the left or right (depending on whether you press the left or right button) at a speed determined by the shuttle wheel. In other words, if you have moved the shuttle wheel to the extreme (left or right) and let go of it (which will stop the play line), then the Jog buttons can move the line to the left or right at the same quick speed that was last used by the Shuttle wheel.

CAUTION

Since the Jog buttons are dependent on the setting of the Shuttle wheel, if the Shuttle wheel is in its neutral position (straight up at 12 o'clock), the Jog wheels won't do nothin'!

Saving Your Work

You might be ready for a break! Now might be a good time to talk about how to save your work and shut down the application. Why not just hit "Save?" Because if you simply save a standard MIDI file like the one included with this book, you might lose certain aspects of the file, like track sounds and MIDI channel assignments. Saving the file in the program's native format is the way to go at this point, and here's how to do it.

 NOTE

You'll learn more about standard MIDI files (SMFs), what they do, and how to use them in Chapter 7.

Using Cakewalk Home Studio

The process of saving your work begins at the File drop-down menu, as shown in Figure 4.48.

Figure 4.48

1. **Click** the **File** drop-down menu.

2. **Click** the **Save As** menu item. The **Save As** window will appear (see Figure 4.49).

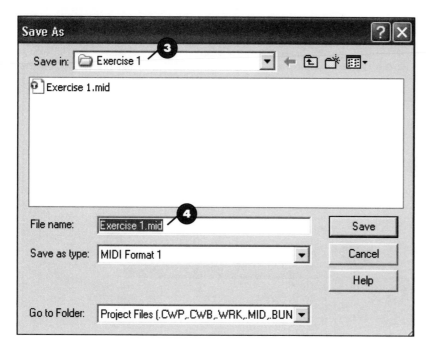

Figure 4.49

3. **Navigate** to the **drive** and **folder** where you want to save your file (if you've ever saved a file in Windows XP, this is exactly the same process).

4. **Name** your **file**. Again, this is the same as saving any file in Windows. After that, though, you have the option of saving in a number of different ways, as shown in Figure 4.50.

Figure 4.50

5. **Choose** the **format** of the file you're going to create. **Click** the arrow button to the right of the **Save as type** field to see a list of options.

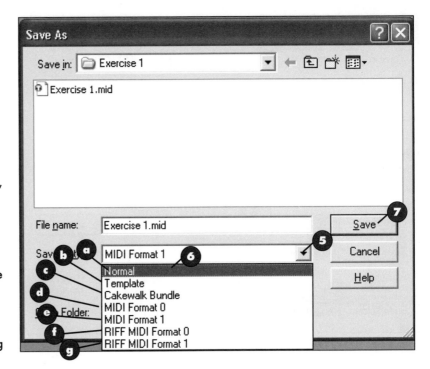

a. **Normal:** This file saves all session settings, MIDI, and points to audio files on your hard drive (if your session includes audio).

b. **Template:** A template file is commonly used as a basis for a new file. If you like the settings in a particular session, saving them as a template will allow you to use those settings when creating a new session.

c. **Cakewalk Bundle:** Instead of pointing to audio files, digital audio is incorporated into the Cakewalk file. The good news is that you'll only have one file to worry about—the bad news is that the single file could be *huge* if you've got a lot of digital audio in your session. Saving a file in this way is generally reserved for backing up your work.

d. **MIDI Format 0:** Standard MIDI file with all MIDI data contained in a single track.

e. **MIDI Format 1:** Standard MIDI file that maintains separate tracks.

f. **RIFF MIDI Format 0:** Standard MIDI format 0 that improves compatibility with certain programs.

g. **RIFF MIDI Format 1:** Standard MIDI format 1 that improves compatibility with certain programs.

6. **Click** the **desired format**. Generally, the Normal format does the trick.

7. **Click** the **Save** button. That's it!

> ❋ **NOTE**
>
> You'll learn more about standard MIDI files and how to use them in Chapter 7.

Once you've saved, you can exit out of Cakewalk Home Studio just as you would close any other application.

Using Quartz AudioMaster Freeware

AudioMaster uses sequence files as its proprietary file format. Here's how to save your work as a sequence file (see Figure 4.51).

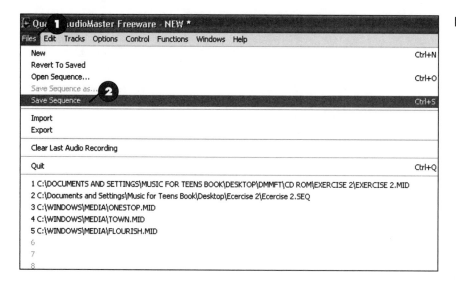

Figure 4.51

1. **Click** the **Files** drop-down menu.

2. **Click** the **Save Sequence** menu item. The Save As window will appear, as shown in Figure 4.52.

Figure 4.52

3. **Navigate** to the **drive** and **folder** where you want to save your file (if you've ever saved a file in Windows XP, this is exactly the same process).

4. **Name** your **file**.

5. Don't worry about the Save as type field. You can only save as a sequence.

6. **Click** the **Save** button.

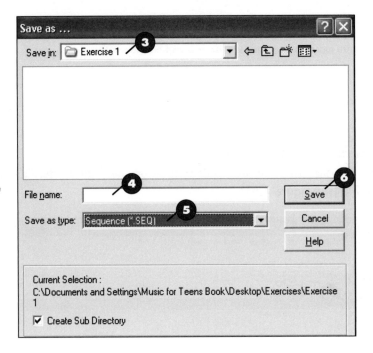

You can save as other types of files, however. Here's how to do it (see Figure 4.53).

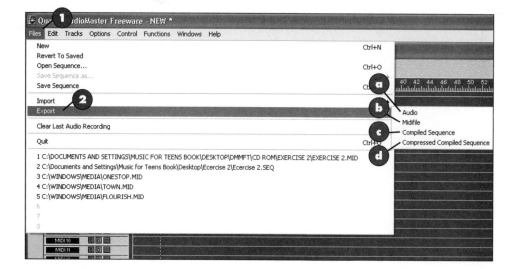

Figure 4.53

1. **Click** the **Files** drop-down menu.

2. **Click** the **Export** menu item. A submenu will be selected, with the following options.

a. **Audio:** Audio in your session will be mixed together and rendered down to a single audio file.

b. **MIDI file:** This will save your session as a standard MIDI file, or even a—ugh—Karaoke file (which you can use in a Karaoke player).

c. **Compiled Sequence:** Saving as this sort of file will save MIDI and digital audio into a single file (much like Home Studio does with bundle files). You even have the option of documenting your session with a title and other information, and you can choose selectively which MIDI and audio tracks will be included in the file.

d. **Compressed Compiled Sequence:** Same as a compiled sequence, but with lossy data reduction to help keep the file size small (though keep in mind that sonic quality may well suffer).

That's about it! Once you've saved your work, you can exit the program just as you would any other Windows program. Good work—now take a break, clear your head, and meet me back here when you're ready for more MIDI madness!

5 The Language of MIDI

Now you should have an idea of the role of MIDI and how it relates to the job of the composer. The next step is to understand how MIDI controls devices and expresses musical ideas. There are a number of ways in which MIDI can convey these musical ideas, but your earlier understanding of traditional written music will really come in handy here. In this chapter, you'll learn:

* How notes are created and how to manipulate them.

* How to change sounds on a synth module from the comfort of your computer screen.

* How MIDI can control hardware and how to use MIDI to keep all the members of your MIDI setup working together.

MIDI Channel Messages

MIDI messages fall into two families. First, there are channel messages, which are the most basic messages in MIDI and communicate performance data to the instruments that are being controlled. Beyond that, there are system messages, which are a bit more related to MIDI hardware and more technical issues. Let's start with the channel messages.

MIDI Voice Message

Channel messages also have two families—voice messages and mode messages. Voice messages are perhaps the most musically relevant, referring to individual notes and other kinds of expression, whereas mode messages are more oriented to the overall control of a MIDI device. As you read through the descriptions of voice messages, put yourself in the mindset of a performing musician, and you'll see how these messages, more than any other type, relate to the reading of written music and playing of a MIDI instrument!

Note on

Let's go back to the ol' player piano example. The actual roll of paper that you loaded into the player piano would be riddled with tiny punched out holes. As the piano roll scrolled its way over the reading mechanism, the holes sent a message to the piano to press a key and play a note. The position of the hole on the piano roll determined not only the timing of the notes, but also the pitch, like Figure 5.1.

Figure 5.1

How a player piano works.

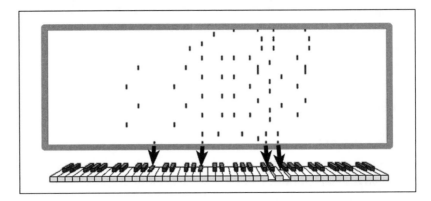

A MIDI note on message, the most basic command of the MIDI language, works a lot like the holes in a player piano roll. To transmit a note on message, all you have to do is *press a key* on a keyboard. It's that easy! A MIDI device that is receiving note on information will respond by playing a note, but there's more. Remember that MIDI data is serial data, which means that information is sent in a string. So what information should be sent with a note on message? Well, it would be nice to know what pitch is needed, for starters. Keep in mind that MIDI is also digital data, so notes aren't going to be described in letters but rather in numbers (digits). Each note on the keyboard is assigned to a specific note, similar to Figure 5.2.

Figure 5.2

Note numbers.

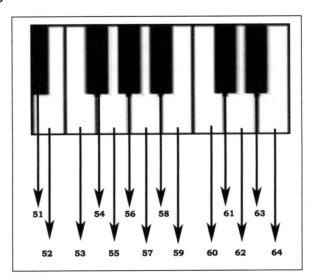

We have a MIDI note on message, which tells the destination device to play a note, which includes a note number, which determines *which* note to play, so what is next? Well, how hard (or most specifically how *fast*) was the key pressed? That's where a velocity message comes in. MIDI velocity information ranges from a value of 1 to 127, with a value of 1 being a key being pressed *very* slowly and 127 representing a key being struck fast (see Figure 5.3). Naturally, a low velocity value will tend to be a very soft sound and a high velocity will be louder, but in addition to the volume change, the tonal quality of the instrument can change as well.

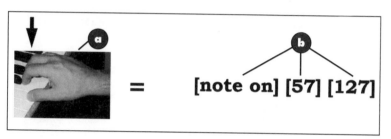

Figure 5.3

Note on!

a. **The Cause:** A MIDI musician plays an "A" below middle "C" really hard!

b. **The Effect:** A MIDI note on message, including a MIDI note number of 57, and also a MIDI velocity of 127.

Note off

Of course, a note that only starts and never ends is no good, so MIDI has to have a way of stopping the note. A MIDI note off message does exactly that. A MIDI note off message simply sends a command to stop playing a certain MIDI note number. This message is sent whenever a pressed key is released. Better yet, some MIDI keyboard controllers actually have mechanisms that can sense not only that a key has been released, but also how fast that key has been released, or its note off velocity. Note off velocity is sometimes used to further manipulate a MIDI module's sound after the key is released (for example, with a sound decay slowly or quickly). Here's how MIDI uses note off messages:

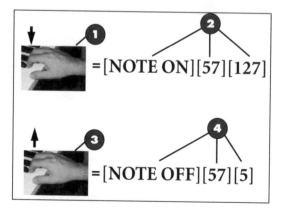

Figure 5.4

Note on/note off.

1. **The Cause:** A MIDI musician plays an "A" below middle "C" really hard, just like before.

2. **The Effect:** A MIDI note on message, including a MIDI note number of 57, and a MIDI velocity of 127.

3. **The Cause:** The musician releases that key very slowly.

4. **The Effect:** A MIDI note off message, including a MIDI note number of 57 and a MIDI velocity of 5, indicating that the key has been released slowly, which *may* change the way the sound ends, depending upon the MIDI device being controlled and the setup of the sound.

Note on and note off data is all well and good (and certainly central to the job of MIDI), but let's start to delve into some of the features that make MIDI a really cool way to work.

Pitch Bend

You can't do pitch bend with a piano. When you press a piano key, the pitch you start out with is the pitch you end up with, but life's different with a MIDI controller. Pitch bend does what you probably think it does—it bends (or shifts) the pitch of a note over time. With pitch bend, you can get the subtle effect of a slur, or the most impressive of glissandos. The vast majority of MIDI keyboards have a cool little controller, usually in the form of a wheel or lever, like Figure 5.5, that can generate pitch bend data:

Figure 5.5

Experiment with pitch bend to create some awesome sounds.

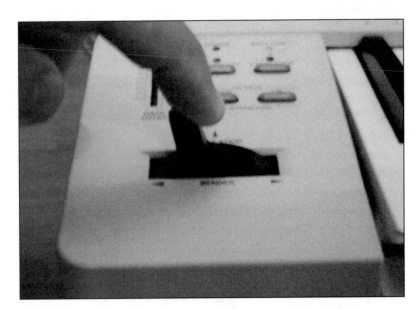

Now here's a new little tidbit about the MIDI language: MIDI values have a range of 128 different values (note on velocity data, for example, can have values of 1–127, plus a value of 0, which indicated note release). This creates a problem, because our human ears are very sensitive to changes in pitch. If you tried to create a pitch bend with only 128 different steps, it just wouldn't sound smooth. Good thing the programmers of the MIDI language were really smart—they figured out a workaround.

First, a pitch bend command is sent. Then, instead of only one parameter to describe how much pitch bend, there are two parameters that work together to give us smooth pitch bending. First, there's a coarse pitch bend message and also a fine pitch bend message. Each one of these parameters has a range of 128 values, and when they combine forces, those values are multiplied together. That makes

128 × 128 and gives us a grand total of 16,384 different values. That amounts to a very smooth pitch bend (see Figure 5.6).

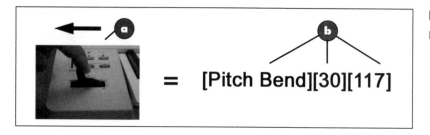

Figure 5.6

Bending a pitch.

    a. **The Cause:** A MIDI musician moves the pitch bend wheel.

    b. **The Effect:** A MIDI pitch bend message is sent, including a coarse pitch bend value and also a fine pitch bend value.

Of course, this string of commands would only be a single pitch bend value (which would only sound like the note was slightly sharp or flat). During the course of performing, though, a pitch would need to shift up and down smoothly. This means that as you move the pitch bend wheel, an ever-changing stream of pitch bend commands are sent.

> ❋ **TIP**
>
> So, what do you want the range of your pitch wheel to be—a small pitch change or a large one? Actually, you can configure the pitch bend range in the MIDI device being controlled. In fact, different sounds in a single device can be set to have different ranges.

Program (Patch) Change

I've got this friend named Brian who plays woodwind instruments. Not just one of them, mind you, but pretty near all of 'em! This means that I can put some music in front of him and say "play this on a tenor sax," and after that, he could play the same music on the clarinet, or soprano sax, piccolo, you name it! MIDI sound modules are similar to musicians like Brian, but in a much bigger way. Instead of playing a handful of woodwind instruments, it's not hard to find a MIDI synth module that can emulate *hundreds* of instruments. More than that, synthesizers routinely play sounds of every type of instrument—woodwinds, brass, percussion, keys, and many more.

Now in the old days (*my* days), you could get different sounds out of a primitive synthesizer by connecting different electronic components in different ways using cables. This process was called *patching a sound*, and the cables were dubbed *patch cables*, a nickname that survives to this day. This process of "patching" in order to get different sounds out of a synth became so standard in the early days of music technology that different sounds were called "patches"—woodwind patches, brass patches, and so on.

Today's modern synths have many sounds, called *programs* or—you guessed it—patches. Like all MIDI data, each program is represented by a number, which is usually associated with a name. For example, program (or "patch," if you want to sound particularly hip) number 1 might sound like a grand piano. A MIDI controller can send out a MIDI program change message to change the sound of the MIDI device(s) being controlled. There's just a couple things to keep in mind when using program change commands.

※ **Different numbers:** The MIDI language only reserves 128 different values for program change commands. No problem, you might think, every synth will have patch 1 through 128, right? Well, as luck would have it, that depends on the manufacturer. Some synths number their patches from 1 through 128, but others number their patches from 0 to 127. But wait, it gets better— still other manufacturers organize their patches into banks of 32, 64, 99, what have you! This can make organization difficult at times.

※ **Different sounds:** You'll love this—not only are the patches on different synths numbered differently, but also the sounds themselves are different. What that means is that patch number 1 might sound like a grand piano on one of your synths, but that same patch number might sound like a snare drum on another. Good thing you can set up MIDI messages to control only certain specific pieces of gear. (I'll talk about that in Chapter 7.)

> ※ **NOTE**
>
> Wouldn't it be great if there were a standard arrangement of patch names and numbers, so that the same sounds played on the synth you've got at home would work on a friend's synth? Fret not, true believer, General MIDI is for you! To make a long story short, General MIDI was created as a cross-manufacturer default order of sounds, and is implemented in many (although not all) synthesizers of different brands and models. More about General MIDI in Chapter 7.

Controllers

At some point, you'll be bound to take a trip to your local music store for a little well-deserved window-shopping. When you check out the keyboard synths there, you'll notice that some of them are loaded with knobs and levers, buttons, and sliders—way beyond what you've learned so far. These controls are used to sculpt the sounds of the instrument using MIDI control change messages. Often, the knobs and sliders on your keyboard can be assigned to any expressive control (via a controller number) that you want.

So how do control change messages work? Let's say that you want a knob on your keyboard to change the panning of your sound from the left to the right speaker. The first thing you need to find out is which controller number is assigned to pan changes. As you'll see in the list to follow, that controller number is 10. The next step is to configure that knob to generate controller 10 data (each MIDI keyboard has different ways of doing this, so check your gear's documentation). Once you're set, here's what will happen:

- ❋ **The cause:** A controller knob is moved, generating the following string of MIDI data.

- ❋ **The effect:** A MIDI controller message is sent, followed by the specific controller number being adjusted (in this case, controller number 10), followed by a control value (a range of 128 different values that will behave differently, depending upon the controller number).

- ❋ **The effect you'll hear:** As you move the knob from left to right, the controller will send values from 0–127, which when assigned to controller number 10 will cause the sound to move from the left speaker to the right.

> ❋ **NOTE**
>
> MIDI data in general tends to operate in value ranges of 0–127 (or 128 possible values). This is a natural side effect of MIDI being a digital and, more specifically, a binary-based language. At any rate, you'll see this magic number of 128 coming up again and again in MIDI, and controllers are no exception.

The list that follows is a description of all the available continuous controllers:

0.	Bank select	16-19.	General purpose controllers #1-4	71.	Sound controller #2 (default: timbre)	91.	Effects 1 depth
1.	Modulation wheel			72.	Sound controller #3 (default: release time)	92.	Effects 2 depth
		20-31.	Undefined			93.	Effects 3 depth
2.	Breath controller	32-37.	Least Significant Byte (LSB) for values 0-5			94.	Effects 4 depth
						95.	Effects 5 depth
3	Undefined			73.	Sound controller #4 (default: attack time)	96.	Data increment
4.	Foot controller	38.	Data Entry LSB			97.	Data decrement
5.	Portamento time	39-63.	LSB for values 7-31			98.	Non-registered parameter number LSB
6.	Data Entry Most Significant Byte (MSB)	64.	Damper (sustain) pedal	74.	Sound controller #5 (default: brightness)	99.	Non-registered parameter number LSB
		65.	Portamento on/off				
7.	Volume			75-79.	Sound controllers #6-10 (no default)	100.	Registered parameter number LSB
8.	Balance	66.	Sostenuto				
9.	Undefined	67.	Soft Pedal			101.	Registered parameter number MSB
10.	Pan	68.	Legato Footswitch	80-83.	General purpose controllers #5-8		
11.	Expression Controller	69.	Hold 2			102-119.	Undefined
12.	Effect Control #1	70.	Sound controller #1 (default: sound variation)	84.	Portamento control	120-127.	Channel mode messages
13.	Effect Control #2			85-90.	Undefined		
14-15.	Undefined						

Obviously, there are some pretty specific controls. Let's take a moment to discuss some of the most commonly used controllers in greater detail:

* **Controller #0—Bank Select:** Think back on the program change MIDI command. Like most other MIDI messages, there's a limit of 128 values, which would suggest that at most, a MIDI sound module could only have 128 different sounds. That wouldn't do at all, and the bank select controller helps us work around this apparent limitation. The vast majority of synth modules have multiple banks of sounds, with each bank having as many as 128 programs. To access these different banks, just send a bank select command, like the one in Figure 5.7.

Figure 5.7

Banks and patches (or programs).

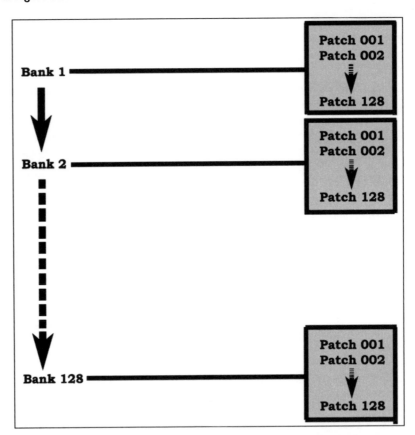

The MIDI language supports 128 different banks. If you do a little math and multiply the maximum number of program values (128) by the maximum number of bank select values (128), you'll find out that MIDI can support a great number of individual programs without cracking a sweat. Just multiply the number of program changes by the amount of banks—that would be 128 × 128 = 16,384 maximum programs (sounds)! Of course, that doesn't mean that you'll ever find a piece of MIDI gear that actually *has* so many sounds (I've never seen one, actually), but it's good to know that the MIDI language isn't holding the hardware back!

❋ **Controller #1—Modulation Wheel:** There's no law saying that every MIDI keyboard *must* have a modulation wheel, but it is an almost universal feature on a MIDI device (particularly keyboard-based devices). A modulation wheel is either a wheel or lever, much like a pitch bend mechanism, that alters (or modulates) the sound. There are different ways that a sound may be modulated. Modulating the frequency of a sound will create an effect called *vibrato*, whereas modulating the amplitude of a sound will create an effect called *tremolo*. Additionally, you can modulate a specific frequency range in a sound, which will give you a *wah wah* effect.

Similar to pitch change messages, MIDI messages generated by the modulation wheel are sent in an ever-changing stream, based upon how far you push the mod wheel. The specific ways in which your sound will be changed depend on how your sound module is set up to respond to these specific MIDI messages.

❋ **Controller #2—Breath Controller:** There are just a few MIDI controllers out there that actually have breath controllers. A breath controller is a little gizmo that is connected to your MIDI controller that you stick in your mouth, and it creates MIDI messages by exerting air pressure on a sensor inside. Breath controllers are generally used for the same kinds of effects as a modulation wheel, but the idea is that with a mod wheel *and* a breath controller, you can alter two different qualities of the sound simultaneously. The breath controller can give you more control over shaping your sound. One word of warning from the voice of experience: Don't try to sing background vocals with one of these stuck in your chops—it just looks stupid.

> ❋ **TIP**
>
> Most manufacturers haven't built breath controllers into their gear, but that doesn't necessarily mean that breath controller data is completely useless in those cases. Breath controller data can be created in other ways (like in a computer-based DAW) and used to affect the sound of a MIDI sound device.

❋ **Controller #4—Foot Controller:** Not to be left out, your feet can also create MIDI data, and in a number of different ways. First on the hit parade are foot controller messages. The particular device that creates foot controller messages looks and acts a bit like a gas pedal on a car, creating higher values the farther down you press the pedal. Like modulation wheel messages, the foot controller may be used to adjust a number of aspects of a program that are assigned and configured in the MIDI device receiving the messages.

❋ **Controller #7—Volume:** This MIDI controller message is probably the most frequently used. Volume messages turn the amplitude of the sound up or down, just like the volume knob on your stereo. On MIDI keyboards, you can usually configure any one of the data sliders or knobs to transmit controller #7 data and act as a volume control.

Remember when we talked about volume versus velocity (in the "Note on" section of this chapter)? Here's where that distinction can really be heard. Remember, velocity refers to how forcefully the instrument is being played (which will not only affect the amplitude of a sound, but also the tonal quality or timbre). Volume messages, on the other hand, will only change the amplitude of the output, just like any volume control.

What this means is that if you want an instrument to really sound like it's being played softly, then sending lower velocity values would be the best way to do it. A patch (like a drum kit, for example) played with high MIDI velocities but low MIDI volume will simply sound like a kit being played hard but with the volume turned down.

MIDI volume messages are particularly useful when mixing many MIDI tracks together, the kind of activity you'd routinely perform in a DAW. Volume will let you balance the various MIDI "instruments" used in your music by adjusting their loudness but leaving their tone color unchanged.

> **NOTE**
> Keep in mind that the volume knob on your synth modules is not a MIDI controller. Any MIDI volume messages that are going to the sound module will adjust the sound before it gets to the volume knob, which will further affect the output volume.

❄ **Controller #10—Pan:** This is probably the next most used controller, after volume. *Pan* (which is short for *panorama*) refers to the "position" of the sound between your left and right speakers. For many, pan is a straightforward term, but the way MIDI treats pan is not quite as obvious. MIDI pan messages have a range of 0 to 127, with 0 being panned "hard left" (signal will only be heard out of the left speaker). And as the value increases, the position of the sound will move toward the right, with a pan value of 127 being panned "hard right."

Panning, like volume, can be manipulated through pan messages to create complex stereo soundscapes, and is a popular favorite (MIDI message, that is) when working with MIDI in a computer-based workstation or sequencer.

❄ **Controller #64—Sustain Pedal:** For those among you who play piano, you already know this, but for those who aren't pianists, there are three foot pedals. Each of these three pedals isn't a gas-pedal style like a MIDI foot controller, but rather on/off switches for three different effects. First, there is the damper pedal (also known as the *sustain* pedal), which holds notes even after the key has been released. This pedal is by far the most used of the three pedals at the pianist's feet.

The damper pedal is commonly used in MIDI as well, particularly in the creation of piano parts. It's worthy to note that this particular controller is either on or off. The only thing that can sometimes come as a surprise to us non-piano players is that once the damper pedal is engaged (pressed), *all* notes that are played from that point on, no matter how brief, will hold until the damper pedal is released.

✳ **Controller #66—Sostenuto Pedal:** This pedal is related to the sustain pedal, but holds down only notes that are already being sustained, allowing subsequent notes to be played normally. A typical use of this pedal would go something like this: Play a bass note while holding down the sustain pedal. Then *also* press the sostenuto pedal and play a series of chords above. The bass note will be held, freeing up the hands of the player to play other musical ideas.

Even on pianos (the real ones, not the synth versions), a sostenuto pedal is considered an option and is not universally found. In MIDI, this pedal isn't commonly used, but for those among you who are also pianists—have at it!

✳ **Controller #67—Soft Pedal:** Next is the soft pedal, which decreases the volume suddenly by roughly one-third. This pedal is not used nearly as much as the damper (sustain) pedal, but again, it's useful for creating realistic-sounding piano parts. Also, like the damper pedal, it is either on or off, and when engaged, affects all notes being played by the patch.

Channel Mode Messages

If you take a look at the last eight controller messages as listed earlier (numbers 120 through 127), you'll see them named as channel mode messages. These final controllers operate in a special way, controlling the MIDI slave device on more of a hardware level than a musical level. Here's a brief rundown of these very useful MIDI commands:

✳ **Controller #120—All sound off:** Imagine that you're in a live situation. All of a sudden, your MIDI sound module starts making some sort of unexpected noises, something not being triggered by the MIDI musician or the MIDI sequencer. What you've got is some sort of hardware failure, and you need the device to be quiet *now*. That's the job of the all sound off command, which will not only stop the playback of any stray MIDI notes that might be straggling along but also brings all volume controls down to zero.

This command is useful not only for MIDI instruments and sound devices, but also to defeat other MIDI-controllable devices, like lighting consoles or sound effects units.

✳ **Controller #121—Reset all controllers:** This message is also a nifty little problem solver. Sometimes, a controller will get "stuck," meaning that a pedal will continue to sound like it's down even when it's up. To quickly reset all controllers to their default (in this case, if the default for the sustain pedal is "up"), just send a reset all controllers message to your MIDI device.

✳ **Controller #122—Local control on/off:** A typical keyboard synthesizer isn't really one piece of gear, but two. On the one hand is a MIDI controller, which is the keyboard that you play, and on the other hand there's the MIDI sound module, which is the sound-generating part of the equation that is equivalent to a MIDI sound module, like Figure 5.8.

Figure 5.8

Inside a MIDI synthesizer.

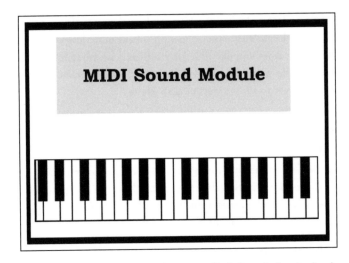

The sound module component of a keyboard synth can be controlled directly by the keyboard of the synth, or it can be controlled externally (like from a MIDI sequencer). That's what local control is all about. For example, with local control set to *on*, the sound-generating electronics inside the keyboard synthesizer will be under the direct control of the built-in (or *local*) MIDI keyboard, as shown in Figure 5.9. Note that the keyboard is sending MIDI commands to the tone generator *and* sending MIDI messages out of the MIDI Out port of the synth.

Figure 5.9

Local control on.

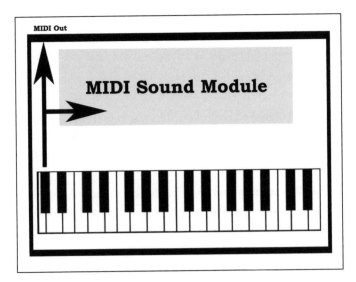

Now, if local control is set to off, then the built-in keyboard doesn't have direct control over the tone generator, and the sounds are only triggered by messages coming into the MIDI In port. The keyboard still is sending MIDI data, but there's no direct connection to the sounds of the synth.

So when do you use the different local control settings? If you're just playing the instrument alone, like in the case of a live performance, then you'll probably want to have local control on. If you're working with a sequencer, however, you'll want to have the sequencer controlling the playback of the sounds. Here's a common setup shown in Figure 5.10 for a sequencer workstation with local control set to *off*.

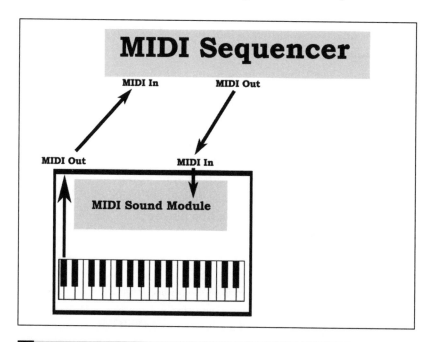

Figure 5.10

Using a MIDI synth with a MIDI sequencer.

> **TIP**
>
> Local control is not only accessible as a MIDI control message, but is also a front panel setting on the vast majority of synthesizers. In fact, it's probably most common to enable or disable local control from the synth's own window (usually in the Global menu, but check your synth's documentation to make sure).

❄ **Controller #123—All notes off:** This message is a close cousin of the all sound off controller, and is also a very useful tool when you need it. You see, every so often a note on message will be received without a note off command, which means that the note will go on *forever!* Sure, it's funny, but after the first half hour or so, it gets a little old. This message sends a note off command on all notes, so that if there are any notes hanging on, they will be silenced.

> **NOTE**
>
> This command is not only an abstract MIDI message. You'll also find it on many MIDI devices (especially MIDI interfaces), and in virtually every sequencer, it can be found as a dedicated "panic button!"

MIDI System Messages

MIDI system messages, contrary to MIDI channel messages, concern themselves with the way that your MIDI setup (or *system*) behaves. For the most part, they affect all the devices in your MIDI studio.

MIDI Common Messages

Even though these messages don't trigger any sounds in and of themselves, they help get your music together and make sure that everything sounds good.

Song Position Pointer

Now that you've got everything set up, it's *finally* time to start playing. To do this, you've got to find a way to stay synchronized (especially if you've got multiple sequences running on multiple devices together), and one way to do this is through the use of a song position pointer (or *SPP* for short). Simply put, SPP counts sixteenth notes. If you've enabled SPP on your sequencer, as soon as playback starts, SPP MIDI messages will stream out of the MIDI Out ports of your workstation at a rate of one per sixteenth note. If you've enabled your MIDI slave devices to follow SPP, then your devices will be locked together as playback goes on. Better yet, when you stop playback on the master device, SPP will stop, and your slave devices will stop as well.

> ❄ **NOTE**
>
> Now that you're learning about the timing of MIDI and synchronizing multiple devices and MIDI sequences, maybe you'd like to know what a *sequence* is in the first place? It's not very mysterious actually, if you think of MIDI in relation to printed music. If you look at the notes on a page of music, you'll see that the arrangement, or *sequence,* of those notes will determine the way the music will sound. A MIDI sequence is a specific arrangement of MIDI data set up in such a way as to play a specific song. With that in mind, a MIDI sequencer is a device that records, edits, and plays back MIDI sequences of MIDI data.

> ❄ **NOTE**
>
> SPP is known as a relative kind of sync code, meaning that it can change its speed *relative* to the tempo of the music. This is particularly useful in music production scenarios, because as your master device's tempo speeds up or slows down, the stream of SPP messages will speed up or slow down accordingly. Since the timing of your slave MIDI devices is dependent upon the speed of the incoming SPP, your slave will follow the tempo changes of your master device. For example, if you've got a sequencer program that's controlling a drum pattern on a drum machine, through SPP you can get the slave drum machine to speed up and slow down to keep in time with the master sequencer. Cool!

MIDI Time Code

Although a song position pointer is one way to get different pieces of gear to lock together, it's not the only way. Here's another way to deal with the timing of the events in your studio—MIDI Time Code (commonly called *MTC*). Instead of measuring the passage of time in terms of sixteenth notes like SPP does, MTC measures time in terms of hours, minutes, seconds, and subdivisions of seconds called *frames*. You can set up this sort of sync in much the same way that you set up SPP. First, you set up your sequencer to transmit MIDI Time Code, and then you set up your slave device to follow MIDI Time Code. Once that's done, the only thing you've got to do is start your sequencer or DAW, and your slave device(s) will follow right along.

> ❊ **NOTE**
>
> MIDI Time Code is a great example of an absolute form of time code. An absolute form of time code, in contrast to relative sync like SPP, does not change its speed depending upon changes in tempo. Instead, the speed of MTC is the speed of time (the speed of time being an absolute value—an hour per hour, a minute per minute, and so on). Because it's not dependent upon tempo to get the job done, this is the time code of choice for working with film and other tempo-less situations.

> ❊ **NOTE**
>
> MIDI Time Code (MTC) is MIDI's version of a timing standard called SMPTE (Society of Motion Picture and Television Editors) time code. There are many forms of SMPTE time code, but they all share the same hours, minutes, seconds, and frames format, and they are all absolute forms of sync. MTC is the only digital form of SMPTE time code, which makes it particularly well suited for working with computer workstations.

Real Time Messages

We're closing in on getting a bead on all the important types of MIDI messages, so stick with me and you'll be in great shape to use MIDI like a pro! The next messages we'll touch on—the MIDI real time messages—help our sequences work in real time.

MIDI Beat Clock

MIDI beat clock is another relative type of sync, meaning that it's a time code based upon tempo. To use MIDI beat clock properly, you'll need to reflect back upon our earlier discussion of written music. Let's take a look at a typical bar of 4/4 time at a tempo of 120 beats per minute with four quarter notes (see Figure 5.11).

Figure 5.11

Four beats.

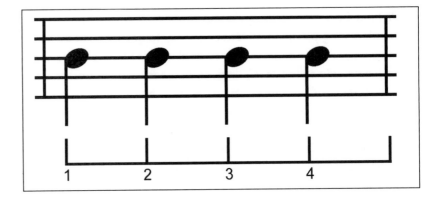

MIDI beat clock can follow our quarter notes, but then it goes even farther and divides each quarter note into a number of parts, commonly known as *ticks*. The number of these parts per quarter note (or PPQN) differs from application to application (ranging from 24 PPQN to hundreds of PPQN in higher resolution products), but no matter how many parts you have, the logic of their use remains the same. For example, if you were to populate a bar with nothing but eighth notes (an eighth note gets a half of one beat), then every other note would be on the beat (tick 0) and every other note would be halfway between beats, at tick 12 (assuming a system that's running at 24 PPQN), like Figure 5.12.

Figure 5.12

Eighth notes and ticks.

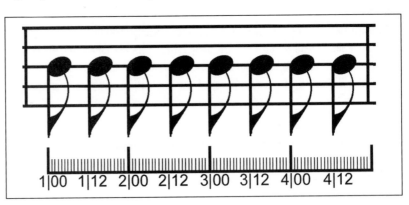

As you can see, MIDI beat clock is arranged in measures|beats|ticks (or PPQN), and even with the lowest MIDI beat clock resolution of 24 PPQN, you can use this way of measuring musical time to represent a wide range of rhythms, as shown in Figure 5.13.

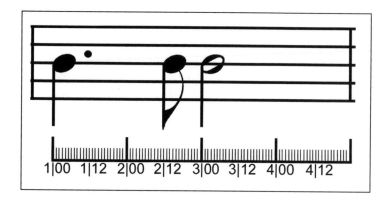

Figure 5.13
MIDI beat clock and rhythm.

Transport Commands

Take a look at your CD player, DVD, VCR, whatever—you'll see transport controls. Transport controls are controls like start, stop, and pause. In the graphic-rich environment of the modern computer-based DAW, you'll see buttons that look similar (if not identical) to the transport controls of those other pieces of electronics. In your computer workstation, clicking these buttons will send MIDI transport commands, and it's worthwhile to briefly touch on how these commands work.

❋ **Start:** Pressing the Start button will not only start your sequencer from its current position but also send a Start command through the MIDI Out port to any MIDI slave devices that might be listening. This way, starting your master sequencer program can also start a slave sequencer (like drum machines, for example).

❋ **Stop:** You guessed it—a MIDI Stop command will not only stop the playback of the master sequencer you're directly using but will also send a Stop command to any slave sequencers as well.

❋ **Continue:** If you want to continue playback from where you stopped, this is the command to use. Again, a Continue command will not only be used internally in your master program but will be sent to the slave sequencers as well.

❋ **NOTE**

More often than not, you won't see a Continue button in the transport section of your sequencer program. Instead, what you will see is a Pause button, which does the job. The first time you click the Pause button, it'll send a Stop command; then when you press it again, it will send a Continue message. It will look and act just like the Pause button on your CD player.

Active Sensing

While this isn't traditionally an entry-level sort of MIDI message, I love this feature—it's just a stroke of genius.

Here's a problem that can sometimes rear its ugly head, especially in live situations. A MIDI setup is completely set up, and the MIDI musician's kickin' it with a rack full of synth modules. So far, no problem. Enter the clumsy guy (someone like me, for example) who, in a fit of emoting, trips over the MIDI cable connecting the slave gear to the controller! Worse yet, the musician was holding out a chord when the gear was unplugged, meaning that the modules received a note on command, but never got any note off command! So you've got these notes just holding on *forever*! Wouldn't it be great if the gear were smart enough to know when it had gotten unplugged? Fear not—that's what active sensing does.

Active sensing, when enabled on a MIDI slave device, allows that device to determine whether it's properly connected. Just enable active sensing on your sequencer or MIDI controller, and an active sensing message will be sent from that master device's MIDI Out port(s) about three times a second if other MIDI data isn't present. Once your synth modules start "hearing" active sensing messages, they will expect these messages, three times a second. If the cable connecting the MIDI out of the sequencer (or controller) to the MIDI In port of the MIDI slave is accidentally unplugged, then these messages will no longer be received by the MIDI module, and it will go silent. Clever, don't you think?

System Reset

This MIDI message is as powerful as it is simple. When sent from a MIDI sequencer or controller, a system reset message commands all MIDI devices attached to it to return to their initial power-up settings.

Exclusive Messages

This is it, the last of the MIDI messages! On top of that, system exclusive (also called *SysEx*) messages can be the most powerful and the most mysterious. These messages are different in form, as well as function, from any other kind of MIDI message. Consider this: All the messages that you've studied up to this point apply to all MIDI gear in the same way. In fact, that was the mission statement of the MIDI language to begin with. However, there was no getting around the fact that different manufacturers and different models of MIDI gear at some point would be unique (or exclusive), and the MIDI language had to find a way to support each device's unique qualities.

What kind of uniqueness are we talking about here? Well for starters, patches. Even though patches, or programs, may be called into action through a standardized program change message, the patches themselves are not necessarily standardized. For example, a Roland synthesizer might have a radically different way of creating a given sound than a Yamaha synth. With system exclusive messages, a more specific message of how to create that sound, tailored to a specific piece of gear, may be sent (and stored in a sequencer program).

Patches aren't the only aspects of a piece of gear that could be considered specific or exclusive. Also high on the list of exclusive qualities are master tuning, output assignments (for devices with multiple outputs), program names, and more. The bottom line is this: SysEx data is designed to speak to the lowest levels of a MIDI device's programming.

This sounds like pretty advanced MIDI use, doesn't it? Well, in a sense it is. It's surprisingly easy to use, and can be a powerful ally. Here's a real-world example of how SysEx may be used to save a custom patch.

Imagine that you have edited and tweaked a sound on your synth. Since this sort of work can be very time consuming, you want to save this custom sound for later recall. Certainly, you can save the patch in your synth module itself, but if the device were ever reset to its factory defaults, your work would be lost. Instead, let's use your MIDI sequencer to record this special kind of data (see Figure 5.14).

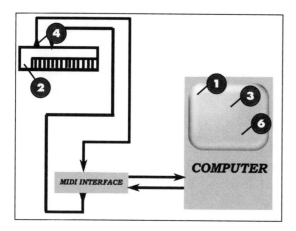

Figure 5.14

SysEx signal path.

1. Set up your MIDI sequencer to record MIDI data from the device (this is a different process for different programs).

2. From your MIDI device's display, prepare to send SysEx data for that particular program (again, this is different for different pieces of gear, but generally this is accessed from either a global menu or a SysEx menu).

3. Begin recording MIDI data on your sequencer.

4. Send the system exclusive data for the patch (there is usually a Send button that you can press, which will initiate the "SysEx dump" or transmission of SysEx data).

5. A SysEx block of data will be sent to the sequencer, consisting of the following elements:

   ✳ A start of exclusive message, indicating that a system exclusive message is on its way.

   ✳ A manufacturer's ID number will be sent. Each MIDI manufacturer has a specific manufacturer's ID number, which differentiates the message from that of other manufacturers.

   ✳ A model ID, which further describes the model of the piece of gear. For example, a Korg M1 and a Korg Triton (two different pieces of gear made by the same manufacturer) will share the same manufacturer's ID but have different model IDs.

   ✳ A device ID, which goes even further and specifies between different individual devices, even if they are made by the same manufacturer and are the same model. For example, if you have *two* Korg Tritons (lucky you!), the system exclusive data will be recorded as having come from either device number one or number two (if you only have one device, that data is set as device one by default). You will need to set up each MIDI synth with a different device ID to have this feature work.

   ✳ Data! Finally, the substance of the message, which includes the specific parameter being saved and any associated data.

   ✳ An end of exclusive message to indicate that the SysEx message is finished.

6. Stop recording MIDI data on your sequencer, and you're done. The SysEx data will be saved on the track, just as if it were any other MIDI data.

Your custom patch is saved. Now that it's been stored on your sequencer, life can get even better. Let's suppose that your synth was reset to its factory defaults. All you need to do is play back the MIDI track that you just recorded. What will play back is the SysEx MIDI data. Since the data has been specified by manufacturer, model, and device, it will be ignored by all other gear (for example, the data you created in the previous example being flagged as Korg data would be completely ignored by a Yamaha synth). When the right device gets the SysEx data, it will become silent, accept the data, and quickly spring back to life, with the patch that you created in its memory.

Each manufacturer has different types of SysEx data that can be stored, but virtually all devices support SysEx to some degree. With SysEx data, you'll eventually be able to store tons of custom-made patches.

> ❋ **TIP**
>
> When looking for new sounds, there's no place to start like the Internet. Seasoned programmers have set up Web sites for just about every MIDI device out there, even vintage gear! Just search the Net for SysEx sounds (and be sure to include the synth model to narrow down the search), and before long you'll have a good number of brand new sounds to try out.

Now that you've got a solid understanding of what MIDI does and how it gets done, let's take a look at how you can wield this power in your computer.

Sequencing Basics

MIDI sequencers have evolved over the years, from the basic recording and playing back of a series (or *sequence*) of MIDI commands, to a powerful workstation for not only recording and playing back but also editing and tweaking each and every MIDI message with a surgeon's precision. Okay, maybe I'm exaggerating a little, but today's MIDI sequencers are pretty sweet.

There are lots of MIDI sequencers to choose from, so how are you supposed to learn them all? Worse yet, the MIDI software that you begin using today will almost certainly not be the application that you'll use a few years from now (at the very least, the app you're using now will be upgraded a version or two). The good news is that the majority of MIDI workstations follow some time-tested conventions. In fact, if you look at the most popular software titles, you'll notice an immediate visual similarity in the way that things are laid out and organized.

In short, the best idea is to get a feel for how these applications *think*, so that you can figure out any new software with a minimum of effort. Let's take a look at the primary windows of some common MIDI production environments.

Multitrack MIDI

The idea that makes any professional MIDI sequencer work (or DAW for that matter) is that if individual musical elements can be recorded to individual separate parts, then they can be edited and mixed with much greater efficiency. For example, if you can record a bass part to one area of the software and a piano part to another, then editing each instrument individually is easy. And not only can the parts be tweaked, but they can be mixed together and blended with great precision.

Keep in mind that music is a time-based art, so these separate parts will have to be arranged in such a way that they can be played together. How about a series of horizontal strips of data that each includes the MIDI data for a specific musical part? Maybe the window would look something like Figure 5.15.

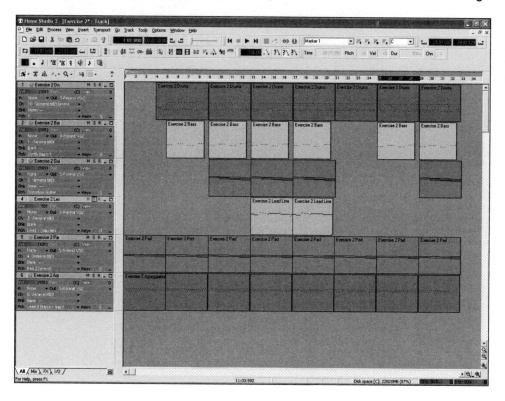

Figure 5.15

A typical multi-track MIDI window.

Or it might look like Figure 5.16.

Figure 5.16

Another multitrack MIDI window.

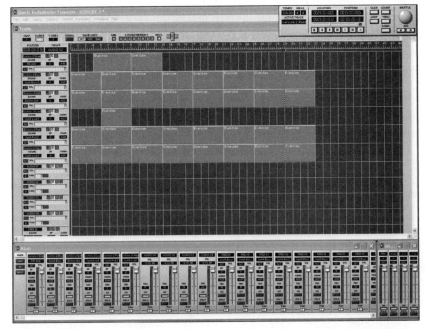

Or it even could look like Figure 5.17.

Figure 5.17

Do you see the similarities?

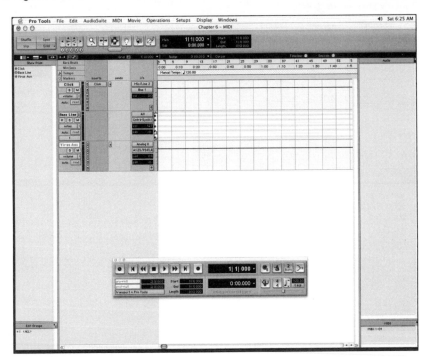

Virtually every sequencer and DAW has a window like this, and whether the software calls this window the Track window, Regions window, or Edit window, the layout and function of these windows are uncannily similar. Here are a few of the common elements and what they do:

❋ **Track information:** Look to the leftmost end of each horizontal track. You'll see critical information about that specific track, such as things like track names, the volume and panning of the track, and track inputs and outputs.

❋ **That long vertical line:** This line goes by many names, but it always does the same thing. As your song plays, this line will move from left to right, showing you the specific data being played back at any given time. As you fast forward or rewind, this line will move accordingly to show you where you're going in order to help you navigate through your project.

❋ **MIDI regions:** On the tracks, you'll see boxes of *stuff*. That stuff is actually MIDI data, and the box is a MIDI region. The idea of using regions to manage data within a track is particularly useful to composers and producers, as they can easily move, copy, and paste these boxes to other locations.

> ❋ **NOTE**
>
> Here's a term for you: nonlinear. This became a popular buzz-word early on in the days of computer music production. Nonlinearity is in stark contrast to the earlier ways of recording music to audio tape—tape being a linear mode of storage. You see, the way tape works, it's impossible to cut a section out of one track and just drag it to another section of the tape. (The best you could do was to physically cut a segment of tape and then insert it at another point, but that affects *all* tracks for that section of time.) When you work with regions in a computer-based workstation, it's easy to grab them with a mouse and move them anywhere in time and even to other tracks, which is the very definition of nonlinear.

The Big Event (List)

While the Track window is immensely useful, especially when it comes to dealing with large chunks of data, it's not the only window you'll use to do your work, particularly when it comes time to do some real tweaking. The best place to go for doing specific editing on MIDI messages is the MIDI Event List window, and the good news is that nearly every MIDI application has one.

The MIDI Event List is the closest that most people ever get to directly operating on the MIDI code itself. MIDI essentially boils down to specific messages being sent along specific channels at specific points in time. The Event List strips away all the software window dressing, and you can just get your hands dirty with the actual messages. Here's a great example of what a MIDI Event List looks like in Figure 5.18.

Figure 5.18

A MIDI Event List.

1. **Track:** The Track column tells what track the MIDI data is on. The MIDI Event List can show messages on many tracks in one window.

① Trk	② HMSF	③ MBT	④ Ch	⑤ Kind	⑥ Data	⑦
4	00:00:10:27	6:03:882	1 Note		E 6	116
1	00:00:10:29	6:04:008	1 Note		Ride Bell	55
1	00:00:10:29	6:04:008	1 Note		Electric Snare	127
1	00:00:11:02	6:04:248	1 Note		Acoustic Bass Drum	124
4	00:00:11:05	6:04:402	1 Note		D 6	119
1	00:00:11:06	6:04:488	1 Note		Ride Cymbal 2	61
1	00:00:11:09	6:04:728	1 Note		Ride Cymbal 2	65
1	00:00:11:13	7:01:008	1 Note		Acoustic Bass Drum	127
1	00:00:11:13	7:01:008	1 Note		Ride Bell	67
1	00:00:11:20	7:01:488	1 Note		Ride Cymbal 2	61
1	00:00:11:24	7:01:728	1 Note		Ride Cymbal 2	61
1	00:00:11:24	7:01:728	1 Note		Acoustic Bass Drum	119
1	00:00:11:27	7:02:008	1 Note		Electric Snare	127
1	00:00:11:27	7:02:008	1 Note		Ride Bell	61
1	00:00:12:04	7:02:488	1 Note		Acoustic Bass Drum	121
1	00:00:12:04	7:02:488	1 Note		Ride Cymbal 2	54
1	00:00:12:08	7:02:728	1 Note		Ride Cymbal 2	63
1	00:00:12:12	7:03:008	1 Note		Ride Bell	64
1	00:00:12:15	7:03:248	1 Note		Electric Snare	102
1	00:00:12:19	7:03:488	1 Note		Acoustic Bass Drum	69
1	00:00:12:19	7:03:488	1 Note		Ride Cymbal 2	60
1	00:00:12:22	7:03:728	1 Note		Acoustic Bass Drum	72
1	00:00:12:22	7:03:728	1 Note		Ride Cymbal 2	62

2. **Timing:** This column is named **HMSF**, for Hours, Minutes, Seconds, and Frames (frames are divisions of a second). This column gives the exact location of each MIDI message in time.

3. **And More Timing:** Displaying location in terms of time (as a clock tells time) is all well and good, but sometimes that isn't enough. Knowing an event's location with regard to tempo might be much more useful. That's why most Event Lists will allow you to view (and edit) a specific message's location in terms of measures, beats, and ticks (ticks are subdivisions of a beat), as shown here in the **MBT** column.

4. **Channel:** This column tells you what channel a data message is using.

5. **Message Type:** In any decent Event List, there will be a column (in this case, called *Kind*) that tells you what type of MIDI messages are being sent (note data, program change, pitch bend, whatever).

6. **Message Value:** Every type of MIDI message has its own specific parameters. This column lets you know what that parameter's value is. For example, if a given MIDI message's type was note data, the value might be D-sharp.

7. **More Message Values:** In many MIDI messages (in the case of this figure, note messages), there are a number of different values communicated together. In the case of note data, this second value column shows the velocity at which the note is being played.

Of course, this window doesn't only *show* you the MIDI events, but alters those events as well. That's what really makes this window so unique and powerful. When you really need to tweak a MIDI message down to the digit, all you need to do is click on the field that you want to change and type in a new value.

Two Ways to Look at the Music (Staff and Piano Roll)

The multitrack window deals with larger blocks of MIDI data, and the MIDI Event List deals with different parts of individual messages, but those aren't the only ways to work with MIDI data. In fact, there are usually at least a couple of environments where you can graphically edit (instead of the numeric editing of the Event List) notes and other MIDI messages within a MIDI region.

Staff Window

If you learned to read music in school, you're gonna love this window (and if you didn't learn how to read music notation before, this might fire up your interest). Here's the Staff window in Figure 5.19.

Figure 5.19

The Staff window.

1. **Pencil/Eraser:** Since this is a graphic editing environment, you can use the Pencil tool to create new notes or the Eraser tool to delete a note. It might be the long way to go about composition, but you can conceivably create an entire song without ever touching a MIDI keyboard.

2. **Snap to grid:** Virtually every program has a way to limit the creation and movement of regions, notes, and other kinds of MIDI data to certain locations in time. For example, in this program (Cakewalk Home Studio), clicking this grid icon will automatically snap notes to the nearest grid line. You get to set what kind of grid you want to use (beats, measures, and so on), and even if your timing is off a little bit with the mouse, the note will automatically be moved to the correct timing.

3. **The play line:** Just as in the Track window, there's a long vertical line that will progress across the music as it's being played, to let you know what notes are playing at any given time.

4. **Staff/Page Setup:** Many (but not all) programs will customize each staff with whatever staff names, clef symbol, and other display options you want, in order to make working with the notes easier. In some applications, these features are so advanced that you could very well print up this page and use it for live musicians.

5. **Dynamics:** When working with written music, you use dynamic markings (like piano, forte, etc.) to tell the musicians how forcefully to play their instruments. You can add these markings to your music in this window and print music for live musicians to play!

6. **Chords and Lyrics:** This isn't universally supported on all applications, but when it is, you can make your MIDI sequence even more suitable for printing and live performance by adding lyrics (song words for vocalists) and chord symbols (for guitarists).

For those with a more traditional music background, this is a great window to use during the composition phase of production. You can really see the interrelationship of harmony and melody when they appear together on a multitrack staff.

Piano Roll Window

You might have noticed earlier in the book that I compared a player piano (and the piano roll that makes it work) to the MIDI language. This window, commonly called the *Piano Roll* window, is another great graphical way to look at musical information. It has some particular editing strengths (see Figure 5.20).

Figure 5.20

The Piano Roll window.

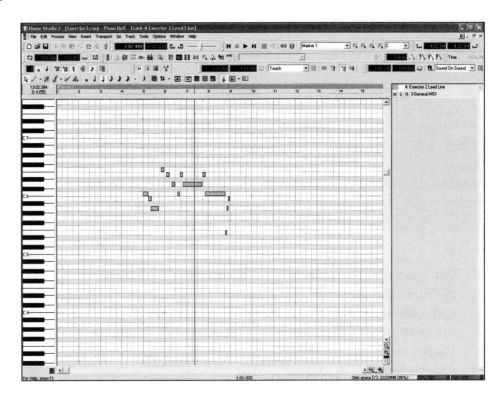

The trick to understanding this window is to figure out the layout. The key is to understand that the piano keyboard is on its side. Notes that are higher on the screen (or to the right-hand side of the keyboard if you were looking at it the right way) are higher in pitch.

To the right of the keyboard, you'll notice a gridded area. The rows to the right of each key represent the pitch of that key, and the columns represent units of time (this can be different depending on how you set up your timing "ruler" and timing grid). If your track has music on it already (as you saw in the previous figure), you'll see small rectangles. These rectangles represent MIDI note commands just as the punched-out holes in a real piano roll would command the piano to play. This particular graphic representation is not only a bit more user-friendly to non-music readers, but it is the editing environment of choice for a number of editing operations (see Figure 5.21).

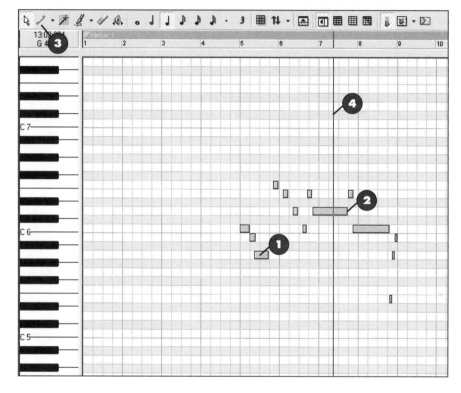

Figure 5.21

A closer look at the Piano Roll.

1. **Drag:** One of the big advantages of this window is its ability to drag a pre-existing note not only earlier or later in time (by moving the note left or right), but also to different pitches as well (by dragging up or down).

2. **Change Duration:** In this window, you can change the length of each note. Usually, this is accomplished by moving your cursor to the end of the note and adjusting the note's boundary left or right.

3. **Create:** This window has a Pencil tool, just like the Staff window did, and it does the same thing. Use this tool to create notes where before there were none. You'll note that on the top of the screen there are note values to help you create quarter notes, whole notes, or whatever you want.

4. **Playback/Navigation:** Here's another old friend. Remember the vertical line that shows you what's presently playing (found in the Track window and the Staff window, too). That line is here as well, thankfully, and as it passes over the squares of MIDI data, you'll hear them play.

No matter what the application, you'll notice that many of the features and modes found in the Score view have their own places of honor in the Piano Roll view as well. For example, if an application supports any sort of Snap to Grid mode (most do), then a similar-looking icon will appear in both windows. Personally, I like to use the Piano Roll window a good bit (even though I know how to read music), as I find that tweaking note positions and durations is a *lot* easier and more accurate than in the Staff window (for all the plusses of the Staff window, it's bound by the limitations of written music).

 NOTE

The Piano Roll view might lead you to think that it can't show more than one track at a time, but it can. Generally, when you select more than one track in the Piano Roll window, different tracks will be displayed in different colors. Take care, though, because having an entire band appearing together on one keyboard can get pretty complex.

6

Exercise 2: Working with Multitrack MIDI

As you've played the standard MIDI file in Exercise 1, you've probably noticed that it sounds *horrible*. There's nothing but piano there, and that top track sounds like somebody is playing that piano with a hammer! Trust me, there's nothing wrong with the file that you can't fix, but before you can solve the problem, you've got to *understand* the problem. In this chapter, you'll learn:

❈ How to set up your sounds.

❈ How to customize the speed of your song.

❈ How to fix wrong notes.

> ❈ **NOTE**
>
> For the purposes of this exercise, you can use the files you saved at the end of Exercise 1, or you can use the files included with the CD-ROM that accompanies this book. To locate the Exercise 2 file for Cakewalk Home Studio, navigate to your CD-ROM drive and then open the Exercise folder. From there, go to the Ex_02/Cakewalk folder and open up the Ex_02.cwp file within with Cakewalk Home Studio. The Quartz AudioMaster Freeware file is in the Exercise/Ex_02/Quartz folder, and it is named Ex_02.SEQ.

Changing Instruments

Here's what's happening. Each of these tracks has no defined program change data, which means that the software will just choose a default sound (in this case a piano sound). Furthermore, all the tracks in this song are assigned to the same MIDI channel. To solve the problem, first, you need to assign each separate MIDI track to its own individual MIDI channel (you've got 16 of them to work with, and you'll lean more about how they're used in Chapter 7). Once that's done, you can assign each channel to its own program ("patch"). Then things will sound a *lot* better. Let's go!

> ❄ **NOTE**
>
> If you decide to use both applications, that's fantastic, but make sure you save your work in an application-specific format before switching programs, so you don't lose valuable work. To learn how to do this, refer to the "Saving Your Work" section in Chapter 4. Simply saving your work as a standard MIDI file will cause you to lose specific session settings.

Using Cakewalk Home Studio

The layout of the Tracks window makes setup a breeze (see Figure 6.1)!

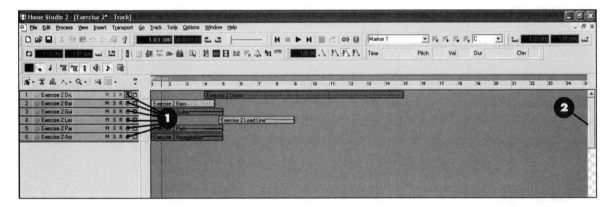

Figure 6.1

1. First, let's **open up** each **track**, so you can configure it. On each track, **click** the **Restore Strip Size** button to expand the track.

2. After you expand the fourth or fifth track (depending on your screen resolution, you'll need to use the scroll bar to shift your view downward and expand the remaining tracks.

When you're done, scroll back up to the top of your track list, and your screen will look something like Figure 6.2.

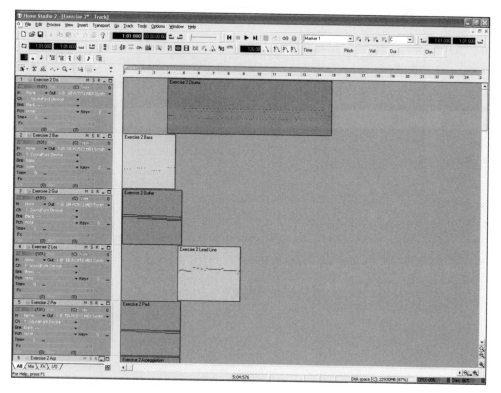

Figure 6.2

Let's start out by setting up the drums to actually sound like *drums*.

> ✳ **NOTE**
>
> There's nothing wrong with this track that a couple of simple changes can't fix. Truth is, the drum track is just fine, and the notes are all correct. The problem is that instead of the drum part playing a drum sound, it is playing a piano sound. Changing this situation will immediately fix the problem.

Setting up your output and MIDI channel will make this track sound *much* better (see Figure 6.3).

Figure 6.3

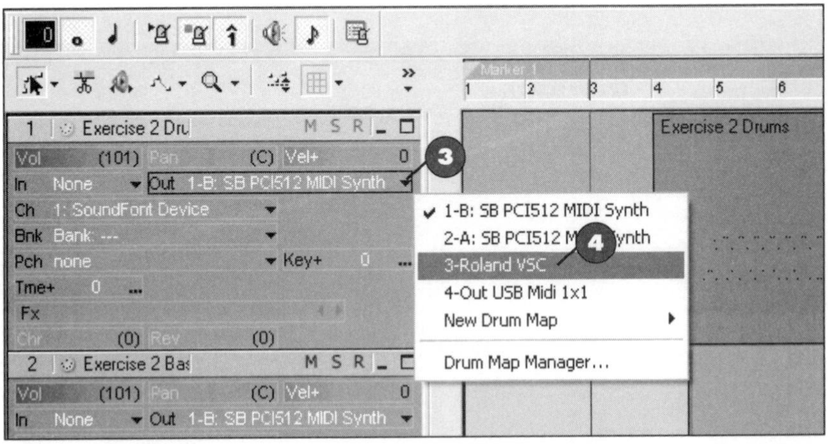

3. **Click** the **arrow button** at the right side of the Out (for Output) area. A drop-down list of possible MIDI output devices (which you set up when you configured your MIDI devices in Exercise 1) will appear.

4. **Click** the **device** you want to assign to the

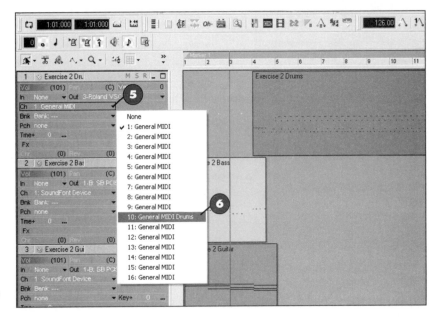

playback of this track. In this case, I've chosen the Roland VSC, my General MIDI software synth. (Your output may already show this output, particularly if the VSC is your only MIDI output device.)

Next, let's set the MIDI channel (see Figure 6.4).

Figure 6.4

5. **Click** the **arrow button** to the right of the Ch (for MIDI Channel) area. A drop-down list of possible MIDI channels will appear, assigned to the program setup you configured when you set up the MIDI instruments for each channel.

6. **Click** the **desired MIDI channel** for the track. In this case, choose MIDI channel #10, since this is a General MIDI drum track (note that the instruments are already set up for the job).

TIP

General MIDI, a standard that you'll learn more about in Chapter 7, always has drum sounds assigned to MIDI channel #10, which can make setting up a drum track a breeze.

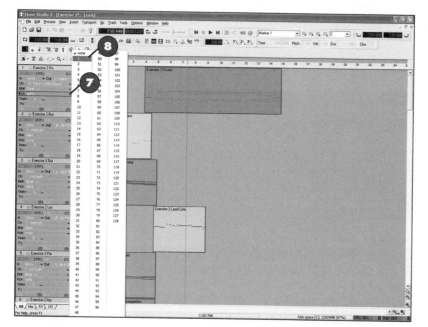

Figure 6.5

7. **Click** the **arrow button** to the right of the **Pch** (for Patch) area. A drop-down list of program numbers will appear.

8. **Click** the **desired patch number** for this track. In this case, choose patch #1.

Let's listen to this track and see how our patch selection sounds. To do this, it would be nice to hear *only* the drum track (those other tracks are just distracting at this point). That's where the solo feature (present in all DAW applications) will really help out. When you solo a track, you will hear only that track.

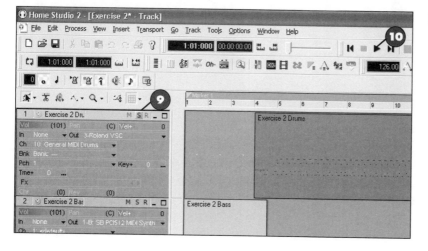

Figure 6.6

9. **Click** the **Solo** button (marked with an "S"). The solo button will turn green, indicating that it will be the only track heard.

10. Begin playback. Hey, the drum track actually sounds like drums! Let's do another track (see Figure 6.7).

Figure 6.7

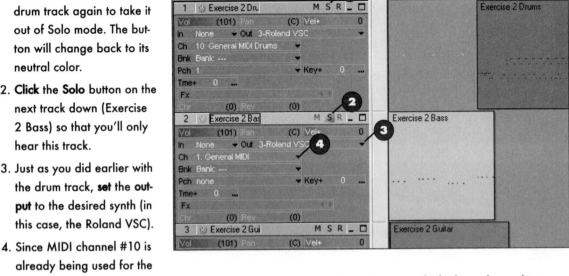

1. **Click** the **Solo** button on the drum track again to take it out of Solo mode. The button will change back to its neutral color.

2. **Click** the **Solo** button on the next track down (Exercise 2 Bass) so that you'll only hear this track.

3. Just as you did earlier with the drum track, **set** the **output** to the desired synth (in this case, the Roland VSC).

4. Since MIDI channel #10 is already being used for the drum track, choose another MIDI channel for the bass part. It doesn't matter which channel you choose, just so long as it isn't channel 10. I've chosen MIDI channel #1 for simplicity's sake.

Figure 6.8

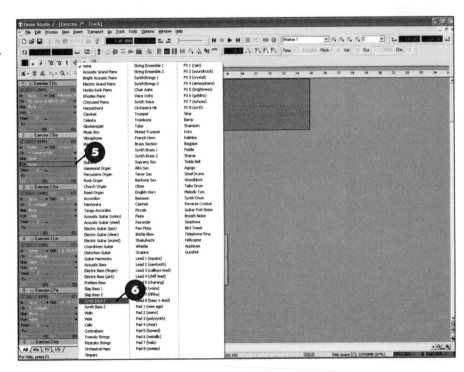

5. **Click** the **arrow button** to the right of the Pch (for Patch) area. A drop-down list of program names will appear.

6. **Click** the **desired patch number** for this track. I found that **Synth Bass 1** works pretty well for this track, but feel free to experiment.

> **❋ NOTE**
>
> You might wonder why there's such a large list of patch names here, where there were only numbers in the drum track. You can take credit for that—by identifying your General MIDI synths as such to Cakewalk, Home Studio now gives you a more descriptive list of patches, as opposed to just patch numbers. See how a little preparation can really pay off?

Now you can flesh out the rest of this sequence. Here are the steps:

1. **Solo** only the **track** that you want to set up (just a suggestion).

2. **Change** all the **track outputs** to be the MIDI device that you want to hear.

3. **Assign** a **different MIDI channel** to each of the tracks. Again, it doesn't matter which channel you use, but each track's MIDI channel must be different from any others in order to hear a different instrument on that track.

4. Finally, **pick a patch** that suits the track. Use the track's name as your guide. Here's what I've chosen (see Figure 6.9).

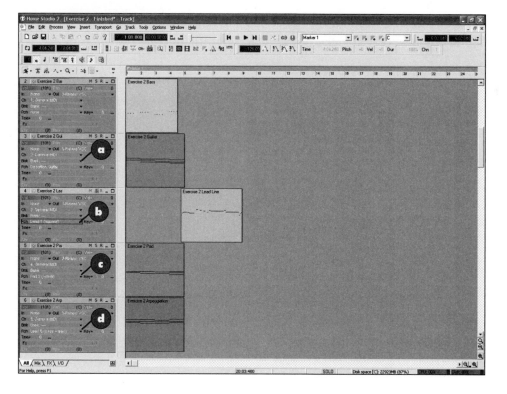

Figure 6.9

a. For the Exercise 2 Guitar track—Distortion Guitar.

b. For the Exercise 2 Lead Line track—Lead 1 (square).

c. For the Exercise 2 Pad track—Pad 2 (warm).

d. For the Exercise 2 Arpeggiation track—Lead 8 (bass + lead).

❄ **TIP**

When soloing a track and picking a patch, you might want to listen to the track over and over without having to manually go back to the beginning again and again. This is a great time to use loop playback to your advantage. Here's a trick: Click on the region that you want to set up. The corresponding time will be selected on the timeline. All you have to do at that point is just capture that selection using the Set Loop to Selection button, which will automatically put you into loop mode, Just hit play, and you're set.

❄ **TIP**

Could you imagine trying to assign sounds to unnamed tracks? Thank goodness the track names are there to give you an idea of what the track is doing musically. When you create your own music, you should get into the practice of naming your tracks. One of the most important skills of any computer artist or producer is good documentation habits. Naming your tracks (for starters) will really pay off in the long run, especially when you archive your sessions.

Using Quartz AudioMaster Freeware

Getting the job done in AudioMaster is even easier than it was in Home Studio (mainly because you only have a single MIDI device to work with in this freeware version). There are a few ways to get the job done (see Figure 6.10).

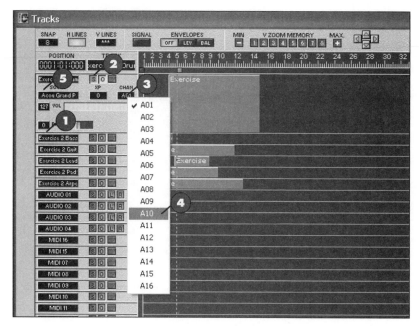

Figure 6.10

1. **Click** and **drag** the **bottom boundary** of a track to reveal more information about that track.

2. **Click** the **Solo** button to solo the track. Note that not only will the track go solo, but all the other tracks will turn off (the green "on" lights on the track in the Track window and the Mixer window will go out).

3. **Click** the **Chan** (for MIDI Channel) display. A list of MIDI channels will appear.

4. Again, since this is a General MIDI situation and this is a drum track, **choosing channel A10** is the right choice for this particular track.

5. **Click** the **Sound** display (which will change to STANDARD as soon as you click). The Sound Names window will appear (see Figure 6.11).

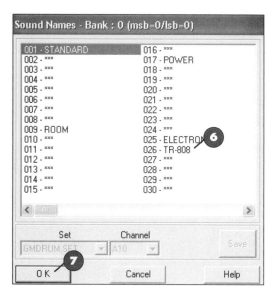

Figure 6.11

6. **Choose** the **desired sound** for your drum kit. In this case, I chose the TR-808 drum patch. Kinda fun!

7. **Click OK.** That's all!

Here's another way to do the same thing, this time using the Mixer window (see Figure 6.12).

Figure 6.12

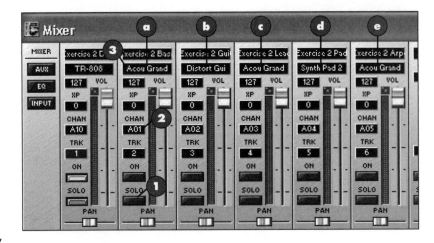

1. **Click** the **Solo** button for the channel you want to modify

2. **Click** the **Chan** display to select your MIDI channel.

3. **Click** the **Sound** display (which is unlabeled in the Mixer window) to choose your sound. Clicking this button will give you the same sound name window

that you saw when you chose a patch from the Tracks window, and the process of choosing a sound is the same.

Now you can set up all the rest of your tracks. Remember, don't assign any two tracks to the same MIDI channel if you want them to have different sounds associated with them. As far as patch names go, try these for starters:

a. For the Exercise 2 Bass track—Synth Bass 1.

b. For the Exercise 2 Guitar track—Distort Guitar.

c. For the Exercise 2 Lead Line track—Synth Lead 1 (square).

d. For the Exercise 2 Pad track—Synth Pad 2 (warm).

e. For the Exercise 2 Arpeggiation track—Synth Lead 8 (bass + lead).

❊ **CAUTION**

For some reason, changing MIDI channels and sounds using the Mixer window isn't always reflected in the display. The changes are being made, but the window doesn't always change to reflect this. Closing and opening the Mixer window updates the display.

Changing Tempo

Hope you're having fun! Your song may not sound like much yet, but it's actually well on its way! Let's see how we can work with the tempo (the speed of your song).

Using Cakewalk Home Studio

There's one window that tells us about the tempo of our session, not surprisingly called the Tempo display (see Figure 6.13).

Figure 6.13

This display tells you that your session is set to play at 126 beats per minute. Changing the tempo is easy.

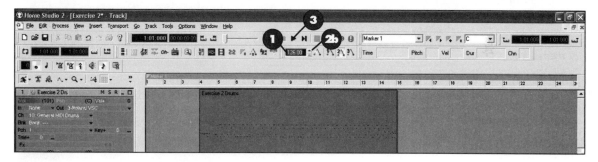

Figure 6.14

1. **Click** the **Tempo** display window. The number will be highlighted.

2a. **Type** in the **tempo** that you want to use. Higher values will be a faster tempo, while lower numbers will mean a slower song, or

2b. **Use** the **incremental buttons** to the right of the tempo display (marked with a plus and minus sign) to change the tempo.

3. **Press** the **Enter** key to confirm your choice.

4. **Begin playback**. You'll hear the music at a the new tempo.

> ❀ **TIP**
>
> Try entering a radically different number than the 126 beats per minute that the session originally was. Notice that the pitch doesn't change, only the speed of the music.

Follow the steps in Figure 6.15 if you want to change tempo somewhere in the song.

Figure 6.15

1a. **Click** the **Insert Tempo** button to the right of the tempo display window, or

1b. From the Insert drop-down menu, **choose** the **Tempo Change** menu item.

Either way, the Tempo window will appear (see Figure 6.16).

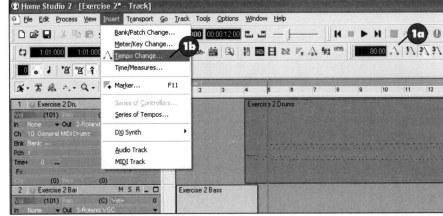

Figure 6.16

2a. **Type** the **desired tempo** in the Tempo display, or

2b. **Click** the **Click here to tap tempo** button according to the tempo you want for the song. (This is particularly useful if you don't know the number of the tempo you want, but you do know the speed.) The tempo display will change according to the speed of your mouse clicks.

3. **Click** the **Insert a New Tempo** radio button.

4a. **Type** a **location** into the Starting at Time display (the format of the display is bars:beats:ticks), or

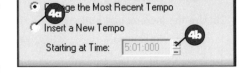

4b. **Click** the **incremental button** to the right of the Starting at Time display to change the time of the new tempo.

5. Once you're done, **click OK**.

6. **Start playback**, and you'll hear the change in speed at the point in time that you inserted the tempo change.

❄ **TIP**

The initial location shown in the Starting at Time display is based upon the current location of the play line. Sometimes the easiest way to insert a tempo change is to move the play line to the point where you want the tempo to change *before* you begin the tempo change process.

Let's say that you want to have a gradual change in tempo (speeding up or slowing down). Does that mean that you have to insert a bazillion individual tempo changes? Nope—read on (see Figure 6.17).

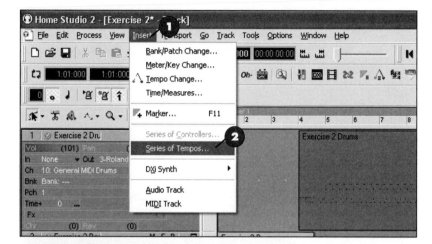

Figure 6.17

1. **Click** the **Insert** drop-down menu.

2. **Click** the **Series of Tempos** menu item. The Insert Series of Tempos window will appear (see Figure 6.18).

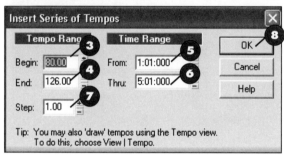

Figure 6.18

3. **Use** your **cursor** to select the Begin value and **type** the **tempo** that you want to start off with. Just for fun, I've chosen to enter 80 beats per minute.

4. **Use** your **cursor** to select the End value and **type** the **tempo** that you want to wind up with at the end of the gradual tempo change. I've entered 126 beats per minute (the original tempo of the MIDI sequence).

5. Now **select** the **From value** and **type** in the **point** at which you want to start your tempo change. Since I want to begin the song with this strange tempo change, I've chosen 1:01:000 (the first bar, the first beat).

6. **Type** a **value** into the Thru area to tell Cakewalk Home Studio when to end the tempo change. I want to reach 126 BPM by the beginning of bar 5, so I've entered 5:01:000. This will give me a gradual tempo change over the first four bars of the song, *ending* at the beginning of measure 5.

7. The Step value determines how frequently (in beats and ticks) a tempo message will be inserted. The way it's set up now, there will be a different tempo value created every beat between the From and Thru point.

8. **Click OK** to apply the tempo changes.

9. **Play** the **session** back to hear what you've done. If you've followed what I've done, you'll hear the song start *painfully* slowly and change gradually to the regular tempo of 126 beats per minute. If you watch the Tempo window on Home Studio's desktop, you'll see the tempo change on the beat (watch your Now display to see the beats passing).

That wasn't too hard, but there's an even easier way to change tempos. Here's a hint: Take a look at the tip at the bottom of the Insert Series of Tempos window (see Figure 6.19).

Figure 6.19

1. **Click** the **View** drop-down menu.

2. **Click** the **Tempo** menu item. The Tempo window will appear (see Figure 6.20).

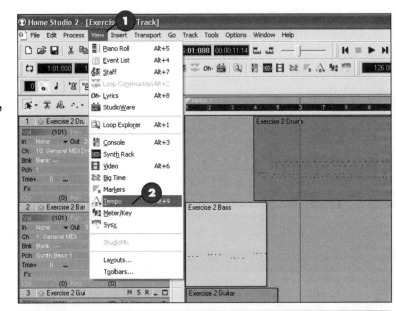

Figure 6.20

a. The numbers on the left edge of the window indicate tempo in beats per minute. Again, the higher the number, the faster the music.

b. The numbers on the top edge of the window indicate time in bars and beats. Time is displayed from left to right.

c. This line represents the tempo of the song over the course of time. In this case, you can actually see the beginning tempo of 80 beats per minute as it ramps up to 126 beats per minute by the beginning of measure 5.

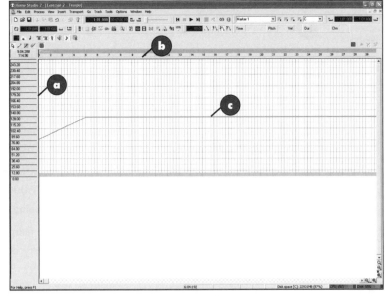

Let's change that beginning ramp-up in tempo (see Figure 6.21).

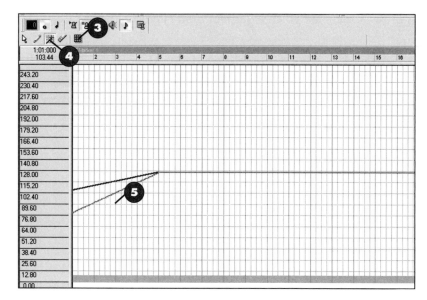

Figure 6.21

3. For now, make sure the **Snap to Grid** icon is **not depressed** (physically, not emotionally).

4. **Click** the **Draw Line** icon. With this feature activated, you can draw in a linear tempo change.

5. **Click** and **drag** in the **Tempo window** to create a new tempo line. Since the tempo ramp-up used before was a little too extreme, I've made the ramp a little more shallow. Once I let go, the tempo will change to start at a faster tempo (about 103 beats per minute) and ramp up to 126 beats per minute.

❄ **TIP**

If you want to draw a tempo change to the beginning of a song, it's much easier to do it if you draw it *backwards* (in other words, click where you want the tempo change to end and drag to the left). It's very difficult to click right at the beginning of the song with the Draw tool, and if you don't catch the very beginning of the song, you'll wind up with an old tempo value that you can't get rid of.

That was really easy. So, now let's draw in some tempo changes that *aren't* in a straight line (see Figure 6.22).

Figure 6.22

1. **Click** the **Draw** tool button.

2. **Click** and **drag** across the Tempo window to "draw" new tempos. As you draw, the area that you're affecting will be shown in blue.

3. **Release** the **mouse** to enter your tempo changes. The window will look something like Figure 6.23.

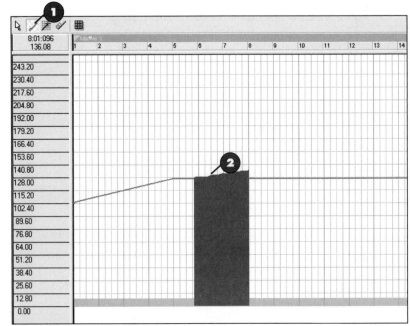

Figure 6.23

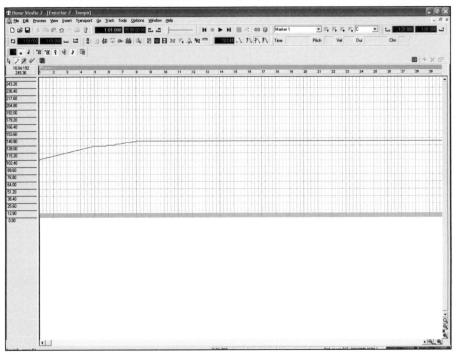

❄ **TIP**

I'm sure it comes as no surprise by now for me to say that MIDI is a great way to create electronic kinds of music. MIDI is also good for creating music that *doesn't* sound electronic as well! In fact, you probably hear MIDI every day, but it sounds completely real. It's the mark of a truly advanced MIDI user to create such "real" sounding work using MIDI, and a big part of creating the illusion is to put yourself in the mindset of a "live" musician.

Put yourself in the role of a live drummer. As the song progresses, isn't it natural that it should rise and fall in energy? Assuming that it does, might that not send the adrenaline kicking in at certain points, naturally resulting in a small increase in tempo? Sure it would, and you can emulate that very effect by changing tempo *slightly* when the power of the song increases (choruses, for example). When the energy goes down, you can make the band "relax" by inching the tempo down a bit.

This is a nuance effect, really perceived only subconsciously, so you don't need to go crazy with big, perceptible tempo changes. With some experimentation, you'll be pleased at how even a couple of beats per minute can breathe life into your MIDI sequences.

There are a couple buttons left to talk about before tackling AudioMaster. These buttons aren't really tempo changes, but they will allow us to listen to our music at different speeds. Just to the right of the tempo display on the Home Studio desktop, there are three Tempo Ratio buttons. Check out what they do in Figure 6.24.

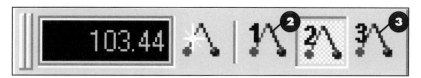

Figure 6.24

1. **Begin playback** of your song from the beginning.

2. During playback, **click** the **Tempo Ratio 1** button. Note how the speed of the song decreases dramatically, but the tempo value (as displayed in the tempo window to the left) remains unchanged.

3. While still playing, try **clicking** the **Tempo Ratio 3** button. Now the song will speed up (the tempo value still doesn't change).

These buttons allow you to hear your song at different speeds *without* having to change the tempo of the song. This is a useful production tool, and I personally use the slower playback ratio quite often. These buttons are even configurable (see Figure 6.25).

Figure 6.25

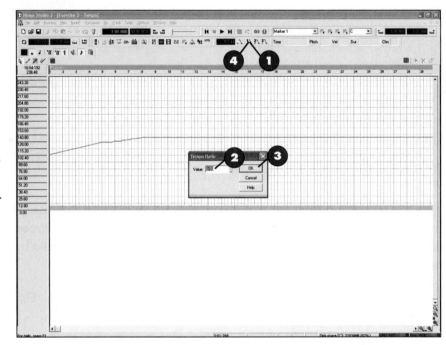

1. Holding the Shift key, **click** the **Tempo Ratio 1** button. The Tempo Ratio window will appear.

2. Right now the Tempo Ratio 1 button is set to play back at a speed of .5 of real time (half-speed). Let's make it *really* slow, and change it to play back at .25 speed (one quarter of real time). To do this, **type** the **desired ratio** (in this case, .25).

3. **Click** the **OK** button to confirm your choice.

4. Now, **click** the **Tempo Ratio 1** button and begin playing your song. You'll see that now your song is playing back at one quarter of real time.

> **TIP**
>
> Remember to leave at least one of the Tempo Ratio buttons with a value of 1. You'll need that button to play back your song at normal speed.

Using Quartz AudioMaster Freeware

Tempo is not quite as advanced in AudioMaster Freeware as it was in Cakewalk Home Studio, but there are still a number of things you can do with it (see Figure 6.26).

Figure 6.26

1. On the Control window, **click** the **Tempo** display. The Tempo window will appear (see Figure 6.27).

Figure 6.27

2. **Type** the **desired tempo** for the song.

3. **Click OK.** Your setting will be applied, and the Tempo display will be updated.

What if you want to change the tempo in the middle of the song? In AudioMaster, you'll have to get your hands a little dirty with the MIDI Event List (see Figure 6.28).

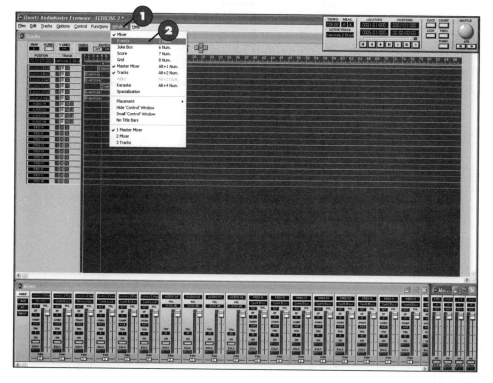

Figure 6.28

1. **Click** the **Windows** drop-down menu.

2. **Click** the **Events** menu item. The MIDI Event List window will open, looking something like Figure 6.29.

Figure 6.29

What you're looking at is a list of individual MIDI messages on a single track. Tempo messages, however, are global messages, affecting all the tracks. Let's take a look at a global Event List instead.

3. **Click** the **Master** button. The master MIDI Event List will appear (see Figure 6.30).

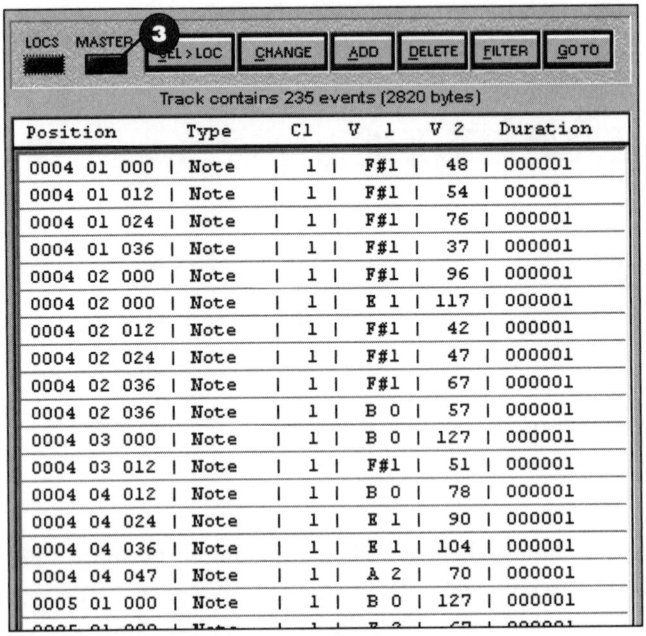

Figure 6.30

This relatively short list is more concerned with the song as a whole rather than any single track.

a. **Time Signature** (in this case, 4/4)

b. **Key Signature** (in this case, the key of C major)

c. **Tempo** (in this case, 125 beats per minute)

Note that all of these messages start at the beginning of the song (in the Position column, all messages are at bar 1, beat 1, tick 0). So what if you want to change any of these global aspects later in the song? (See Figure 6.31.)

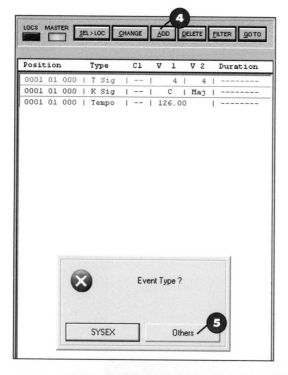

Figure 6.31

4. **Click** the **Add** button. The **Event Type** window will open.

5. Since this isn't a system exclusive message (device-specific control data), **click** the **Others** button. The MIDI Event window will open (see Figure 6.32).

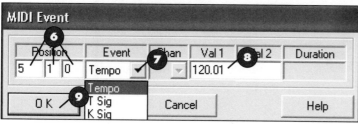

Figure 6.32

6. **Type** the **desired location** (in bars, beats, and ticks) of the new MIDI message.

7. If the desired type of MIDI message isn't showing in the Event display, just **click** the **arrow button** to reveal a drop-down list of possible global messages (tempo, time signature, key signature). **Click** the **type of message** you want to create (in this case, you will make a Tempo message).

8. **Type** the **desired value** in the value field.

9. When you're done, **click** the **OK** button. Your MIDI message will be created.

> ❋ **NOTE**
>
> Notice that the channel and duration fields are filled in. This is because these types of messages apply to all MIDI channels, and their duration is permanent (or until the next MIDI message of the same type).

If you want to change messages that are already on the list, it couldn't be easier. In fact, I'll set the initial tempo to 80 beats per minute. See Figure 6.33.

Figure 6.33

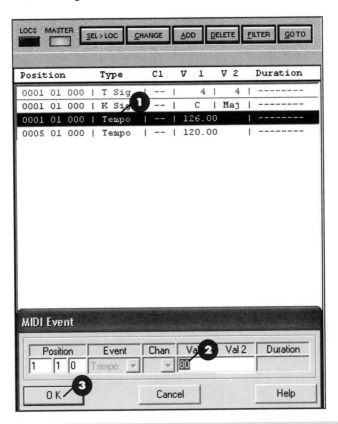

1. **Double-click** the **MIDI message** that you want to change. The MIDI Event window will open.

2. **Type** the **new value** in the appropriate field. In this case, I want to change the tempo value to 80 beats per minute, but I could just as easily change the location or even the type of the message.

3. When you're done, **click OK.** That's it!

> ❄ **NOTE**
>
> Unfortunately, there's no easy way to create a gradual tempo change with the AudioMaster Freeware. If you really want that sort of musical effect, you'll have to do it the hard way, by creating a ton of individual MIDI tempo messages. Look at the bright side, though—you'll be an old hand at creating MIDI events!

Fixing Notes

Sometimes, notes are just *wrong*. The wrong finger goes on the wrong key, and the wrong note is recorded. In fact, there are wrong notes in the lead line. Not a problem—there are a lot of ways you can fix your mistakes (see Figure 6.34).

Using Cakewalk Home Studio

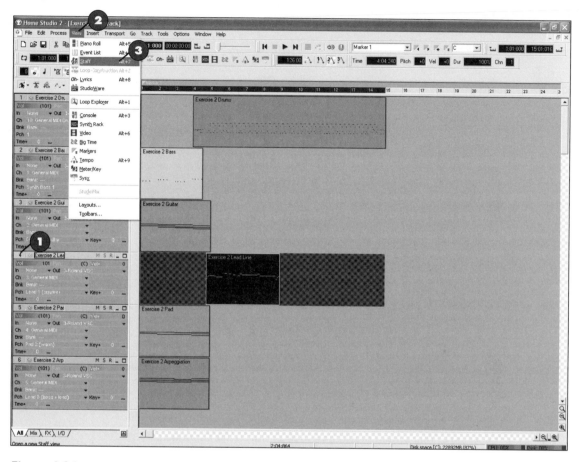

Figure 6.34

1. In the Track window, **click** the **Exercise 2 Lead Line** track number. The track will become highlighted.

2. **Click** the **View** menu.

3. **Click** the **Staff** menu item. The Staff window will appear (see Figure 6.35).

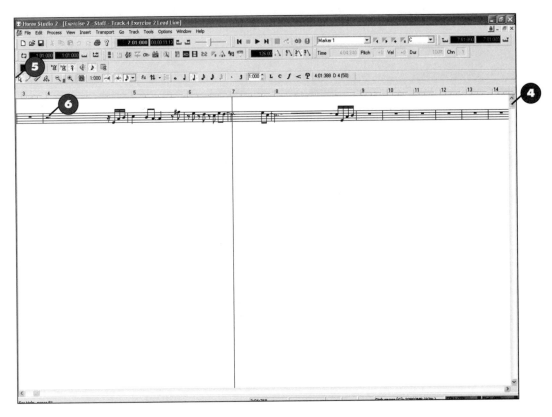

Figure 6.35

4. Use the scroll bar or the arrow keys at the bottom of the Staff window to center the melody in the window. Your screen should now look similar to this illustration.

5. You'll notice that all the notes are blue. That means that they are all selected, and any editing process will be applied to all of them. Since you'll be editing individual notes, you'll need to deselect them. **Click** the **Select** tool.

6. After the Select tool has been chosen, **click anywhere** in the Staff window to deselect the notes.

First thing to do is remove the first three notes (after I played them, I decided they didn't work). See Figure 6.36.

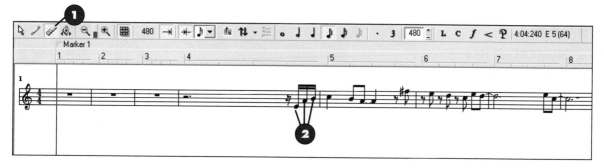

Figure 6.36

1. **Click** the **Erase** tool.
2. **Click** the **note head** (the round part) of the note(s) you desire to remove.

That was easy! Next, let's change the pitch of the note at the end of measure 5. For example, I don't know what pitch will work, but I *do* know that what it is now (F-sharp) ain't it! See Figure 6.37.

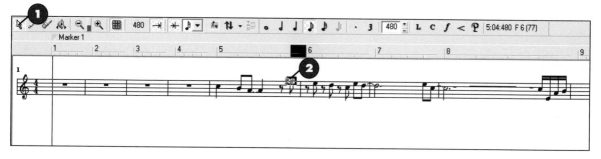

Figure 6.37

1. **Click** the **Select** tool.
2. **Click** and **hold** on the **note head** of the note you want to change.
3. **Drag** the **note** up or down to the desired pitch. When you release the note, the Drag and Drop Options window will appear (see Figure 6.38).

Figure 6.38

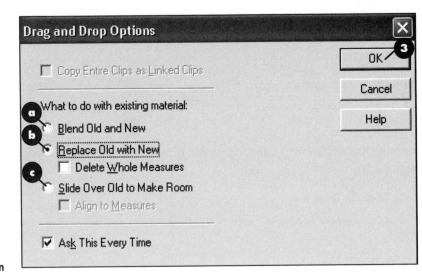

a. **Blend Old and New:** Choosing this option will place your note without adjusting any other notes.

b. **Replace Old with New:** This will delete any existing notes at the location to which the note has been moved.

c. **Slide Over Old to Make Room:** This will cause any pre-existing notes to slide later in time to make room for your moved note.

3. After you've selected your option (Replace Old with New works in this case), **click** the **OK** button.

Also very easy, but what if I want to change the note to F-natural, which is on the same line? Here's another way to change a note that might work better in this particular case (see Figure 6.39).

Figure 6.39

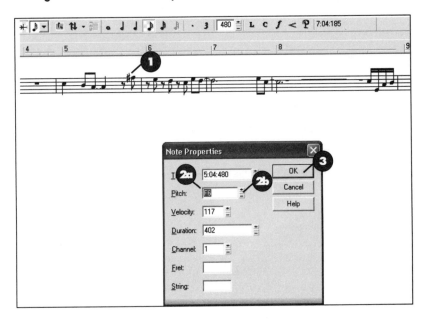

1. **Right-click** on the **note head** of the note that you want to change. The Note Properties window will appear.

2a. **Type** the **desired pitch** into the Pitch area, or

2b. **Use** the **arrow keys** to the right of the pitch display to move the pitch up or down.

3. When you're done, **click** the **OK** button, and your changes will be applied.

> ❊ **NOTE**
>
> You'll notice that in the world of MIDI, note names have numbers after them. This number, along with the note letter, describes the pitch of the note. To learn more about the meanings of these numbers, refer to Appendix B.

If you don't want to work in the Staff window, you can do the job in the Piano Roll window (see Figure 6.40).

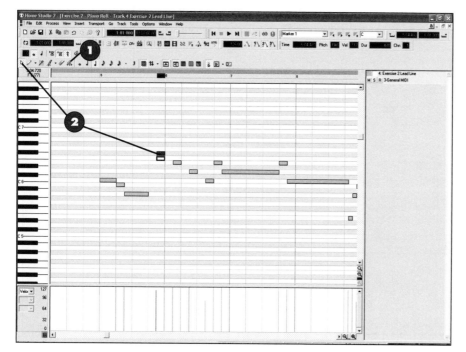

Figure 6.40

1. **Click** the **Erase** tool to remove notes, just as you did in the Staff window. After that, simply click on the notes that you want to remove.

2. **Click** the **Select** tool to move notes again just as you did a moment ago in the staff view. To move notes, **click** and **drag them.** There's a familiar window that you'll see when you release your mouse (see Figure 6.40).

3. After you've selected your option (Replace Old with New works in this case), **click** the **OK** button.

Now listen to your music, and you'll see that it sounds much better. After the pitches have been fixed, you might notice that some of the notes are too quiet in relation to the melody in general. From our earlier discussion about MIDI, you know that that problem can be fixed by adjusting the velocity of the offending notes (see Figure 6.41).

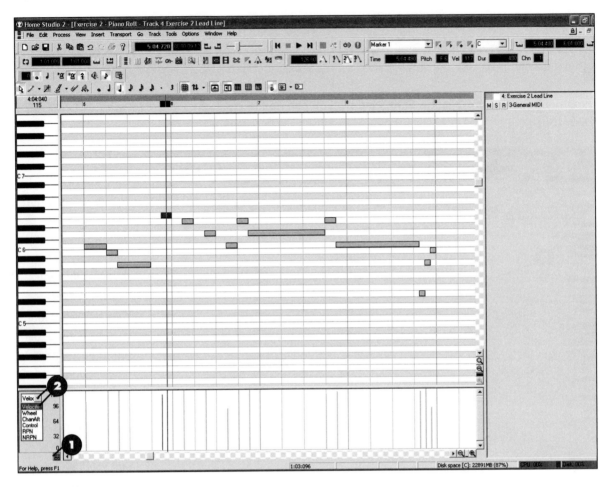

Figure 6.41

1. If it's not showing already, **click** the **Show/Hide Controller Pane** icon to reveal the controller section of the Piano Roll window.

2. Since we want to work with note Velocity, make sure that Velocity is showing in this display. If it's not, you can click the arrow button to the right of the display to show a list of controllers, and **click Velocity (see Figure 6.42)**.

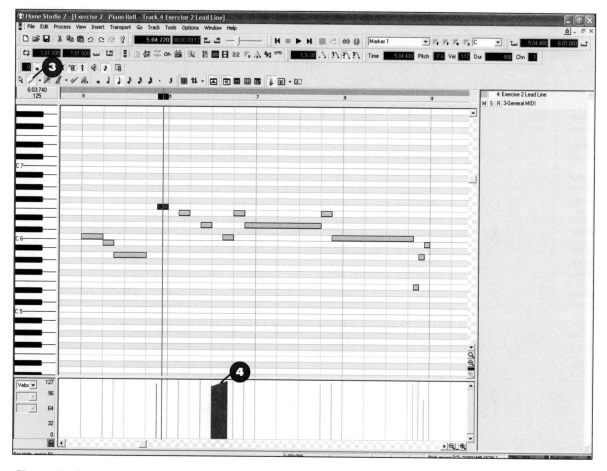

Figure 6.42

3. **Click** the **Draw** tool button. Your cursor will turn into a pencil.

4. **Click** and **drag** over the **velocity** (or velocities) that you want to change. As you draw, you'll create a filled area as shown in Figure 6.43.

   After you let go of your mouse, any velocity messages included in that filled area will be changed, like Figure 6.43.

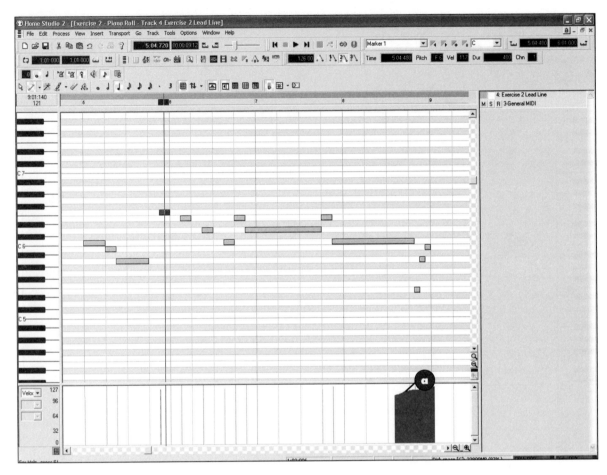

Figure 6.43

  a. You can also modify a number of velocity messages by clicking and dragging with the Draw tool over a
  series of controller messages.

Using Quartz AudioMaster Freeware

Unfortunately, the Staff window in the Quartz AudioMaster Freeware isn't particularly useful. Tracks
aren't labeled, clefs can't be changed, and the only editing you can do can be done more effectively
in the Grid window or MIDI Event List. With that in mind, going into the Grid window (which is
AudioMaster's name for a Piano Roll window) makes editing a snap!

Before you start:

1. **Select** the **lead track**. This is easily done by **clicking** the **Trk** button in the Mixer window (the track number for the lead track is 4).

2. From the Windows drop-down menu, **select** the **Grid** menu item. If you don't see any notes in this window, use the scroll bars at the bottom and right edge of the window to navigate until your window looks something like Figure 6.44.

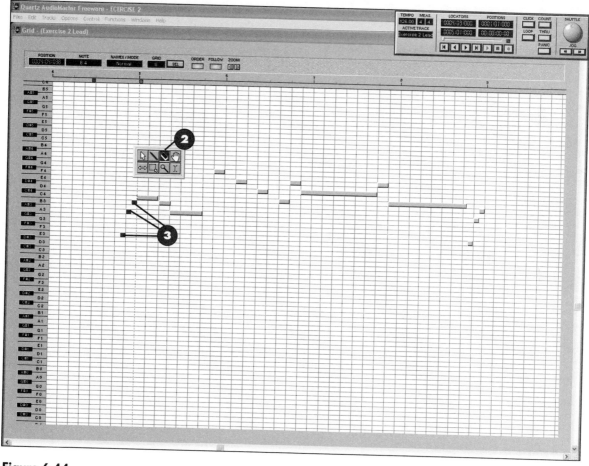

Figure 6.44

1. **Right-click** in the **Grid window** to show the toolbox.

2. **Click** on the **Eraser** tool. Your cursor will turn into an eraser.

3. **Click** on the **notes** that you want to delete.

Changing a note's pitch is also very easy (see Figure 6.45).

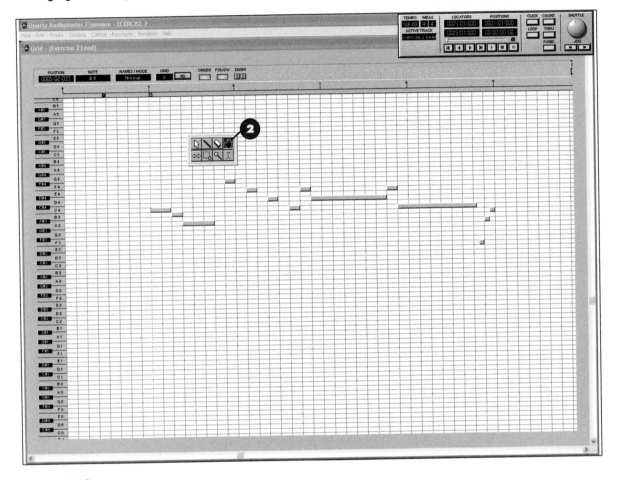

Figure 6.45

1. **Right-click** in the **Grid window** to show the toolbox.
2. **Click** on the **Move** tool.

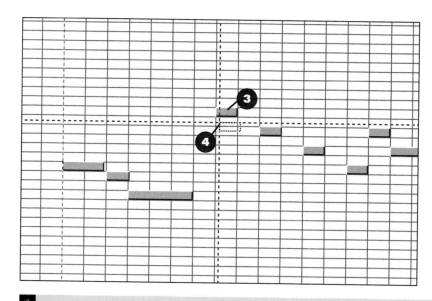

Figure 6.46

3. **Click** and **hold** on the **note** that you want to change.

4. Still holding the mouse, **drag** and **drop** the **note** to the desired pitch.

 TIP

Getting hold of a desired note with the Move tool can be a trick sometimes. Try grabbing the note with the fingers of the hand icon to get more reliable performance.

TIP

The point at which the dotted lines intersect will determine the point on the grid where the note will be deposited.

To change velocities, let's go back to another old friend, the Event window. Before you start, do the following:

1. If the lead line track isn't selected, please do so now. This is easily done by **clicking** the **Trk** button in the Mixer window (the track number for the lead track is 4).

2. From the Windows drop-down menu, **select** the **Event** menu item.

3. If the Master button in the Event window is still lit, **click it** to get back to the normal Event List.

As you learned earlier, there are two values that are relevant to every note message, which are pitch and velocity. You can see the pitch in the V1 column, and in the V2 column is a number representing each note's velocity. There are two notes with relatively low velocity values (both of them are 88). Basically, it means that these notes were played a little too gently. Here's how to fix them (see Figure 6.47).

Figure 6.47

1. **Double-click** the **MIDI message** that you want to change. The MIDI Event window will appear.

2. **Click** the **arrow button** to the right of the Val 2 display. A drop-down list will appear.

3. **Scroll** and **click** the **desired new velocity value**.

4. **Click** the **OK** button. Your changes will be applied.

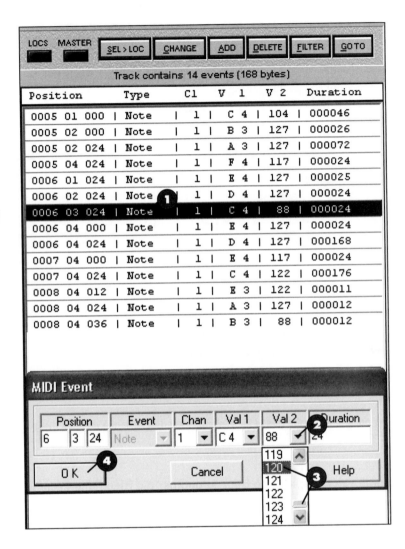

7 The MIDI Studio

Here's where it all comes together. All the theoretical knowledge you've taken the time to learn will finally make sense when you see the features of today's MIDI workstations. In this chapter, you'll learn:

※ How to set up your MIDI devices to get the most out of your gear.

※ Different types of synthesizers and when to use them.

※ How sequencer programs work.

※ Common MIDI operations and how to use them, regardless of the application you're using.

More About MIDI Signal Flow

Brace yourself, 'cause life is about to get a *lot* better. By now you're starting to get a sense of how powerful MIDI can be, but we haven't even talked about MIDI channels yet. While you *have* set up tracks using MIDI channels, there's much more to this aspect of the MIDI language than what you've worked with so far. Truth is, through MIDI channels, a single MIDI plug can trigger not one sound but up to *16*.

MIDI channels operate in some ways like radio channels. Here's a mental picture for you: You're tuning your radio. How many radio stations will you hear at a time—one, right? Even though you're only listening to one, though, aren't *all* the radio stations in town broadcasting? So, in effect, when you choose a radio station, aren't you also choosing to ignore all the other stations that are buzzing around in the air?

MIDI works in much the same way. According to the MIDI spec, a single MIDI cable can carry up to 16 channels of MIDI data. That means that not only can you have more than one MIDI device connected to a single MIDI Out port of a sequencer (through the magic of the MIDI thru port), but each device can play completely different MIDI parts. It's easy as pie to set up (see Figure 7.1).

Figure 7.1

A typical MIDI setup.

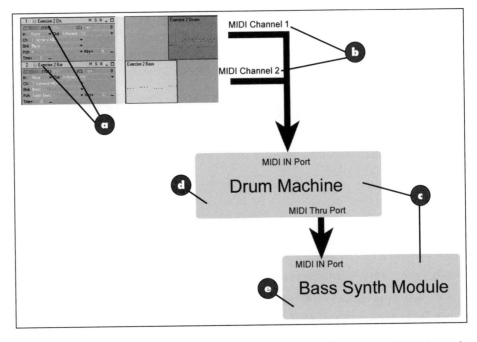

a. Your sequencer program is set up to play a number of different musical parts, for example a bass and drum part. Each part is on its own track, much like each part would be written on separate musical staves of manuscript (written music).

b. Both tracks are assigned to be sent out of a single MIDI port, but each is assigned to its own MIDI channel (numbered 1 through 16). For example, let's say that the drum part is assigned to MIDI channel 1, and the bass part is assigned to MIDI channel 2.

c. On the receiving end, there are two MIDI sound modules. One might be a drum machine as shown here, and another might be a device with a particularly sweet bass sound that you're interested in using.

d. Set the device to react only to data coming in on MIDI channel 1. Basically, you've matched the drum machine's receive channel to the drum track's transmit channel.

e. Now all you need to do is also set up the other synth module to react to any MIDI messages that are transmitting on MIDI channel 2.

Here's the really cool part about MIDI channels: Not only will the gear play the part that it's assigned to, it'll *not* play any MIDI data that's assigned to any other channel. That way, you can have your drum machine playing only the drum part and your bass synth module playing only the bass part. By using all the MIDI channels available on only one MIDI Out port, you can get up to 16 different musical parts to play together, each triggering its own sound.

> ❋ **NOTE**
>
> You might be tempted to daisy-chain 16 MIDI slaves together in order to take full advantage of these MIDI channels, but unfortunately there's a problem with that idea. Due to the way MIDI cables and plugs are designed, there can be data transfer problems with long MIDI chains. In fact, daisy-chain configurations of over three slave devices are specifically discouraged in the official MIDI specifications. Don't worry, because this limitation isn't as significant as you might think, and there are workarounds.

If you have a MIDI interface with more than one MIDI Output port, then these 16 channels are multiplied by the number of ports. Each MIDI cable not only has 16 channels, but 16 discrete channels, different from the 16 channels in the other cables. So, if you have a MIDI interface with two MIDI Output ports, then you would have a grand total of 32 different MIDI channels you could use. The interfaces for MIDI Out port #1 would have 16 channels, and MIDI Out port #2 would have another 16. A typical routing setup with a 2 in/2 out MIDI interface might look like Figure 7.2.

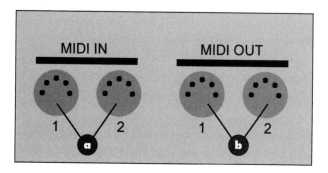

Figure 7.2

Multiple Ins and Outs.

a. Each of the two MIDI In ports on the MIDI interface supports 16 channels, giving a grand total of 32 different channels of input. Keep in mind that multiple devices can be set up in a MIDI chain as shown in Figure 7.1, opening the possibility of multiple controller devices being attached to a single MIDI In port.

b. Each of the two MIDI Out ports supports 16 channels. Take those 16 channels and multiply that by two ports, and you've got 32 different output channels. An added bonus to multiple output ports: You can have more slave devices attached to your system. Instead of one daisy chain of three slave devices (sharing 16 channels), you can now have *two* daisy chains, giving you six slave devices sharing 32 channels.

To use a multiport MIDI interface is easier than you might think. In the environment of a multitrack MIDI sequencer, any given track's output can be assigned. All you have to do is choose the output port for that track and then the channel upon which the data will be sent.

❋ ❋ ❋

Synthesizers and MIDI

You've got a good conceptual understanding of how the MIDI language works and the kinds of things that can be done with this powerful tool, but there's still a little to discuss before moving on to some hands-on music making. Let's talk a little more about the devices that make the sounds—the synthesizers.

Monophonic versus Polyphonic

Back in the day when synthesizers were in their infancy, analog synthesis ruled the earth. These giant behemoths relied upon primitive tone-generating oscillators. These oscillators would work together, combining their massive sound-creating power to give the musician... one note. No kidding—you could let the cat run across the keyboard, and you'd only hear one note at a time! With many synthesizers, this is still the case. These synthesizers are called *monophonic* (meaning "one sound") synthesizers.

On the other hand of the spectrum are polyphonic synthesizers. Whereas a monophonic synth can only play one note, polyphonic synths can play more than one. How many notes can a polyphonic synth play? There is no set answer. Different models of synths boast different levels of polyphony, from two notes on up. The polyphony of a synth (a good spec to check up on when shopping for gear) determines the maximum number of notes (also called "voices") you will be able to play (and hear) at one time. For example, if you had a synthesizer with eight-note (or eight-voice) polyphony, and you played a monster chord with all 10 of your fingers, you would only hear eight of the ten notes of your music. If you held down the sustain pedal and hit eight more notes, then the eight notes you originally played would be cut off in favor of the new notes that you played. A limitation to be sure, but not one that can't be worked around.

Let's put the idea of polyphony aside for a second and talk about the tones that can be played.

Monotimbral versus Multitimbral

We use the word *timbre* (pronounced tam-burr) to describe the tonal quality of a given sound. For example a tuba playing a "C" would have a different tone color, or timbre, than an alto saxophone playing the same note. In synthesizers, the concept of timbres is taken to the extreme, as sounds are crafted that no traditional instrument could ever play. The idea of timbre, however, goes even farther to the heart of a synthesizer's tone-generating engine.

Some synths are monotimbral, meaning that they can only play one timbre at a time. Early synthesizers were not only monophonic, but also monotimbral as a result. Now, this doesn't necessarily mean that a monotimbral synth can play only one kind of sound, but it can only play one kind of sound at a time. If a synthesizer can create more than one timbre at a time, then that synth is called *multitimbral* (multitimbral meaning "many timbres"). A multitimbral device is by definition polyphonic—in fact, many synths can play a different sound on each of its notes.

These days, most sound-producing MIDI gear is multitimbral and polyphonic to some extent, although some vintage-style analog modules are monophonic and monotimbral. As for the multitimbral devices, the allocation of tones can be approached in a number of ways. Do you want a lot of different musical parts to be played at once? No problem—simply assign each timbre to respond to its own MIDI channel (for example in a single multitimbral synth, you could have a bass sound playing the MIDI messages coming in on MIDI channel one, a piano making sound as determined by MIDI channel two, and so on). In this way, the module can effectively become a band in a box. The only limitation would be the device's polyphony and the maximum number of programs that can be active at once. Here's how it might work with a synth module with an eight-voice multitimbral and polyphonic synth (see Figure 7.3).

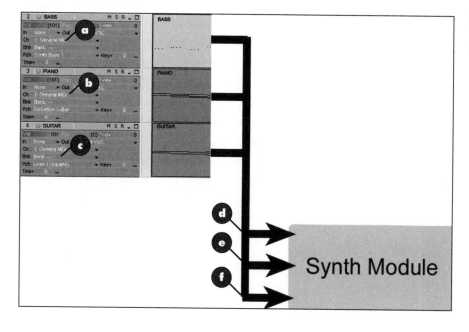

Figure 7.3

Using a multitimbral synth.

a. The bass part is transmitted as MIDI data on MIDI channel 1.

b. The piano part is transmitted on MIDI channel 2.

c. The guitar part is sent on channel 3.

d. The synth module is set to a bass patch on channel 1. Since the bass part has only one note playing at a time, it uses only one voice of the module's eight-voice polyphony.

e. A piano patch is set on MIDI channel 2. Since the piano part calls for four notes to be played at once, four more notes of polyphony are gobbled up.

f. Last, a guitar patch has been assigned to make sound when MIDI data on channel 3 comes along. These power chords have three notes being played at a time, using up the last three voices of polyphony that the MIDI module has to give (1 voice for the bass part plus 4 voices for the piano part, plus 3 voices for the guitar = 8 voices).

With some synths, there's another way to go. Instead of having a greater number of notes of different timbre, you can go for quality over quantity. There are some devices that have exactly that kind of mode. This mode is called by different names by different manufacturers (for example, Korg devices call it *Combination mode*), but the idea behind it is the same. Instead of dividing the module's sound-generating horsepower to make more notes, the synth's electronics cooperate to give fewer notes, but at a higher quality. These sounds are meant to be more layered and complex and more sonically interesting to the ear. To get this boost in performance, the synth's multitimbral qualities are left behind, and even the polyphony can be decreased.

General MIDI and SMFs

Let's discuss General MIDI. Originally, there was a problem, especially with computer-based workstation and sound card synthesizer engines, particularly when playing MIDI files from the Internet. The problem was one of program numbers—on one synth patch #1 might be a piano, but on another it might be a drum set. That means that any given MIDI sequence might sound fine on my system, but if I e-mailed the sequence file to you, all the wrong instruments might play all the wrong MIDI parts. That's no good.

What we needed was a standardized list of program names and numbers, so that if I wanted to call up a piano program on one synth, I could use the same program number on another synth that subscribed to that standard. Of course, the quality of that piano sound might vary from device to device, but at least the instrument would be the same. That's a big part of what General MIDI is, namely, a broadly usable table of patch numbers. Here is a list of the General MIDI sounds, taken directly from the MMA MIDI specification:

1. Acoustic Grand Piano	14. Xylophone	27. Electric Guitar (jazz)
2. Bright Acoustic Piano	15. Tubular Bells	28. Electric Guitar (clean)
3. Electric Grand Piano	16. Dulcimer	29. Electric Guitar (muted)
4. Honky-tonk Piano	17. Drawbar Organ	30. Overdriven Guitar
5. Electric Piano 1	18. Percussive Organ	31. Distortion Guitar
6. Electric Piano 2	19. Rock Organ	32. Guitar Harmonics
7. Harpsichord	20. Church Organ	33. Acoustic Bass
8. Clavinet	21. Reed Organ	34. Electric Bass (finger)
9. Celesta	22. Accordion	35. Electric Bass (pick)
10. Glockenspiel	23. Harmonica	36. Fretless Bass
11. Music Box	24. Tango Accordion	37. Slap Bass 1
12. Vibraphone	25. Acoustic Guitar (nylon)	38. Slap Bass 2
13. Marimba	26. Acoustic Guitar (steel)	39. Synth Bass 1

40. Synth Bass 2	71. Bassoon	102. FX 6 (goblins)
41. Violin	72. Clarinet	103. FX 7 (echoes)
42. Viola	73. Piccolo	104. FX 8 (sci-fi)
43. Cello	74. Flute	105. Sitar
44. Contrabass	75. Recorder	106. Banjo
45. Tremolo Strings	76. Pan Flute	107. Shamisen
46. Pizzicato Strings	77. Blown Bottle	108. Koto
47. Orchestral Harp	78. Shakuhachi	109. Kalimba
48. Timpani	79. Whistle	110. Bagpipe
49. String Ensemble 1	80. Ocarina	111. Fiddle
50. String Ensemble 2	81. Lead 1 (square)	112. Shanai
51. SynthStrings 1	82. Lead 2 (sawtooth)	113. Tinkle Bell
52. SynthStrings 2	83. Lead 3 (calliope)	114. Agogo
53. Choir Aahs	84. Lead 4 (chiff)	115. Steel Drums
54. Voice Oohs	85. Lead 5 (charang)	116. Woodblock
55. Synth Voice	86. Lead 6 (voice)	117. Taiko Drum
56. Orchestra Hit	87. Lead 7 (fifths)	118. Melodic Tom
57. Trumpet	88. Lead 8 (bass + lead)	119. Synth Drum
58. Trombone	89. Pad 1 (new age)	120. Reverse Cymbal
59. Tuba	90. Pad 2 (warm)	121. Guitar Fret Noise
60. Muted Trumpet	91. Pad 3 (polysynth)	122. Breath Noise
61. French Horn	92. Pad 4 (choir)	123. Seashore
62. Brass Section	93. Pad 5 (bowed)	124. Bird Tweet
63. SynthBrass 1	94. Pad 6 (metallic)	125. Telephone Ring
64. SynthBrass 2	95. Pad 7 (halo)	126. Helicopter
65. Soprano Sax	96. Pad 8 (sweep)	127. Applause
66. Alto Sax	97. FX 1 (rain)	128. Gunshot
67. Tenor Sax	98. FX 2 (soundtrack)	
68. Baritone Sax	99. FX 3 (crystal)	
69. Oboe	100. FX 4 (atmosphere)	
70. English Horn	101. FX 5 (brightness)	

NOTE

You might notice that the preceding list has lumped similar sounds together. The instruments are grouped by families, as shown here.

1-8.	Piano sounds	41-48.	Strings	81-88.	Synth Lead
9-16.	Chromatic Percussion	49-56.	Ensemble	89-96.	Synth Pad
17-24.	Organ	57-64.	Brass	97-104.	Synth Effects
25-32.	Guitar	65-72.	Reed	105-112.	Ethnic
33-40.	Bass	73-80.	Pipe	113-120.	Percussive
				121-128.	Sound Effects

On MIDI channel 10, every General MIDI synth has at least one drum set (also called *drum kit*). Each MIDI note is assigned to a different sound (for example, one key might be a kick drum, another might be a snare, and so on), so you can play an entire drum part in one program.

TIP

It can be time consuming to hunt around for the right drum sound. It would be convenient to have a map of the sounds as they're laid out on the keyboard, wouldn't it? Look no further, you'll find just such a map in Appendix B: MIDI Notes, Names, and Numbers.

NOTE

While the drum sounds shown here are the General MIDI spec, many General MIDI-compliant synths feature additional drums in their kits and even other drum kits (rock kit, techno kit, jazz kit, and so on).

There are a few more requirements that must be met if a device can be called General MIDI compatible. Among these requirements is that a General MIDI synth must have at least 24-note polyphony (including drum sounds). Also, GM devices must be able to support at least 16 different instruments (meaning that they must be multitimbral on the order of 16 timbres).

General MIDI has proven to be a valuable common ground between MIDI devices, given that General MIDI has become the *de facto* program set for not only entry-level synthesizers, but also virtually every sound card synth engine on the market. With this the prevailing standard, the Internet has capitalized on the small file size of MIDI files, and much of the music that you hear on the Net is brought to you in the form of General MIDI–compatible files. Curious to find a song? Just search the Internet, and you'll probably find tons of MIDI files that'll sound fine on your computer, thanks to the introduction of General MIDI.

For producers, the benefits of General MIDI go even farther. For example, I have used General MIDI files to collaborate with other musicians, and as you start using MIDI more and more over the years, you'll find it reassuring to know that your MIDI files will sound almost the same on any computer as they do on yours. In fact, General MIDI turned out to be such a great concept that it was even expanded in 1999 in the form of the General MIDI 2, which is essentially an expansion of the original General MIDI spec. How prevalent GM2 will be in the future is anybody's guess, though, and the original GM spec is still by far the more common.

Whereas most MIDI sequencers have one or two proprietary file formats that they can use, virtually all MIDI applications support SMFs, or standard MIDI files.

There are some advantages to proprietary formats, or there would be no need for them. Proprietary file types are designed to work specifically with a single application or a small family of apps. Because they're custom designed by the same programmers who created the application, the files are designed to capitalize on the specific features of the programs. Still, for wide cross-application and cross-platform usefulness, SMFs can't be beat.

Standard MIDI files come in three flavors. First, there's file type 0 (zero). This particular file contains all the MIDI data for the song in one large track. This doesn't mean, however, that the file type is limited to only one timbre—this single track may have MIDI data on all 16 MIDI channels, complete with note data, program changes, and everything else the song needs to run with musically independent parts. Because this type of file is simple to create, store, and transmit, it's a popular favorite for Web site and Internet MIDI files.

On the other hand, there's standard MIDI file type 1. With this kind of file, a multitrack arrangement is maintained. What this means is that when you open up a type 1 SMF, you'll see all the individual tracks that originally existed in the MIDI session, even if the file was created by a completely different application. Each track uses only one MIDI channel (typically), making it the smart choice for transporting a MIDI project from one application to another. As for meter and tempo, that data is encoded on the first track and determines the tempo and time signature of the entire set of tracks.

NOTE

Regardless of the type of standard MIDI file, the file extension (.mid) remains the same.

Transforming Your MIDI

You're just about done with MIDI and MIDI sequencers, but before we move on, let's take a look at some common MIDI processes that you can apply to your MIDI notes within the workstation environment. These certainly aren't the only things you can do to MIDI, but these are standard functions in most MIDI workstations.

Control Freak

Nestled in the Piano Roll window, there's a great tool for graphically editing controller data and other types of data, too (see Figure 7.4).

Figure 7.4

Piano Roll with a controller pane at the bottom.

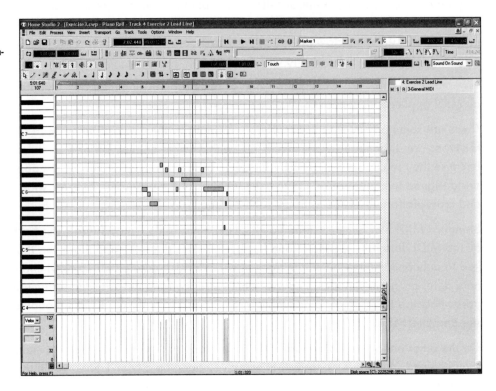

In this case, the Controller pane is an optional view of the Piano Roll window. The controller data is revealed in the bottom of the window. Let's take a closer look at Figure 7.5.

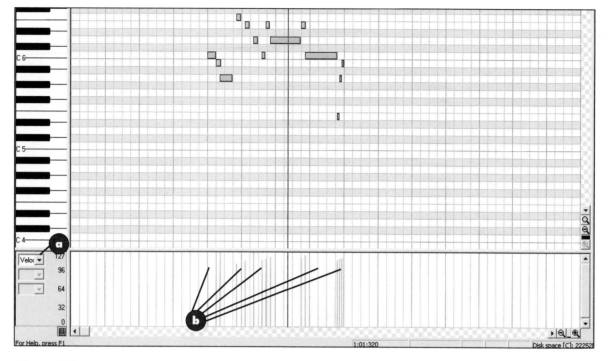

Figure 7.5

A closer look at the controller pane.

a. **Data Type:** Typically, you can only see one type of data at a time, which is usually fine, since you'll normally be working on only one at a time anyway. In this case, you're seeing the velocity values for each note.

b. **Data Value:** Under each note, you'll see a vertical line in the data area. In this particular case, you're seeing the velocity values for each note. The taller the line, the greater the value is (in this case, the greater the velocity of the note).

Velocity is only one of the many MIDI messages that you can tweak in the controller pane (which is ironic since velocity messages aren't actually controller messages). Refer to the list of controllers in Chapter 5 to get an idea of what can be done in this area. Knowing which MIDI messages do what and how to edit them can really breathe some life into otherwise lifeless music. The Pencil tool will really help you out here (see Figure 7.6).

Figure 7.6

Drawing data.

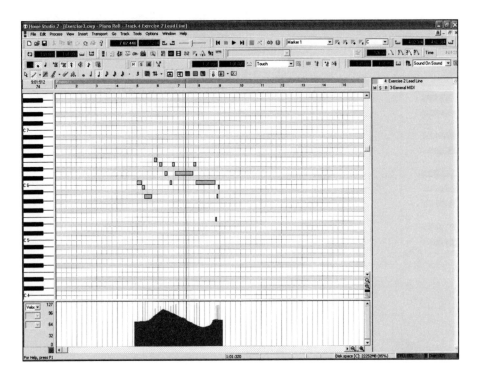

Just select the Pencil tool and click and drag to draw a new line as shown above. What you'll wind up with is something like Figure 7.7.

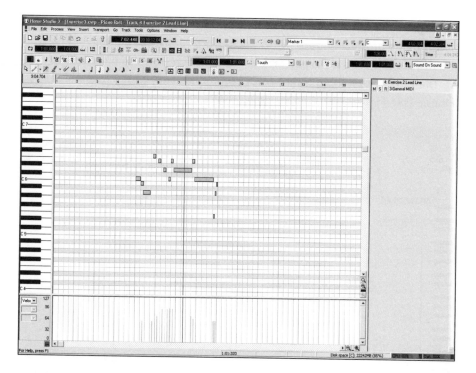

Figure 7.7

The altered velocity.

You'll notice that the velocity values have changed to match the line that was drawn.

> ❀ **TIP**
>
> Even the steadiest of hands might have a difficult time drawing a perfectly straight line. Not to worry—a straight line tool (sometimes a separate tool, sometimes a variation of the Pencil tool) is pretty standard equipment.

> ❀ **TIP**
>
> When you start really tweaking your music, you'll want to edit the controller for a single note. It's not difficult—all you need to do is zoom way in and just draw over a single controller value.

Transpose

Here's a scenario: You work tirelessly to get your MIDI song just perfect. Patch choices, melody, harmony, everything is just right. You're finally ready to have the vocalist come in to your studio to do a dry run through the song and then disaster! The song is too high or low for your singer to sing! You're going to have to change the entire key of the song—every single pitch will have to be changed. Before you start shopping around for another singer, hold on—MIDI's transpose can help.

Transpose really takes advantage of the nature of MIDI. Remember that MIDI data isn't audio, but rather digital data that controls audio-producing gear. MIDI pitches are really just note numbers, so to change the pitch, all the software needs to do is perform a little addition (to raise the pitch) or subtraction (to lower the pitch). The really great thing is that MIDI can do this very easily and without changing the speed of the music (see Figure 7.8). Just try doing that with audio!

Figure 7.8

Transpose notes easily.

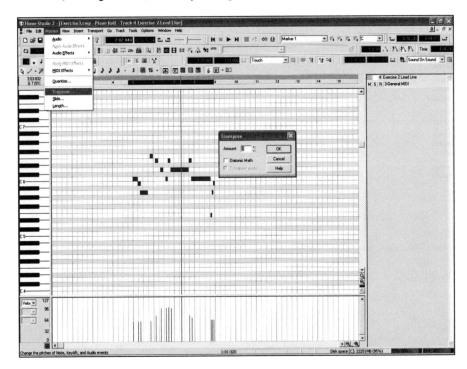

The process is really straightforward: Simply select the note(s) you want to change and choose the Transpose function (commonly under the Edit menu, but not always). In the window that opens, you'll choose by how many half steps the pitches will be moved one way or another. So, let's say that the song right now is in the key of C, and it needs to be changed to the key of D. Once you select the notes to be changed and transposed, you can raise the pitch by two half steps (the difference between C and D).

> ❄ **TIP**
>
> When using the Transpose feature, you don't need to change the pitch of a whole song. In fact, some really cool musical effects can result from changing keys during the course of a song. Just select the area of the song that you want to change (like a verse or chorus), and see if changing the key adds interest and excitement to your music. It doesn't always work with every song, but it's often a great compositional tool.

> ❉ **CAUTION**
>
> When using Transpose, be careful with the drum kit tracks. Remember that most drum patches have different drums assigned to different MIDI note numbers. Applying Transpose to drum tracks usually has the nasty effect of moving the drum sounds you want to the drum sounds you don't want.

Quantize

Truth time: If I had to be a professional keyboard player for the rest of my life, I'd starve to death. Not only can I *not* play fast, but even when I play slowly, my timing is all over the road. My shortcomings really come out when I'm working on drum parts—I think those little wind-up monkeys with the cymbals have better timing than I do! Thank goodness for *quantize*, a cool little feature that can fix sloppy timing.

Here's the *before* shot in Figure 7.9.

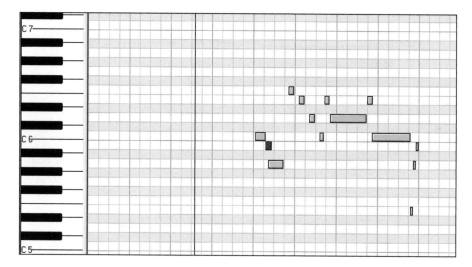

Figure 7.9

Before quantization.

Notice that none of the notes are on the grid lines. With quantize, you just select the notes that you want to fix and choose the resolution of your quantization. In many ways, it's just like using the Snap to Grid mode of operation. Just as pitches are MIDI note numbers, time locations are just part of the MIDI data stream that can easily be manipulated. All you have to do to fix the timing (effectively snapping the note messages to a grid) is select your notes and then choose quantize from your software's list of MIDI processes. A Quantize window will open. They look different from application to application, but aside from any program-specific bells and whistles, they all operate much the same (see Figure 7.10).

Figure 7.10

The Quantize window.

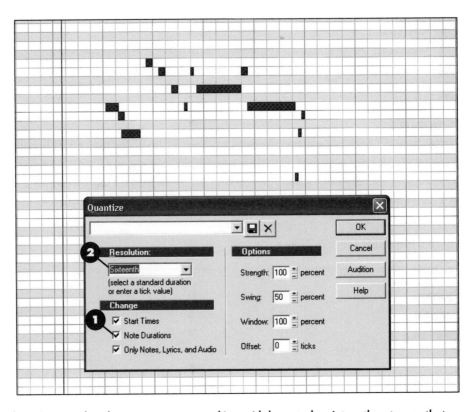

1. Choose what you want to quantize. Most programs will allow you to quantize the note start times, note end times, or both.

2. This is the important part. Choose your quantization resolution. For example, if you choose sixteenth notes as your level of quantization, then your notes will snap to the *nearest* sixteenth note increment. This doesn't mean that the notes you are working with have to be sixteenth notes, or that the notes you've selected will automatically become sixteenth notes. What it does mean is that the notes you've selected will be rounded off to the nearest sixteenth note (in this example).

What you'll wind up will look something like Figure 7.11.

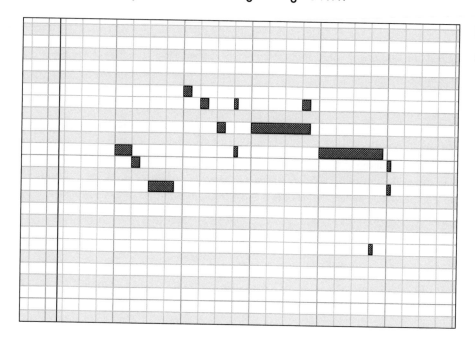

Figure 7.11

After quantization.

See how the notes are all right on the grid? That translates into more mathematically accurate timing, a real godsend for keyboard players like me!

> ❋ **TIP**
>
> Quantization is a great tool for fixing poor performances, but its usefulness should be tempered by an understanding of when *not* to use it. For example, quantize away when you're dealing with music that you want to sound electronic—techno, some house, and 80s retro are all styles that benefit from the mathematical perfection of aggressive quantization. Jazz, funk, and pretty much any music that you want to sound *live* can often be damaged by too much quantization. Consider this—is a human drummer mathematically perfect in his timing? Not by a long shot. In fact, a drummer's pushing and pulling of the beat is a big part of what gives us a sense of a phat groove!
>
> Does that mean that you can't quantize at all if you want something to sound live? Fortunately, that's not the case. First, there's a feature called *groove quantize* that is supported in many MIDI products, which quantizes your notes to a "grid" that has the imperfections of timing of a specific feel (swing, salsa, and so on). Next, nearly every quantize function will allow you to choose the strength of your processing. For example, let's say that you want to clean up your parts, but not make them absolutely perfect. Just choose a quantization strength of a certain percentage (100% being absolute quantization, 0% being no quantization at all), and you can keep a little bit of that human error in your music.

Arpeggiate

This is a really great way to add interest to your music and can immediately compensate for a lack of keyboard skills. But before we talk about what arpeggiate does, we've got to understand what an arpeggio is.

When playing a keyboard, you can plunk down your fingers and play a number of notes at the same time. For example, let's say that you play a C major chord, as shown in Figure 7.12.

Figure 7.12

Before arpeggiation.

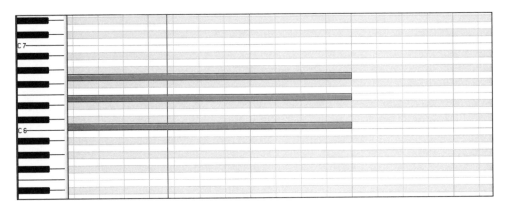

Instead of playing all the notes together as a chord, the notes can be played as a series of notes, called an *arpeggio*, like Figure 7.13.

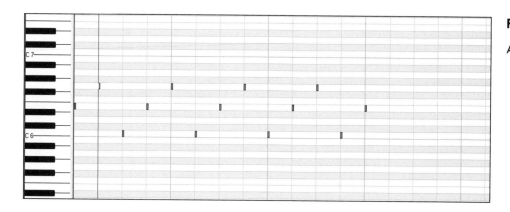

Figure 7.13

After arpeggiation.

An arpeggio can have a number of different patterns (up, down, up/down, or even a random series of notes) and can be played back at any number of speeds (quarter notes, eighth notes, and so on). The arpeggiate process in a MIDI workstation changes a chord (or any number of notes that are played together) into an arpeggio. The process is very straightforward:.

1. Select the simultaneous notes that you want to arpeggiate.

2. Choose the Arpeggiate option from your sequencer's list of MIDI processes.

3. In the Arpeggiator window that appears, choose the pattern of the arpeggio and the speed of the arpeggio (usually that involves choosing a musical value, like an eighth note).

That's it! The sequencer will generate a series of notes. This is a great way to add a degree of complexity to your music. It works particularly well with electronic-sounding music, and you'll hear it crop up in tons of songs.

This winds up our whirlwind tour of MIDI and its power in the hands of a creative person. Now let's turn to more MIDI sequencing.

8 Exercise 3: Transforming MIDI

Now that we've got the basics down, let's take a look at this file and see what can be done to improve it even more. You'll notice immediately that the instruments don't exactly sound like a song, but rather more like a portion of a song. With the power of your workstations, you'll be able to use these track to create a more substantial work. In this chapter, you'll learn:

❄ How to use the different windows of a DAW to their best advantage.

❄ How to construct a song out of smaller MIDI blocks.

❄ How to use MIDI effects.

❄ The ins and outs of recording MIDI data.

❄ **NOTE**

For the purposes of this exercise, you have the option of continuing with the files you created at the end of Exercise 2 or using files that have been created in the Exercise/Ex_03 folder of the accompanying CD-ROM. There are sub-folders named *Cakewalk* and *Quartz* containing files for each of the applications. You'll note that these Exercise 3 files have regions named "Exercise 2 Drums," "Exercise 2 Bass," and so on, so that no matter if you continue with the Exercise 2 files or start fresh with the Exercise 3 files, what you see will match the figures in this exercise.

If you do want to continue working with the session that you've already created in Exercise 2, that's great, but some of the extreme tempo changes might not really work with this style of music. There's a quick way to strip away the tempo changes. (Don't worry, you can create new tempo changes when you're done with the exercise if you want.) The steps are outlined in the next section.

Using Cakewalk Home Studio

Here's how to remove the tempo changes you created in Exercise 2, starting at Figure 8.1.

Figure 8.1

1. From the View menu, choose the **Tempo** window. This is optional, but it will give you a better graphic idea of what you're doing.

2 **Click** the **Edit** drop-down menu.

3. **Click** the **Select** menu item. A second drop-down menu will appear.

4. **Click** the **All** menu item. An area of the Tempo window will be highlighted (see Figure 8.2). This represents your entire song—so far.

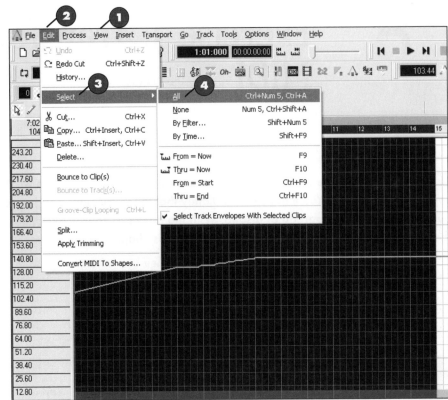

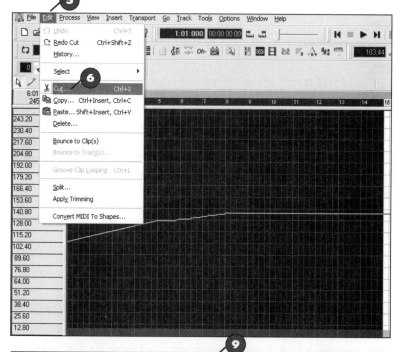

Figure 8.2

5. **Click** the **Edit** drop-down menu.

6. **Click** the **Cut** menu item. The Cut window will appear (see Figure 8.3).

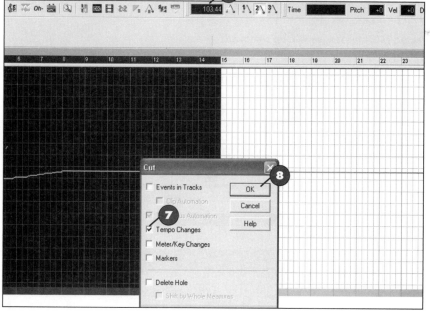

Figure 8.3

7. Since you only want to cut tempo changes, **deselect** all the **check boxes** except the Tempo Changes box.

8. **Click** the **OK** button. The window will disappear, leaving a flat tempo line as a result.

9. To enter a new static tempo, **click** the **Tempo Display** window and **type** the **desired tempo** (the original tempo is 126).

10. **Press** the **Enter** key to confirm your new tempo. That's it!

✽ ✽ ✽

Using Quartz AudioMaster Freeware

To remove tempo changes in AudioMaster, you'll have to go back to the Events window, as shown in Figure 8.4.

Figure 8.4

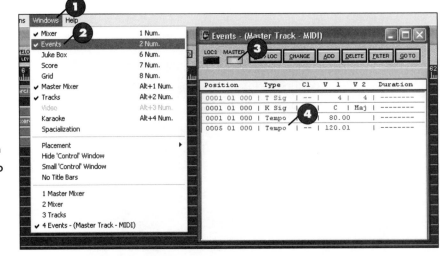

1. **Click** the **Windows** drop-down menu.

2. **Click** the **Events** menu item. The MIDI Event List will appear.

3. **Click** the **Master** button in the MIDI Event List to look at global MIDI messages.

4. **Click** on the **tempo changes** you want to cut. Holding the Control key while clicking will allow you to select multiple MIDI messages. Remember, don't select the first tempo message—you'll need that one to set your new tempo.

5. **Click** the **Delete** key. The selected MIDI messages will be removed.

Here's how you can change the value of the tempo message that's left (see Figure 8.5).

Figure 8.5

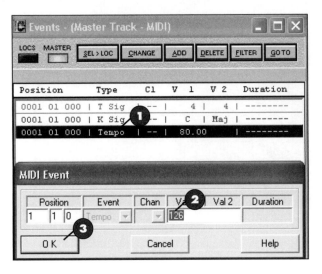

1. **Double-click** the **tempo message** that you want to change. In this case, the tempo message has a location of measure 1, beat 1, tick 0, indicating that this is the tempo message at the beginning of your song. The MIDI Event window will open.

2. **Type** a **new tempo** into the value area of the MIDI Event window. In this case, I've chosen the original tempo of 126 beats per minute.

3. **Click** the **OK** button to apply your change.

Quantizing

I *told* you that I wasn't a very good keyboard player, and the lead line track proves it! There are some pretty serious timing problems, but don't worry, using the MIDI Quantize feature can fix things in a hurry.

Using Cakewalk Home Studio

The Piano Roll window is a great environment for watching quantize do its stuff, so let's go back to that very useful window (see Figure 8.6).

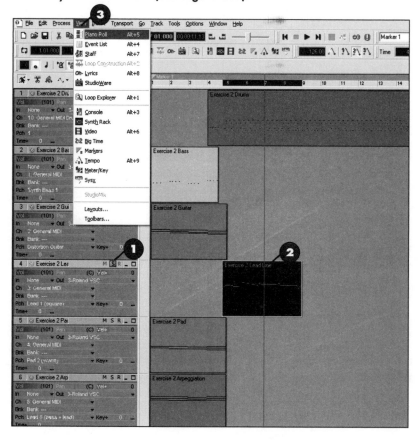

Figure 8.6

1. So we're not distracted by any other tracks, **put the Exercise 2 Lead Line** track into solo. Listen and you'll hear some pretty serious timing problems, particularly around measure 6.

2. **Click** the **Exercise 2 Lead Line** MIDI region. After the region is selected, you can process it.

3. Let's take a look at the individual notes. The best window for this sort of job is the Piano Roll window. **Click** the **View** drop-down menu; then **choose** the **Piano Roll menu item.** The Piano Roll window will appear (see Figure 8.7).

Figure 8.7

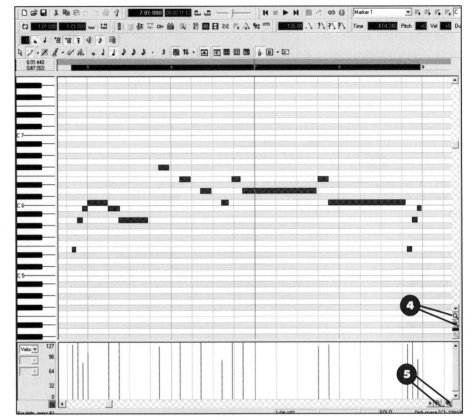

4. If you can't see all of the melody, it might be hard to work on it. **Click the Horizontal Zoom In or Horizontal Zoom Out** button to see more or less of your song's total time. When you're done, your screen should look similar to this one.

5. You can zoom in on the keyboard as well. **Clicking the Vertical Zoom In and Vertical Zoom Out** buttons will let you see a narrower or wider range of notes. Again, when you're done, your screen should look like this one.

❋ **TIP**

Between each pair of zoom keys is a small blank area. Position your cursor in that area, and you'll see that your cursor turns into a line with points on either end. Click and drag your mouse to zoom in and out without having to click the zoom keys themselves.

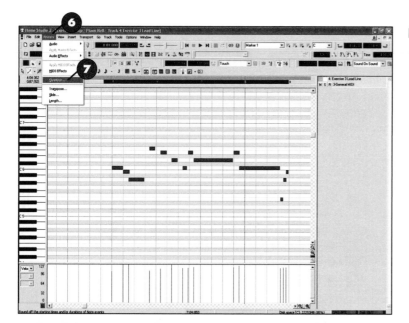

Figure 8.8

6. **Click** the **Process** drop-down menu (see Figure 8.8).

7. **Click** the **Quantize** menu item. The Quantize window will open (see Figure 8.9).

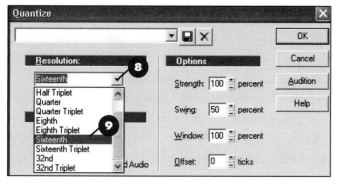

Figure 8.9

8. **Click** the **arrow** button to the right of the **Resolution** display. A Resolution drop-down menu will appear.

9. **Click** the **desired musical resolution**. The value you choose will determine the kind of grid that your notes will "snap" to. Since the smallest musical note in this melody is a sixteenth note (one-fourth of a beat), **click** the **Sixteenth** menu item.

10. When you've set up the Quantize window, just **click OK**.

❄ **CAUTION**

The resolution of your quantization is perhaps the most important parameter of the entire process. It's important to select a value that is small enough to maintain the musical integrity of the musical line, but not so small that notes will snap to an unwanted musical location. For example, if you had chosen Quarter as your quantize resolution, all your notes would have snapped to the nearest beat, and the melody would not sound right. On the other hand, selecting a value that's unnecessarily small, like thirty-second, would possibly cause notes to snap to something other than the desired musical point.

Bottom line: A little familiarity with the melody, combined with a little trial and error, is usually needed when quantizing music.

> ❄ **TIP**
>
> If you're unsure as to the smallest note value in a given bit of MIDI, viewing it in the Staff window can often give you a clue. Refer to the illustrations in Chapter 3 to see what the individual note shapes mean.

Figure 8.10

There are some useful options that can help you when quantizing:

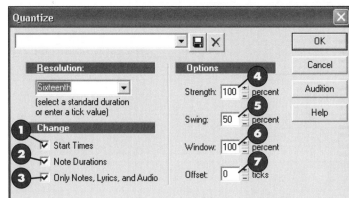

1. **Start Times:** Check this box if you want the *start* times of your notes (and other MIDI data) to move to the selected musical resolution. This option is generally selected.

2. **Note Durations:** Check this box if you want the *end* of your notes to move to the nearest resolution point. This will often change the duration of your musical notes.

3. **Only Notes, Lyrics, and Audio:** Checking this box will move only notes, lyrics, and audio data and leave other MIDI messages (like controllers) alone.

4. **Strength:** This determines how much you want to quantize your music. A value of 100 percent will move your data completely to the nearest resolution value (perfect timing, which can often sound mechanical). Lesser strength values will move notes to a lesser degree (for example, a strength value of 50% will move data halfway to the nearest resolution value), which can preserve some of that "human" feel.

5. **Swing:** The concept of "swing" is a hard one to describe in words (it's much easier to hear), but here goes. This value determines the duration relationship between pairs of notes. If the value is 50 percent as shown here, each note in a pair of sixteenth notes will have the same duration, meaning that they will be equal halves of an eighth note. If you set the value higher, the duration of the first note will be greater (and the second note will be more brief), and as the value dips below 50 percent, the first note in a pair will be quicker and the latter note will have a longer duration. Keep in mind that this is a verbal description of a musical quality, and if you experiment with this setting you'll hear what I'm talking about.

6. **Window:** What if a note is really far from a given quantization point? Sometimes, you might want to leave some notes unquantized. A Window value of 100 percent will quantize all the notes, regardless of how far off the resolution points they may be. As the percentage is decreased, notes that are particularly "off" will be unaffected.

7. **Offset:** This option will allow you to shift the position of the quantization points. A positive value will snap notes to a certain amount *after* a resolution point, whereas a negative value will position your MIDI data *earlier* than your resolution point. A value of zero (as shown here) will snap your notes right to the quantization resolution.

❉ TIP

Playing with offsets can really yield some great results. For example, a snare part that is just a shade late in relation to the other tracks can really give a nice sense of groove. You can quantize your snare and make it a little late at the same time by adding a little offset (try 3 ticks for starters) to your quantize. Of course, you have to select only your snare track and leave the other drums alone to get this effect.

Take a look at what quantization does to your notes (see Figure 8.11).

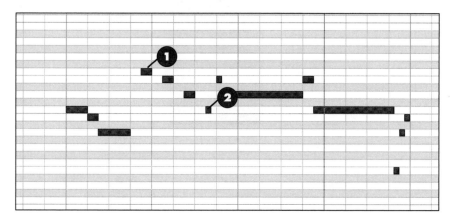

Figure 8.11

1. Note that the timing of some notes has changed slightly. The beginnings of notes have moved to the nearest sixteenth note interval.

2. If you've chosen the settings shown in this example, you'll also notice that some durations have changed as well. The ends of the quantized notes have been moved to the nearest sixteenth note interval as well, which has made some notes longer and some notes slightly shorter.

Listen to this section now that you've quantized it. It's not perfect yet, but it's getting there!

Using Quartz AudioMaster Freeware

Unfortunately, quantization is not included in the AudioMaster Freeware, so it's going to be a good bit more difficult to get the job done. You'll have to fix the timing manually, but you can at least use the Piano Roll view to help out (see Figure 8.12).

❉ NOTE

Although quantize is a nearly universal MIDI workstation feature, Quartz AudioMaster Freeware does not include it unfortunately. The news isn't all that bad, however, because quantize *is* included in the upgraded versions of AudioMaster.

Figure 8.12

1. **Click** the **Options** drop-down menu.

2. **Click** the **General** menu item. The Options (General) window will appear (see Figure 8.13).

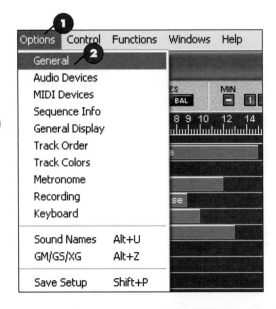

Figure 8.13

Here's what you're looking for: The MIDI Resolution area tells you how many subdivisions are within a single beat. In other words, the distance between any given beat and the next beat can be broken down into evenly divided incre-

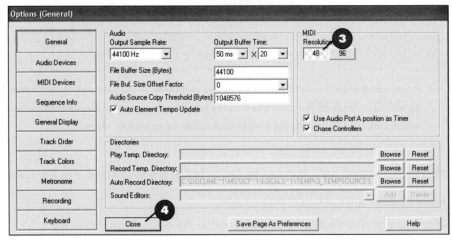

ments, and the number of these increments is up to you.

3. As shown here, the MIDI resolution is 48. If this setting isn't selected, **click** the **48** button to select it now.

4. **Click** the **Close** button, and you're ready to move on (see Figure 8.14).

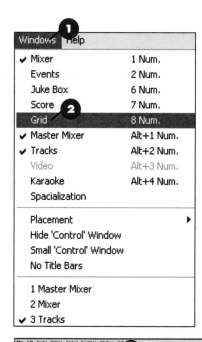

Figure 8.14

1. **Click** the **Windows** drop-down menu.
2. **Click** the **Grid** menu item. The Grid window will appear (see Figure 8.15).

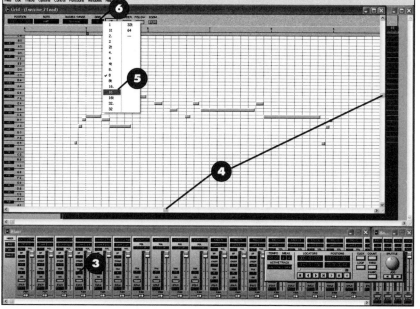

Figure 8.15

3. **Click** the **Trk** (for Track) button on the lead line track in the Mixer window. The button will turn blue.

4. **Use** the **scroll** bars or **arrow keys** to center the MIDI notes in your grid (which is also commonly called the *Piano Roll*) window.

5. Let's change the grid resolution to help see the music more accurately. **Click** the **Grid** button to reveal a drop-down menu of possible resolutions.

6. Viewing the music in terms of sixteenth notes will work best here, so **click** the **16** menu item. The grids will change to look a bit more like Figure 8.16.

Figure 8.16

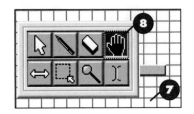

7. **Right-click anywhere** in the grid field. The toolbox will appear.

8. **Click** the **Move** tool. The toolbox will disappear, and the cursor will turn into a hand (see Figure 8.17).

Figure 8.17

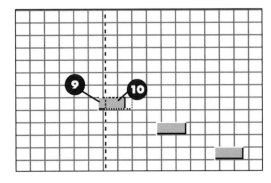

9. **Click** and **hold** on the **note** you want to change. The note's beginning time will be represented by a vertical dashed line.

10. Still pressing on the mouse, **drag** the **note** to the desired location and then **release** the **mouse**. The note's position will be changed, like Figure 8.18.

Figure 8.18

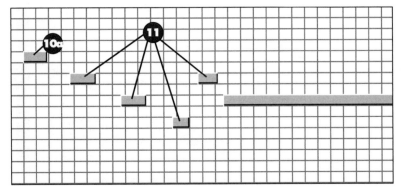

10a. The note's starting point has moved to the nearest grid marker.

11. Repeating Steps 9 and 10, **move** the **rest** of the offending notes to the correct musical position. You may want to put the track into Solo mode to hear more clearly. (You can do this from the Mixer window.) When you're done, the screen should look something like Figure 8.19.

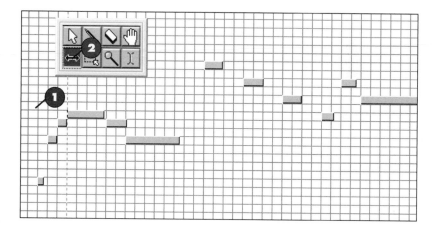

Figure 8.19

If you want to have the ends of notes snap to the nearest grid point, you'll have to use another tool (see Figure 8.19).

1. **Right-click** anywhere in the grid field. The toolbox will appear.

2. **Click** on the **Size** tool. The toolbox will disappear, and your cursor will turn into a double arrow (see Figure 8.20).

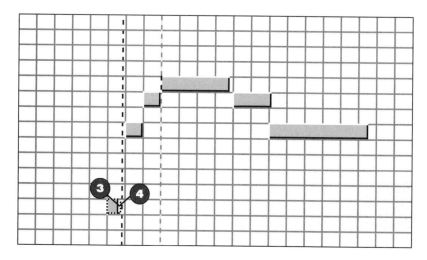

Figure 8.20

3. **Click** and **hold** the note you want to change. The note's beginning time will be represented by a vertical dashed line.

4. Still pressing on the mouse, **drag** the **note** to the desired location and then **release** the **mouse**. The note's ending point will be changed, like Figure 8.21.

Figure 8.21

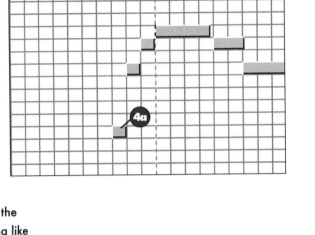

4a. The note's ending point has moved to the nearest grid marker.

5. Repeat Steps 3 and 4 and move the rest of the offending note endings to the correct musical position. Again, you might want to put the track into Solo mode to hear more clearly. When you're done, the screen should look something like Figure 8.22.

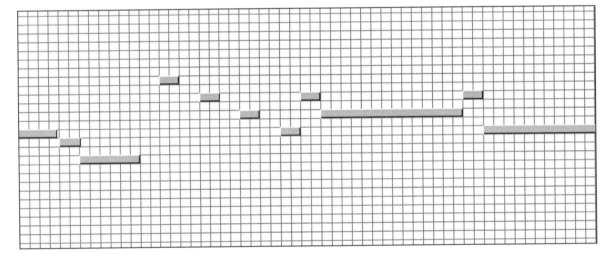

Figure 8.22

❄ **CAUTION**

The Move tool is a bit tricky to work with. I found myself inadvertently changing the pitch of notes by mistake. Don't worry—you'll get the hang of it pretty quickly. Just remember that the tool is very sensitive to vertical motion, and if you need it, you can always undo (from the Edit drop-down menu).

Grid Mode

When editing, having notes, selections, and even MIDI and audio regions snap to a musical mark is a real time saver. We can make this happen by using the Grid function. In fact, you've already used the Grid function to do the job of quantization in Quartz AudioMaster. Let's dig deeper!

Using Cakewalk Home Studio

Let's use the Snap to Grid function to help us fix the melody a little more (see Figure 8.23).

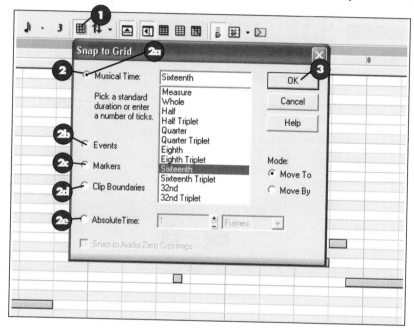

Figure 8.23

1. **Right-click** the **Snap to Grid** button. The **Snap to Grid** window will appear.

2. Like quantization, the first thing to do with the Snap to Grid feature is to establish a grid value. **Click** the desired grid type:

2a. You can choose to have your movements snap to the nearest musical Time value. After clicking this radio button, click the desired grid resolution (let's try working with a sixteenth note grid).

2b. Events: Clicking this radio button will have your motions constrained to the nearest MIDI event (like a note on message, for example).

2c. Markers: If you have set up markers in your session (a feature we'll talk about in Chapter 12), you can have your motions snap to the nearest marker.

2d. If you're working with non-musical material, tempo probably has no meaning to the job at hand. You can click the Absolute Time radio button and then choose a grid based on samples, seconds, or even frames of film.

2e. Mode: This determines whether your notes or regions will move to the nearest grid point or move by the grid increment. If you select Move by, the objects you grab will always maintain their relative distance from any grid point.

3. Once you've chosen your grid and how you're going to use it (let's use a musical grid of sixteenth notes and enable the Move to mode), **click** the **OK** button. The new grid will be in action, and the Snap to Grid button will be depressed if it wasn't already.

Now let's use the Grid mode to help fix a problem that quantize didn't take care of:

Figure 8.24

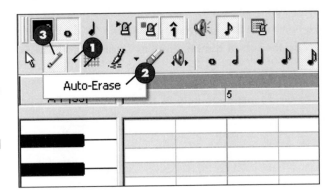

1. **Click** the **arrow** button to the right of the **Pencil** tool.

2. **Confirm** that the **Auto-Erase** option is unchecked. If it is checked, just click on the word Auto-Erase, and it will become unchecked.

3. **Click** the **Pencil** tool.

Figure 8.25

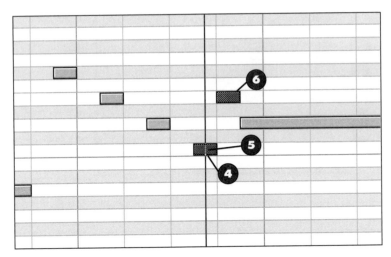

4. **Position** your **cursor** near the end of an existing note to change its duration. As it turns out, quantization cuts this one a little short.

5. **Click** and **drag** your **cursor** to the desired grid point. As you drag, you'll notice that the note boundary snaps from grid point to grid point.

6. **Repeat Steps 5** and **6** for this note and drag out the note ending so that your Piano Roll window resembles this one. Now when you play the melody, these two notes won't sound so unusually short.

Working with the Snap to Grid feature enabled is also very useful in the Track window:

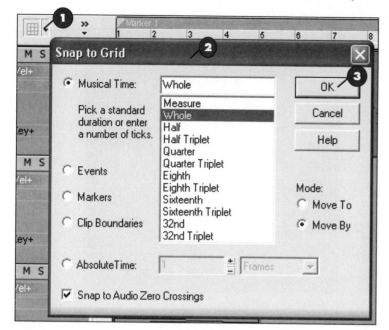

Figure 8.26

1. In the Track window, **click** the **arrow** button to the right of the **Snap to Grid** button.

2. This window should look pretty familiar. Make the desired settings here, just as you did in the Piano Roll window.

3. Once you've made your selections, **click** the **OK** button. Now the Snap to Grid mode is active, and all regions in the Track view will snap to the grid (in this case they will move to the nearest whole note).

✳ **TIP**

Every window that supports a Snap to Grid feature (Piano Roll, Tracks, Staff, and Tempo) supports individual settings. For example, this means that you can have a different grid set up for the Track window than you do for the Piano Roll.

Using Quartz AudioMaster Freeware

You've already seen the power of working with a grid in AudioMaster's grid window, but that's not the only place where you can take advantage of grids.

Figure 8.27

1. In the Tracks window, **click** the **Snap** display. A drop-down list of possible grid resolutions will appear.

2. **Click** the **desired grid resolution**. In this case, clicking the 1 will snap any region movement to the nearest measure.

Figure 8.28

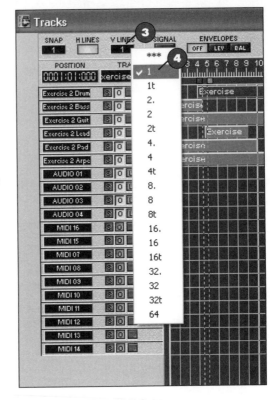

3. It would probably be nice if you could *see* the grid that you were working with. **Click** the **V Lines** (for Vertical **Lines**) display. Another drop-down list will appear.

4. **Click** the **desired resolution** of the vertical lines. In this case, clicking 1 will place a line at every point there is a grid point. When you click a value, your screen will change to reflect your choice.

> ❋ **NOTE**
>
> The values that you set for your grid and vertical lines are not related in any way. In other words, you can have the vertical lines visible, but your grid can be off, and vice versa. It is pretty common to set these two values to be the same for convenience.

> ❋ **TIP**
>
> In AudioMaster, as in Cakewalk Home Studio, you can set different grid values for different windows.

> ❋ **NOTE**
>
> If you want to disable your grid or vertical lines, just set the corresponding value to "—" (for no snap) or "****" (for no vertical lines).

Using the Arpeggiator Feature

An arpeggiator can really spice up a song and add a unique texture to your music. It's also pretty simple to do (see Figure 8.29).

Using Cakewalk Home Studio

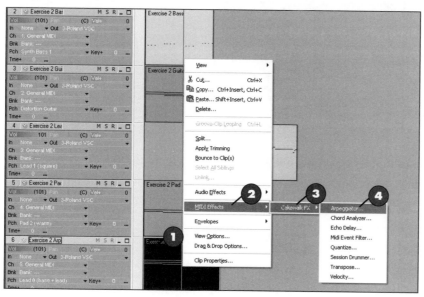

Figure 8.29

1. **Right-click** the **region** that you want to arpeggiate. In this example, it is the MIDI region on the Exercise 2 Arpeggiation track. A menu of processes will appear.

2. **Click** the **MIDI Effects** item. A second menu will open to the right.

3. **Click** the **Cakewalk Effects** item. Yet another menu will open.

4. **Click** the **Arpeggiator** item. The Arpeggiator window will appear (see Figure 8.30).

> **☀ TIP**
>
> Perhaps one of the greatest benefits to a well-designed music application is that there are multiple ways to accomplish the same thing. For example, you could have gone to the Process drop-down menu, then chosen MIDI Effects, then Cakewalk Effects, and then Arpeggiator. This would have brought you to the same window. Exploring these different ways of doing any given task will help you understand the workings of your applications and make you a more efficient user in the long run.

Figure 8.30

5. Start off with a preprogrammed preset. **Click** the **arrow** button to the right of the Preset display. A dropdown menu of options will appear.

6. **Click** the **desired preset.** For this session, 16th Pulse works very well.

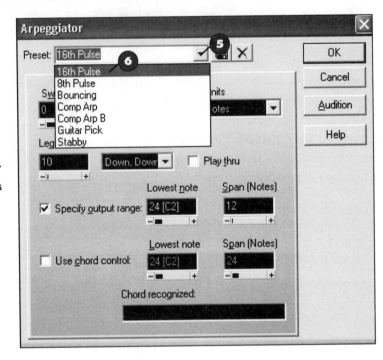

Even though this preset is quite useful, let's tweak it out just a little (see Figure 8.31).

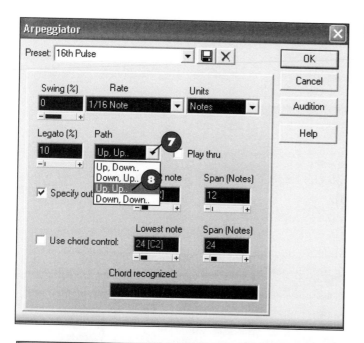

Figure 8.31

7. **Click** the **arrow** button to the right of the Path display. The path tells which direction the arpeggio will go. The list shows you that there are many options.

8. **Click** the **desired direction** for your arpeggio. This will take some trial and error, but I've found that the Up path works well for this session (see Figure 8.32).

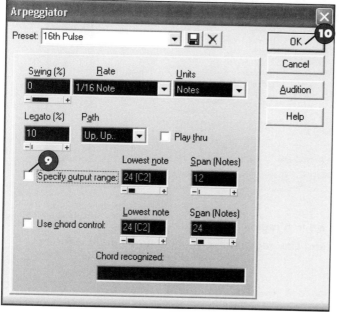

Figure 8.32

9. The **Specify output range** option allows an arpeggio to be created that uses the same note names that are already present in the original MIDI data, but in different octaves. Since you'll be creating an arpeggio using the pitches of the original MIDI, uncheck this box.

10. When you're done, just **click** the **OK** button.

Listen to the part you've created (soloing the track will help you hear what you've done). Pretty cool, huh?

❋ **NOTE**

Unfortunately, arpeggiation isn't available in Quartz AudioMaster.

Cut, Copy, and Paste

Now that you've cleaned up the MIDI a bit, you can begin to assemble your song, and the best window for this is the Track view (see Figure 8.33).

Using Cakewalk Home Studio

Figure 8.33

1. Working with the Snap to Grid feature enabled works well with this sort of song assembling. If this tool isn't enabled, enable it now, and set the grid value to be a measure.

2. **Click OK.**

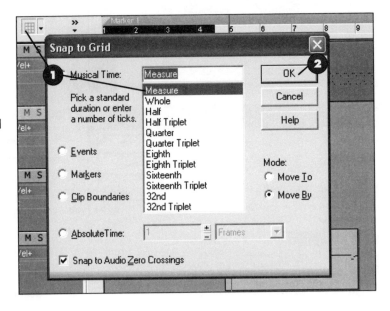

Moving regions is one of the easiest things to do in a region-based workstation, especially when you have the grid enabled. Let's try to move the Lead Line region later in our song by eight measures (see Figure 8.34).

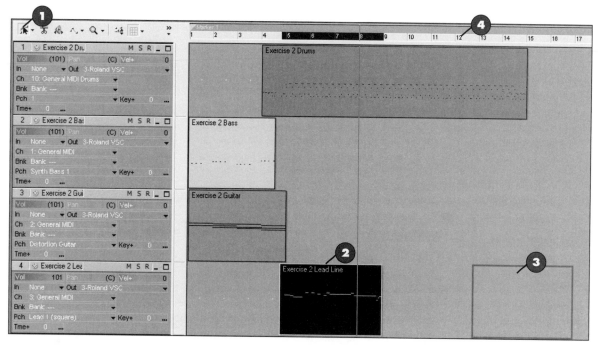

Figure 8.34

1. In the Track window, **click** the **Select** tool.

2. **Click** and **hold** on the **Exercise 2 Lead Line** region.

3. Still holding down the mouse, **drag** the **region** to the right. You'll notice as you drag, a hollow square lets you know where the region will be moved once the mouse is released.

4. Because you're working with a grid of measures, you'll see it snap to the nearest measure as you drag. **Drag** the **region** until it starts at measure 13, as shown here, and then **release** the **mouse** (see Figure 8.35).

Figure 8.35

5. This is the same Options window that you saw earlier when you were moving notes in the Piano Roll window. Since you're simply moving the MIDI region to a new location, choose **Replace Old with New**; then **click** the **OK** button.

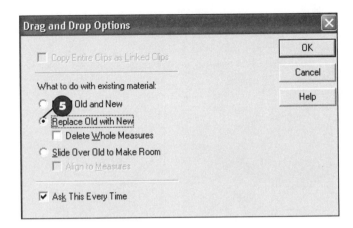

Piece o' cake! Now let's try repeating the bass line a few times (see Figure 8.36).

Figure 8.36

1. Still using the Select tool, **click** on the **Exercise 2 Bass** MIDI region.

2. **Click** and **drag** along the **timeline** to select measures 1 through 4 (ending at the beginning of measure 5). With the grid on and set to one measure, this is fairly easy to do.

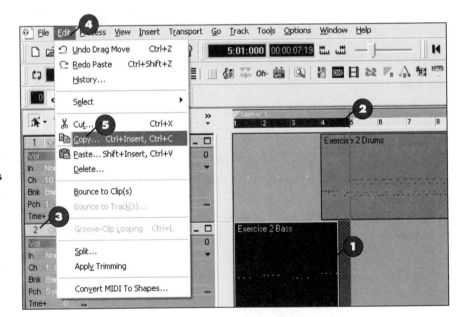

3. **Click** on the **bass track's track number** to select the track. A four-measure block will be selected on that track.

4. **Click** the **Edit** drop-down menu.

5. **Click** the **Copy** menu item. The **Copy** window will appear (see Figure 8.37).

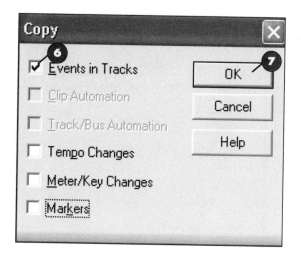

Figure 8.37

6. Since we're only copying MIDI region data, make sure that **Events in Tracks** is the only box **checked**, as shown here.

7. **Click OK (see Figure 8.38).**

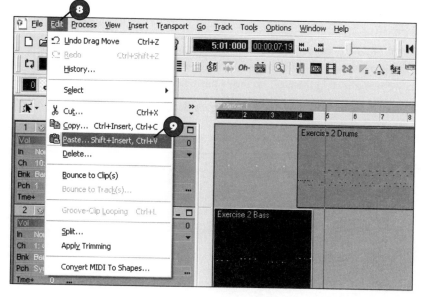

Figure 8.38

8. **Click** the **Edit** drop-down menu again.

9. This time, **click** the **Paste** menu item. The **Paste** window will appear (see Figure 8.39).

Figure 8.39

10. Since this MIDI clip is a four-measure phrase, you'll want to paste a copy of it at the beginning of measure five. **Type** the **desired point** at which the pasted region will start—in this case 5:01:000.

11. **Type** the **number** of times you want to repeat this pasted selection. Since we're building a song, let's try pasting it 7 times.

12. You don't have to paste the region to the track you copied it from. In this case, though, you *do* want to paste the region to the original track. **Type** the **number** of the track you want to paste (or select it from the drop-down list of tracks by clicking the arrow button to the right of the track number).

❈ Checking the **Link to Original Clip(s)** option will apply any changes made to the original region to the copied regions. This is particularly useful if you're using multiple loops of MIDI—changing just one region will change all the repetitions. In this case, you might want to tweak specific regions without affecting them all, so leave this box unchecked.

13. **Click OK.** Your screen should be updated to look something like Figure 8.40.

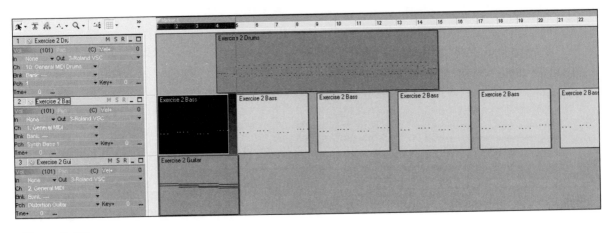

Figure 8.40

The news gets even better—repeating multiple tracks is just as easy as repeating one track (see Figure 8.41).

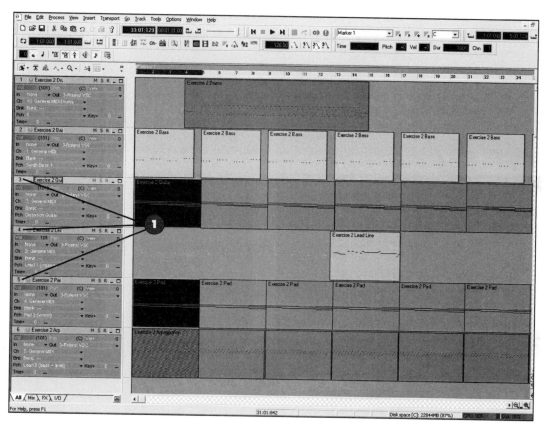

Figure 8.41

1. Holding the Control key on your computer keyboard, **click** the **track number** to select the tracks that you want to repeat. In this example, **choose** the **Guitar, Pad,** and **Arpeggiation tracks.** (Remember to deselect the Bass track before making your selections.)

2. Repeat Steps 4 through 13 that you used to copy a single track. In the Paste window, choose the uppermost track number for the Starting Track (in this case, track 3). When you're done, your song should look like Figure 8.42.

Now your song is starting to take shape, but the drum track needs work. To get the drum track to sound right with the rest of the song, you're going to have to chop up the single large drum region into smaller, more manageable bits (see Figure 8.42).

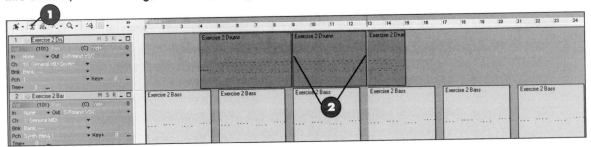

Figure 8.42

1. **Click** the **Split** tool.
2. You want to section off a four-measure segment of the Drum track. With the Grid tool active, it's easy to do. **Click** at the **beginning** of **measure 9** and then at the **beginning** of **measure 13**. You'll see that your MIDI region has been separated into three blocks.

> ❋ **NOTE**
>
> Even though you've sliced and diced this single MIDI region, you haven't changed the MIDI data of the track yet. Just solo the track and listen to it, and you'll see what I mean. It sounds the same as it always did, but now you have different ways of *moving* the data.

You won't be needing that last region, so let's get rid of it (see Figure 8.43).

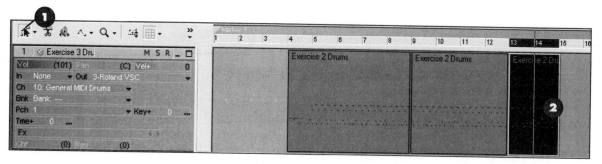

Figure 8.43

1. **Click** the **Select** tool.

2. **Click** the **region** you want to delete. The region will become highlighted.

3. **Press** the **Delete** key on your computer keyboard. The region will disappear.

Now that you've captured a good four-measure block, let's copy it. The process should be getting pretty familiar by now (see Figure 8.44).

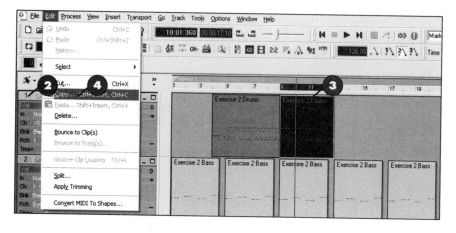

Figure 8.44

1. So you can see more of your song, **click** the **Horizontal Zoom Out** tool a couple of times.

2. **Click** the **desired track number** (in this case, track 1) to select it.

3. **Click** and **drag** along the **timeline** to select from the beginning of measure 9 to the beginning of measure 13 (having the grid on makes this easy).

4. From the Edit drop-down menu, **choose Copy** (see Figure 8.45).

Figure 8.45

5. **Choose** to **copy** only **Events in Tracks**.

6. **Click OK**.

7. From the Edit drop-down menu, **choose Paste** (see Figure 8.46).

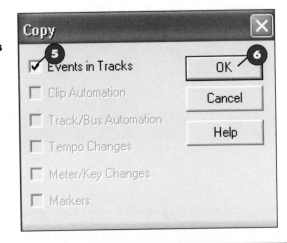

Figure 8.46

8. Make sure you start pasting exactly at the beginning of bar 13 (bar 13, beat 1, tick 000).

9. **Repeat** the **region** five times to match it up with the rest of the song.

10. Make sure that the Starting Track is track 1.

11. **Click OK**. Your screen will now look like Figure 8.47.

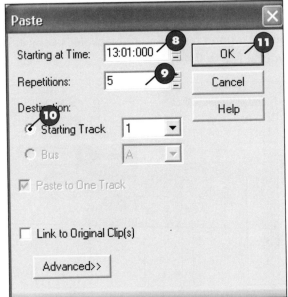

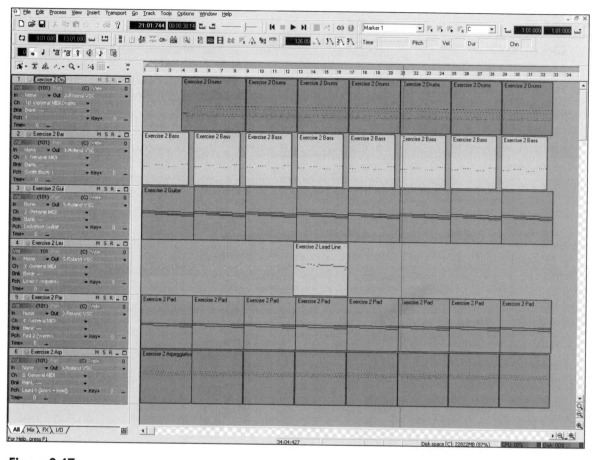

Figure 8.47

Now let's work on that melody (see Figure 8.48).

Figure 8.48

1. **Click** the **arrow** next to the Snap to Grid tool. The Snap to Grid window will appear.

2. Instead of using a musical time grid, let's **snap** to the nearest **event**.

3. **Click OK** (see Figure 8.49).

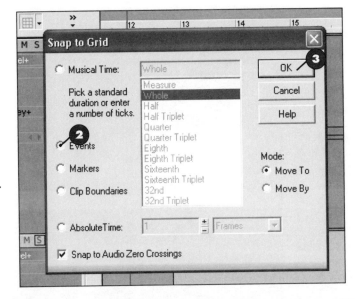

Figure 8.49

4. **Move** your **cursor** very close to the left side of the lead line melody region. The cursor will turn into a small rectangle.

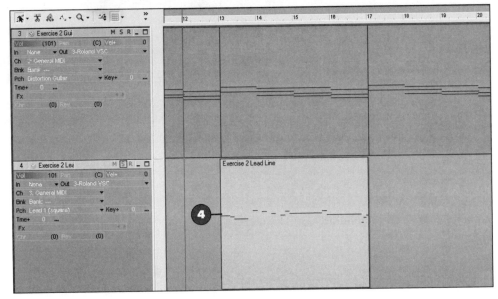

5. **Click** and **drag** your **cursor** to the right until the region boundary snaps to the first note of the melody (which also happens to be at the beginning of the third measure).

6. **Release** the **mouse**, and the region boundary will be changed (see Figure 8.50).

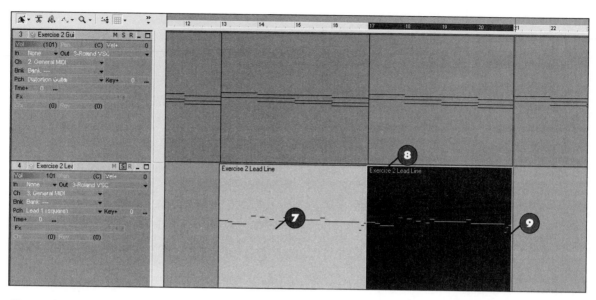

Figure 8.50

7. **Copy** the **region** (using the Events in Track option), just as you've copied regions thus far.

8. **Paste** the **data**, starting at the beginning of measure 17, with 1 repetition only, and on track 4.

9. Now let's get rid of the last three notes of the second MIDI region. **Move** your **cursor** close to the right end of the second region. The cursor will turn into the small rectangle again.

10. **Click** and **drag** your **cursor** to the right until the last three notes of the last region have been removed.

11. **Release** the **mouse**, and the region boundary will be changed. Your track should look like Figure 8.51.

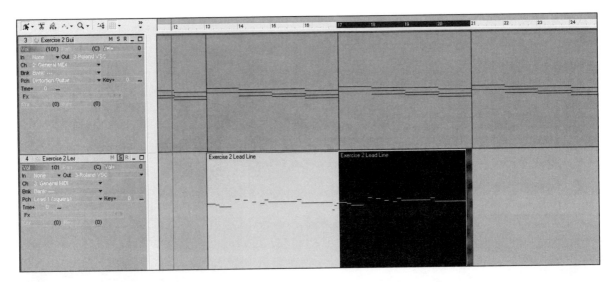

Figure 8.51

❋ TIP

There's a compositional method that works particularly well with workstations like this and especially well with songs like the one you created here.

What you have now is a bunch of regions that are playing at the same time, with a lead line in the middle. However, music works best when it changes over time, so now's a good time to set up your song to introduce different sounds gradually. Try cutting regions so that different sounds come in one at a time, like Figure 8.52.

This isn't the only way to set up your song, so experiment!

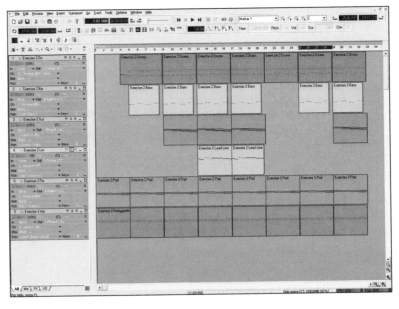

Figure 8.52

Using Quartz AudioMaster Freeware

Editing in Quartz AudioMaster is similar to Cakewalk Home Studio in many ways (see Figure 8.53).

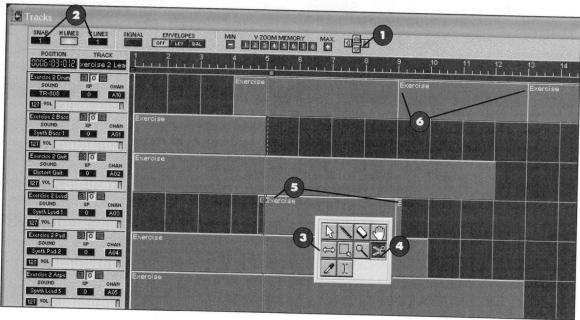

Figure 8.53

1. **Use** the **Zoom keys** to make your tracks taller and longer. This is optional, but it will make editing a bit easier.

2. **Set** your **Snap** and **V Lines values** both to 1 (one measure). This will also make editing more efficient.

3. **Right-click** on any **region**, and you'll see the toolbox.

4. **Click** on the **Scissors tool**. Your cursor will turn into scissors.

5. **Click** on the **Lead Line track** at the beginning of measure 5 and then again at the beginning of measure 9. The region will be separated.

6. **Click** on the **Drum track** at the beginning of measure 9 and then again at the beginning of measure 13.

Now let's get rid of the sections you don't want (see Figure 8.54).

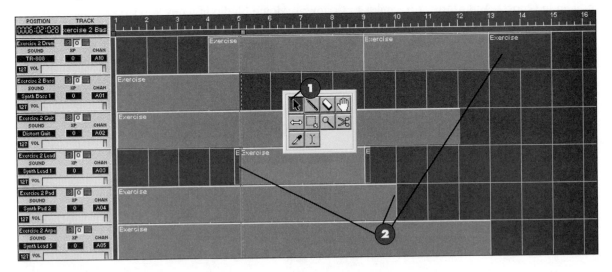

Figure 8.54

1. **Right-click** on any **region,** and the toolbox will appear again. This time, **choose** the **Arrow** tool.

2. While holding down the Control key, **click** on all **regions** that you want to delete.

3. **Press** the **Delete** key on your computer keyboard. The selected regions will disappear.

Copying regions is not hard, but it is a little different from Cakewalk Home Studio. The trick is to remember that the locators determine what will be copied (see Figure 8.55).

Figure 8.55

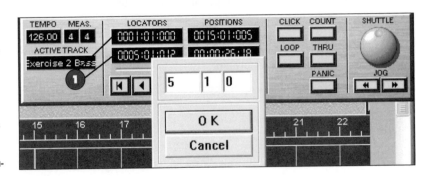

1. **Click** in the respective **locator box** (top is left, bottom is right); then **type** in the **value** (in measures, beats, and ticks). Set the left locator to be measure 1, beat 1, tick 0, and the right locator to be measure 5, beat 1, tick 0 (see Figure 8.56).

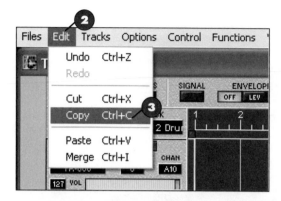

Figure 8.56

2. **Click** the **Edit** drop-down menu.

3. **Click** the **Copy** menu item. The Copy window will appear (see Figure 8.57).

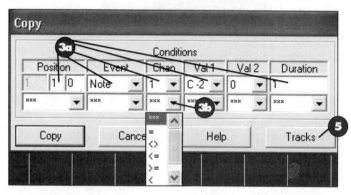

Figure 8.57

3a. The top row of this window should look somewhat familiar. This is the same window that is displayed in the MIDI event window to show the specifics of any given MIDI message. Here it allows you to specify certain data to copy.

3b. Under each aspect of MIDI data is a second row, and each area in that row has a drop-down menu. That menu has certain mathematical functions that allow you to include or exclude certain kinds of data. For example, the = (equals sign) means that only data matching the specific value above will be copied. The ******* symbol means that any value for that parameter will be included in the copying.

4. It's fine to take the values as they are, with * * * in the bottom row.

5. Now you must choose the track(s) you want to copy. **Click** the **Track** button. The Track Select window will appear (see Figure 8.58).

Figure 8.58

6. Holding the Control key, **click** the **Bass, Guitar, Pad,** and **Arpeggiate** tracks.

7. **Click OK.**

8. **Click Copy.**

Now, to paste. The left locator determines the location of your pasted regions (see Figure 8.59).

Figure 8.59

1. **Set** the **Left locator** to the position where you want your pasting to start. In this example, you want to paste starting at the beginning of measure 5.

2. **Click** the **Edit** drop-down menu.

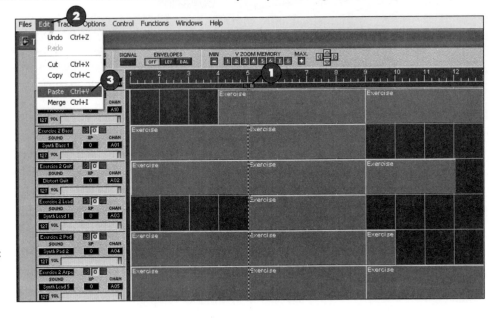

3. **Click** the **Paste** menu item. A dialog box will appear, asking you to confirm that you want to paste.

4. **Click** the **OK** button of the dialog box. The regions will be pasted.

Unfortunately, there's no way to paste multiple copies of regions, so to fill up your song you'll have to move the left indicator at four measure increments and paste. For example, you'll set the left indicator at the beginning of measure 9 and select Paste from the Edit menu. Repeat the process, inching along at four measure blocks until you have eight regions on each of these four tracks. If you zoom out, your session should look like Figure 8.60.

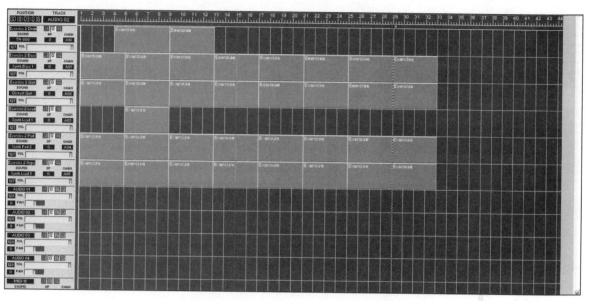

Figure 8.60

The process of copying the drums is straightforward and especially easy since you've already cut the MIDI data that you don't want to use.

1. **Set** the **left locator** to the beginning of measure 9.

2. **Set** the **right locator** to the beginning of measure 13.

3. From the Edit menu, **choose Copy.**

4. In the Copy window, **click** the **Tracks** button.

5. **Click** the **Exercise 2 Drum** track only; then **click OK.**

6. **Click** the **Copy** button.

Now you need to start pasting (again in four-measure increments), this time starting from measure 13. Remember, the left locator determines the starting point of your pastes, so change the location point before you choose Paste from the Edit menu. When you're done, your Track window will look like Figure 8.61.

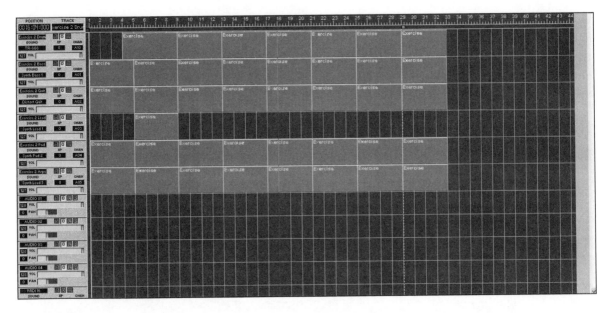

Figure 8.61

Moving regions is very simple:

Figure 8.62

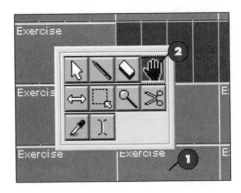

1. **Right-click** in the Track window. The toolbox will appear.
2. **Click** on the **Move** tool. Your cursor will turn into a hand.

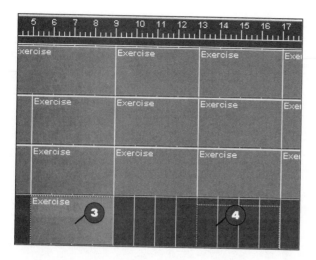

Figure 8.63

3. **Click** and **drag** the **desired region** to the desired position. Dragging left or right will move the region earlier or later in time, whereas dragging up or down will move the region to another track. For the purposes of this example, please drag the Lead Line region so that it starts at the beginning of measure 13. This is made easier with the grid enabled and set to increments of one measure.

4. **Release** the **mouse**, and the region will be moved to its new location.

5. **Copy** the **newly moved Lead Line region** and paste it at the beginning of measure 17. Again, remember to set your location points before copying.

Now, trim the unwanted notes from the second Lead Line MIDI region (see Figure 8.64).

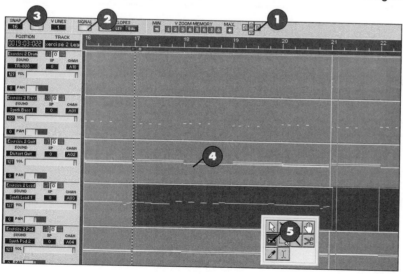

Figure 8.64

1. Use the zoom keys and the scroll bars to get a closer look at the second region of the Lead Line track.

2. **Click** the **Signal** button. You'll now be able to see the MIDI notes within each region. This will help as you attempt to get rid of the last three notes in the last region on the Lead Line track.

3. **Set** the **Snap** resolution to **16**. This will set the grid to increments of sixteenth notes. Since you want to cut the last three sixteenth notes of the last region, this setting will make your work easier.

4. **Right-click** in the **Track window**, and the toolbox will appear.

5. **Click** the **Size** tool. Your cursor will become a double arrow (see Figure 8.65).

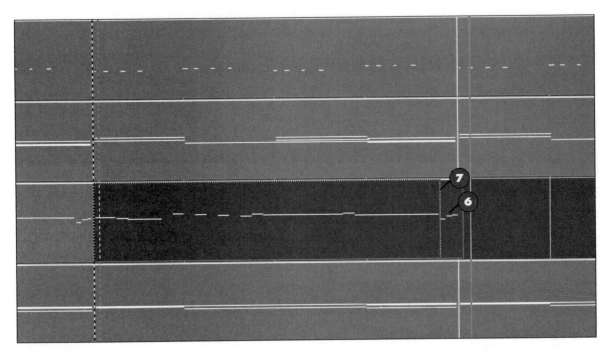

Figure 8.65

6. **Move** your **cursor** to the right end of the last MIDI region on the lead track.

7. **Click** and **hold** your **mouse**, and **drag** the **region boundary** to the left until the last three notes are removed from the region.

8. **Release** the **mouse**, and the region will be changed.

Now all that's left is to delete MIDI regions to give your song some form, like you did with Cakewalk Home Studio (see Figure 8.66).

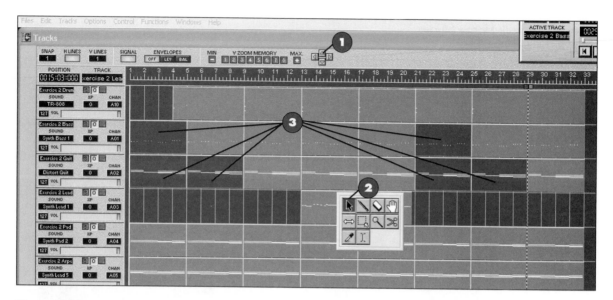

Figure 8.66

1. **Zoom out** until you can see the entire song.

2. **Right-click** to get the **toolbox**; then **choose** the **Arrow tool**.

3. Pressing and holding the Control key on your computer keyboard, **click** the **regions** you want to remove.

4. **Press** the **Delete** key on your computer keyboard. The selected regions will disappear.

Using the Transpose Function

Using Transpose can immediately give your song even more form (see Figure 8.67).

Using Cakewalk Home Studio

Figure 8.67

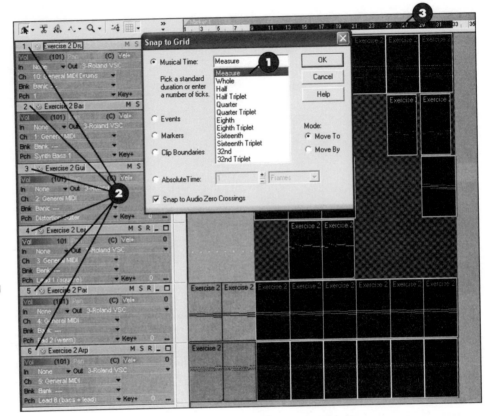

1. While still in Track view, **set the grid value** to be one measure and enable the Snap to Grid feature.

2. Holding the Control key, **select** all six **tracks**.

3. **Click** and **drag** to select from the **beginning of measure 9** to the **beginning of measure 33** in the Track window's time ruler.

4. From the Edit menu, **choose Copy** and copy all Events in Tracks.

5. From the Edit menu, **choose Paste** and paste the copied data starting at 33:01:000, 1 repetition, and starting at track 1 (see Figure 8.68).

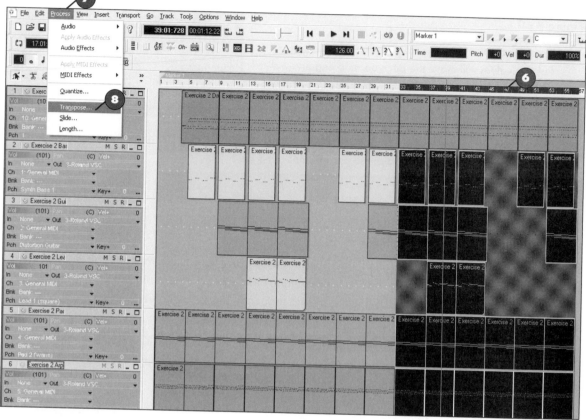

Figure 8.68

6. **Select** the **region(s)** that you want to transpose. In this case, we're transposing all the regions between measures 33 and 57 except the Drum track, so just select the measures on the time ruler and select all the tracks except the Drum track.

7. **Click** the **Process** drop-down menu.

8. **Click** the **Transpose** menu item. The **Transpose** window will appear (see Figure 8.69).

Figure 8.69

9. **Type** the **amount** that you want to change your pitches. Positive values will move the pitch up, and negative values will move them down. The only tricky thing to remember about transposition is that these changes in pitch are counted in half steps. So, if you wanted to change the key of the music from A to B, as you do in this example, that would mean you want to raise the pitch by one whole step or two half steps.

10. **Click OK**. Your changes will be applied.

Using Quartz AudioMaster Freeware

Again, you run into a limitation of the AudioMaster Freeware. There is no transposition process available. However, there *are* workarounds to the problem. First, you could go into the Grid window (or the Score window, or even the MIDI Event List) and manually move the notes. That's arguably a time-consuming process.

Here's another possible solution. Each individual track has its own transposition function. This isn't an editing process, but rather a track-wide configuration. The following procedure will show you how to use this aspect of Quartz AudioMaster to your advantage.

Either way you choose to go—manual editing or track-wide transposition—the first step is to copy a large portion of your song, as you did in Cakewalk Home Studio (see Figure 8.70).

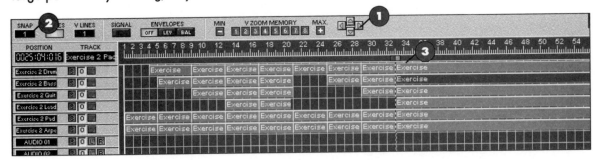

Figure 8.70

1. **Zoom out** until you can **see** your **entire song**.

2. **Set** your **Snap value** to be 1 measure.

3. **Copy** the **data** between the beginning of measure 9 and the beginning of measure 33 for all six tracks and paste it beginning at measure 33. Your screen should look like the one shown in Figure 8.71.

✳ ✳ ✳

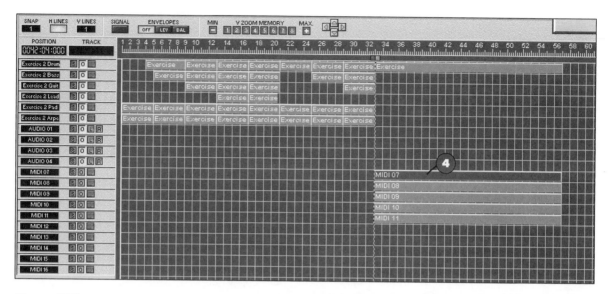

Figure 8.71

4. Using the Move tool, **drag** and **drop** all the **copied regions** except the Drum region to an unused MIDI track. For simplicity's sake, I've moved the copied Bass region to the MIDI 07 track, the Guitar region to MIDI 08, the Lead region to MIDI 09, the Pad region to MIDI 10, and the Arpeggiate region to MIDI 011. Take care to drag the regions vertically only—dragging them left or right will cause timing problems (the grid will help you). See Figure 8.72.

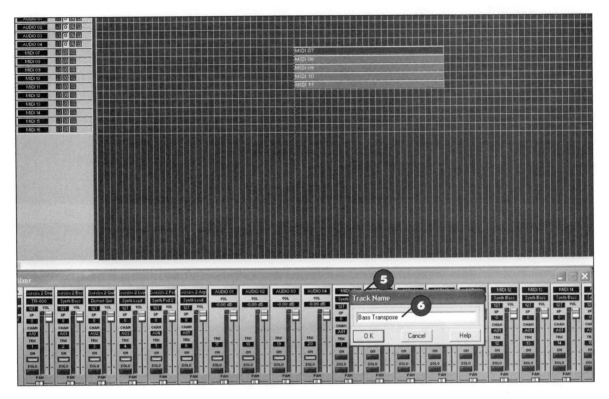

Figure 8.72

5. To name your tracks descriptively, **click** the **track name** you want to change. The Track Name window will appear.

6. **Type** a **descriptive name** for the track. For our purposes, I'm renaming MIDI 07 as Bass Transpose.

7. **Repeat Steps 5 and 6** until all five tracks are named.

You might also want to rename the regions on your newly renamed tracks. There are two easy ways to do this.

1. Double-click the region you want to rename and type in the desired name in the Name area of the Modify MIDI Element window that will appear, or

2. Drag the region you want to rename left or right. The region will automatically rename itself based upon the track name. After that, just drag it back to its original location (see Figure 8.73).

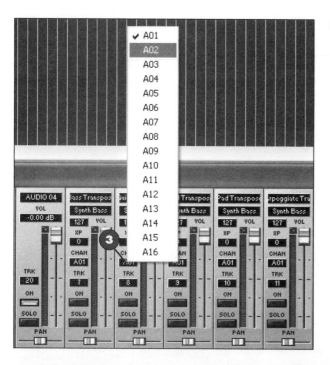

Figure 8.73

3. **Click** the **Chan** display to change the MIDI channel of the track. Change the track's MIDI channel to match the channel of the original track. For example, if the bass track is assigned to MIDI channel A01, then set the bass transpose track's MIDI channel to A01 as well. When you make these changes, you'll note that the patch name automatically changes to match that of the original track (see Figure 8.74).

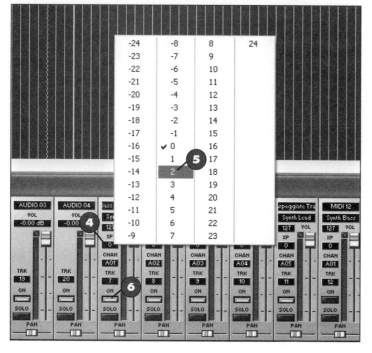

Figure 8.74

4. **Click** the **XP** (for transpose) **display** on each track. This is a track-wide transposition. A transposition drop-down menu will appear.

5. **Click** the **desired transposition value**. In this case, you want to raise the pitch by one whole step, or two half steps, so click on the number 2. Repeat this for all five of the new tracks.

6. **Click** the **On** button to activate the track and make it audible. Now, when you play your song, you will hear the transposed regions.

Recording MIDI

Now that you've created a workable song (or at least a workable beginning to a song), you might want to try your hand at playing your MIDI keyboard and creating some MIDI data of your own (see Figure 8.75).

Using Cakewalk Home Studio

Figure 8.75

1. **Click** the **Insert** drop-down menu.

2. **Click** the **MIDI Track** menu item. A new MIDI track will appear in the Track window (see Figure 8.76).

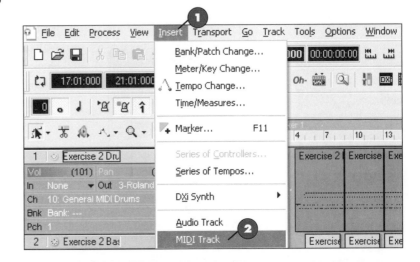

Figure 8.76

3. **Double-click** the **track name** and type a new descriptive name for the track.

4. Where will MIDI data be coming from? To configure that, **click** the **arrow** to the right of the In box. A drop-down list of MIDI channels will appear.

5. **Click** the **MIDI channel** that matches the Transmit channel of your MIDI keyboard. If you are unsure what channel that might be, **choose MIDI Omni**—that way all MIDI data going into your computer will be recorded, regardless of channel (see Figure 8.77).

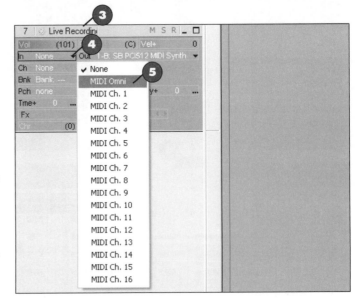

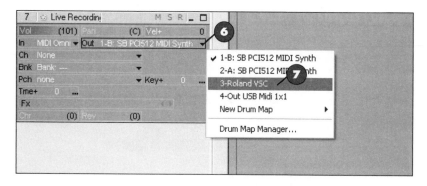

Figure 8.77

6. Where will MIDI be going? **Click** the **arrow** to the right of the Out box. A drop-down list of possible MIDI destinations will appear.

7. **Click** the **MIDI device** that you want to hear when you play your MIDI data (see Figure 8.78).

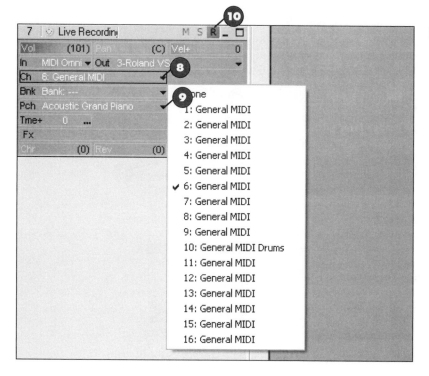

Figure 8.78

8. **Click** the **arrow button** to the right of the Ch (for channel) display. If you want to hear a distinct sound, different from the other sounds you've used so far, you'll have to choose an unused MIDI channel.

9. Once that's done, **pick** a **patch**, again by clicking the arrow key to the right of the Pch and choosing an instrument from the list.

10. The only thing left to do is to arm the track for recording. **Click** the **Record** button. The button will turn red, indicating that the track is ready for recording.

Before you start recording, you should consider setting up a click. Also called a "click track" or "metronome," it is simply a tapping sound designed to give you an idea of the tempo. Here's how to set it up (see Figure 8.79).

Figure 8.79

1. **Click** the **Options** drop-down menu.

2. **Click** the **Project** menu item. The Project Options window will appear (see Figure 8.80).

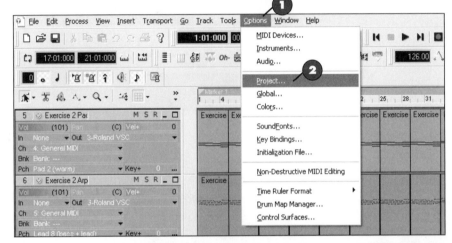

Figure 8.80

3. **Click** the **Metronome** tab. Your click options will appear.

4. **Check** the **appropriate boxes** to determine when the click will be heard. Typically, you don't want to hear it when you're just playing the song, but you *do* want to hear it when you're recording, and you *do* want to hear an accented first beat (so you know when each measure is starting).

5. **Check** the **appropriate boxes** to determine what will make the click sound. You can choose either PC Speaker (your computer will make the clicking sound) or MIDI Note (a note message will be sent to one of your MIDI synths). In this case, using the PC speaker is probably the easiest way to work.

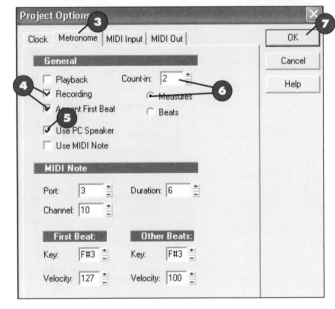

6. A Count-in is a series of clicks played for the musician *before* recording starts. It's standard in the industry to have two measures of click (eight separate clicks and then recording starts).

7. When you've chosen your preferred options, **click** the **OK** button (see Figure 8.81).

✳ **TIP**

If you choose to use the Use MIDI Note option with your click, make sure that you set the port number to match a synthesizer that you're using in your session. (For example, choosing port 1 will send a MIDI note to the first MIDI output device as shown in the MIDI Devices window.)

Figure 8.81

8. **Place** your **Now line** at the point at which you want to start recording.

9. **Click** the **Record** button at the top of your Cakewalk desktop. You will hear your count-in.

10. Once your count-in has completed (in this case, 8 clicks), recording has begun. **Play** your **keyboard**.

11. When you're done, **click** the **Stop** button. A new MIDI region will appear (see Figure 8.82).

✳ ✳ ✳

Using Quartz AudioMaster Freeware

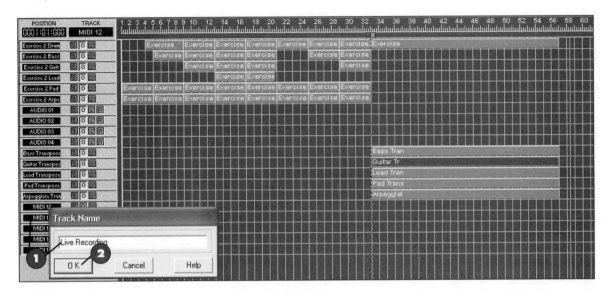

Figure 8.82

1. Let's start by naming a new track. **Click** the **track name** of an available MIDI track. The Track Name window will appear, and you can then type a descriptive name.

2. When you're done, **click OK** (see Figure 8.83).

Figure 8.83

3. In the Mixer window, **click** the **On** button to activate the track.

4. **Click** the **channel box** and **choose** an **unused MIDI channel**.

5. **Click** the **Patch name** box and **choose** a **sound** for your track (see Figure 8.84).

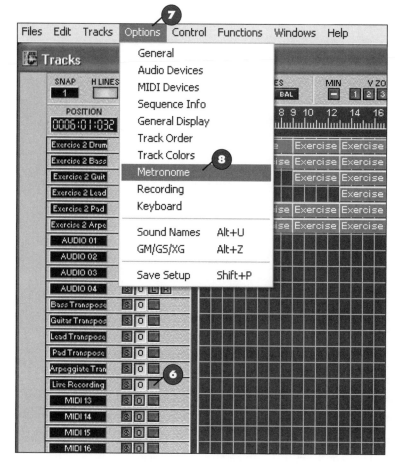

Figure 8.84

6. In the Tracks window, **click** the **Record Arm** button on the track that you want to use for recording your MIDI data.

7. Now let's set up the metronome. **Click** the **Options** drop-down menu.

8. **Click** the **Metronome** menu item. The Options (Metronome) window will appear. These options should look a little familiar compared with Cakewalk Home Studio (see Figure 8.85).

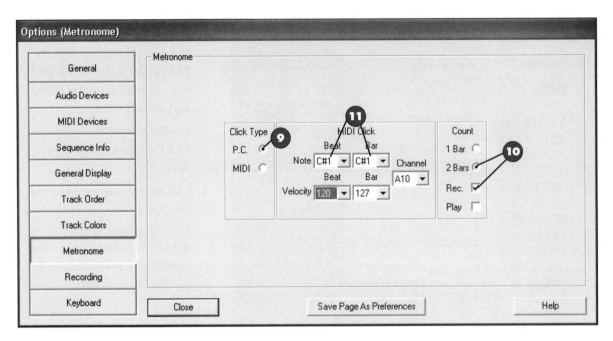

Figure 8.85

9. What do you want to play your click? Choosing PC will have the click coming our of your computer's speaker, whereas MIDI will send a MIDI note message to your synthesizer. **Click one** of the **radio buttons** (you can't have both of these active at one time).

10. Your options with the count-in are a little more limited than Home Studio's, but still very usable. The different check boxes determine if you want to hear the click during playback, recording, or both, and the radio buttons let you choose between a one-bar or two-bar count-in.

11. If you choose MIDI for your Click Type, you can determine the MIDI channel and note number of the click. The Bar column refers to the first beat of every measure, and if you want to accentuate that note, you just increase the velocity for the Beat column. If you're using a General MIDI synth, you can safely leave the note and channel assignments alone (they'll trigger a drum sound). See Figure 8.86.

❋ **NOTE**

The MIDI Click section of the Options (Metronome) window only affects the click if you have MIDI chosen as the Click Type.

Figure 8.86

12. In the Transport window, **click** the **Click** and **Count** buttons to enable your click and count-in. The buttons will light to indicate that they are active.

13. **Click** in the **timeline** at the point at which you want to start recording.

14. **Click** the **Record** button. You'll hear your count-in.

15. After the count-in, you're recording! **Play** your **MIDI keyboard**.

16. Once you're finished, **click** the **Stop** button. A new MIDI region will appear on the track.

Making a Rough Mix

Before we leave the world of MIDI, you might want to change the volume (loudness) or pan (position in the left and right speakers) of your mix. You'll get into this in greater detail when we talk about digital audio in the next section, but for now, here are the basics of bringing your mix into focus (see Figure 8.87).

Using Cakewalk Home Studio

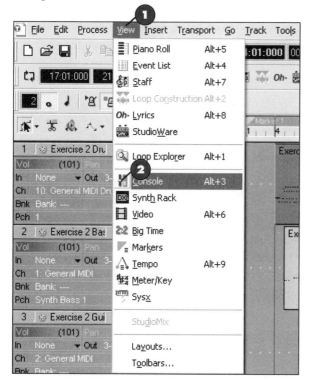

Figure 8.87

1. **Click** the **View** drop-down menu.

2. **Click** the **Console** menu item. The Console window will appear (see Figure 8.88).

Figure 8.88

2a. At the top of each track is the track's name, followed by the output MIDI device, MIDI channel, MIDI bank, and MIDI. Let's start by naming a new track.

2b. Each track has a Volume slider (or "fader"). **Click** and **drag** the **slider** up or down with your mouse to make any individual track louder or softer.

2c. Above the Volume slider is a Pan slider. **Click** and **drag** the **Pan slider** left or right to move the sound between your left and right speakers.

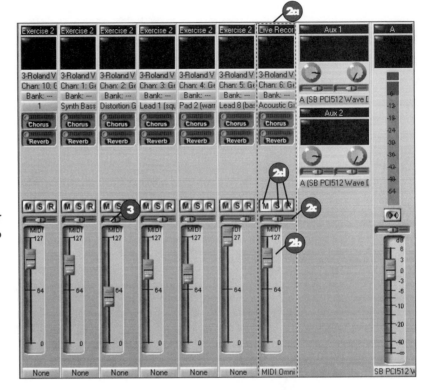

2d. Above the Pan sliders are the Mute, Solo, and Record Arm buttons. **Clicking Solo** will allow you to hear only the soloed track, Mute will make the track inaudible, and Record Arm will record new MIDI data to that track. In this example, I've muted the Live Recording track so that I won't hear it.

3. **Start playback.**

4. **Click** and **drag** to adjust the **Volume** and **Pan** values. If you don't want to hear a track, just **click** the **Mute** button.

Using Quartz AudioMaster Freeware

The Quartz AudioMaster Freeware also has a mixer-like window, just like Cakewalk Home Studio. The layout is similar but not identical (see Figure 8.89).

Figure 8.89

1. **Volume**

2. **Pan**

3. **Solo**

4. There's no **Mute** button in AudioMaster, but if you don't want to hear a given track, just **click** the **On** button to turn it off, making the track inaudible.

5. There's also a **Master** volume control for all the MIDI data. Use this fader to make the entire song louder or softer.

1. While playing, **click** and **drag** the **Volume** and **Pan** sliders, and experiment with different types of mixes. Note that changes you make on the original tracks are reflected on the transposition tracks that share the same MIDI channel number.

There's another window that's specific to AudioMaster, and it takes mixing to a whole new level! See Figure 8.90.

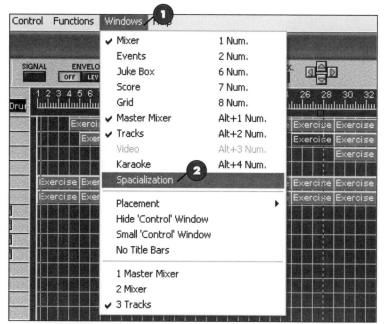

Figure 8.90

1. **Click** the **Windows** drop-down menu.

2. **Click** the **Spacialization** menu item. The Spacialization window will appear (see Figure 8.91).

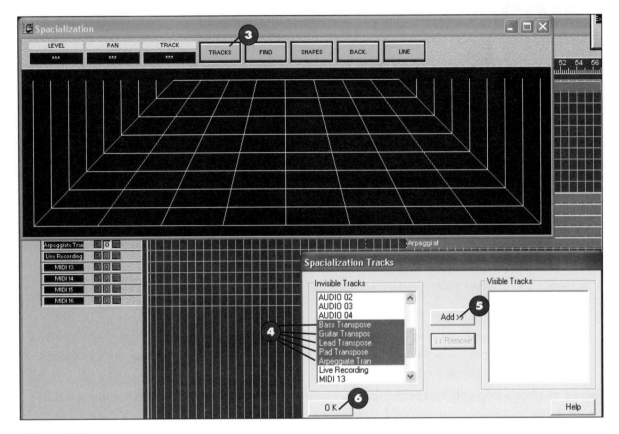

Figure 8.91

3. **Click** the **Tracks** button. The Spacialization Tracks window will appear.

4. Holding the Control key on your computer keyboard, **click** the **tracks** that you want to include in your mix. In this case it will be six Exercise 2 tracks and five Transpose tracks (I'm not including the Live Recording track).

5. **Click** the **Add** button. The selected tracks will move from the left column to the right.

6. **Click** the **OK** button. The selected tracks will now appear as icons in the Spacialization grid (see Figure 8.92).

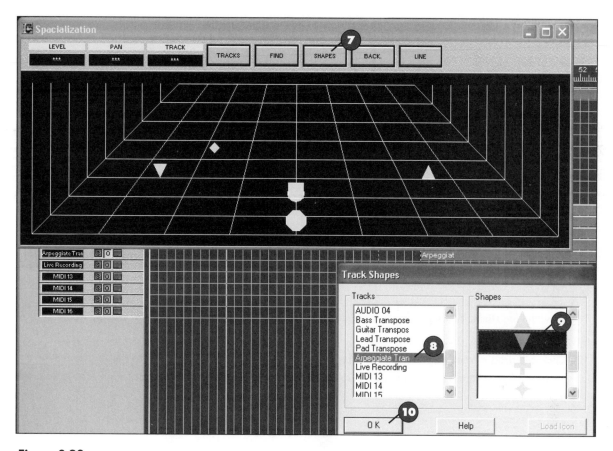

Figure 8.92

7. **Click** the **Shapes** button. The Track Shapes window will appear.

8. **Click** a **track** in the Tracks column.

9. **Click** a shape in the Shapes column to assign that particular shape to that track in the Spacialization window.

10. After you've assigned different shapes to the desired tracks, **click OK**. The shapes will be applied to the track icons (see Figure 8.93).

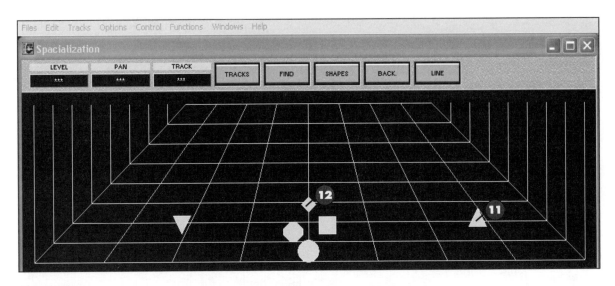

Figure 8.93

11. Now the fun starts. While playing, **click** and **drag** a **track's icon** to the left or right to change its pan value.

12. **Click** and **drag** a **track's icon** up or down (which translates into back and forward in the Spacialization window's 3-D grid) to change the track's volume value. Note that the icon grows or shrinks as the volume is changed.

TIP

Mixing, regardless of the application, is the art of making different sonic elements work together. Like any art, there's a degree of experimentation that must happen, and that goes double for mixing. Listen critically as you change volume and especially when you adjust panning. Generally, the object of the game is to be able to hear all the musical elements distinctly and to have them occupy their own "place" between your left and right speakers. As you experiment with these aspects of your composition, you'll hear your music improve immediately. Enjoy!

9   Studio Setup Tips

We're now ready to start recording and playing back audio. That means we've got to think about getting that audio into and out of your computer at the highest quality sound possible. The environment that you set up in your desktop studio will determine the quality of audio as it is recorded into your system, which will certainly affect the quality of your final product. In this chapter, you'll learn how to:

* Make MIDI and digital audio work together.
* Set up your digital audio studio.
* Choose your digital audio wisely.
* Record audio digitally.

Getting Rid of Hum

There's nothing that can get on your nerves quicker than a persistent hum in your music. Unfortunately, as your studio gets more powerful and complex, the possibility of different kinds of hum being introduced to your setup increases. Worse yet, if you record audio with hum, then that annoying little audio artifact becomes a permanent part of that sound. (There are some hum-reducing features and plug-ins available, but even if the hum can be completely removed, the sound is never really as good as the original.) The bottom line: Hum is important to head off, and the best time is now, *before* you start recording.

Ground Loops

There are many potential causes of hum, but the most common is called a "ground loop." This occurs when multiple pieces of gear are connected by some sort of metal wire (like an audio cable, for example) while at the same time each device maintains its own connection to the earth for grounding. There are a number of potential solutions for this, but usually ground loop problems can be overcome by lifting the ground (disconnecting it from the earth)—a switch sometimes found on the rear of audio components.

Lighting Tips

Unfortunately, ground loops aren't the only hum culprits in studios these days. Lighting can even be a problem. Fluorescent light can create loads of electromagnetic "noise" that can cause even the most protected gear to hum loudly. If you suspect that your fluorescent lights are causing sonic mischief, try turning off the lights—if the noise goes away, it's a safe bet that your lights are the cause of the hum.

Dimmer switches can also be a problem. Because of the way they handle electricity, they can act like a volume knob of hum. Though dimming your studio down to coffeehouse-style intimacy is nice, a CD laden with buzz is just too high a price to pay. If you do have a dimmer, hopefully it'll have a fully on position that bypasses the dimmer's rheostat (the part of the dimmer that actually *dims*), which solves the hum issue. Hey, working in the dark isn't that great for your eyes anyway.

Intelligent Wiring

If you do a little online window shopping, you might be surprised at how much you could spend on just the cables in your studio. Truth is, good wiring *does* make a difference in the quality of audio getting into and out of your gear. Good news, though—you don't have to put yourself into the poorhouse with your cables.

As long as you use middle of the road cables (not the cheapest, but certainly not the most expensive), you should be fine. Beyond that, you should do your best to keep your cables as short as possible. Long cables can act as antennas, especially when coiled. (I've actually picked up *radio* signals this way!)

Taking a moment to thoughtfully arrange your cables can also pay off by giving you less noise. When bundling things together, take special care to keep your audio cables as far away from power cables as possible. Also, make sure that your audio cables are away from your computer screen. Both power cables and your video monitor emit a good amount of electromagnetic noise.

Protecting Your Gear

There are a few things you can do not only to improve the quality of your audio, but also the life of your gear. Check it out.

Voltage

You probably already know that a surge protector can save your computer from power spikes caused by distant lightning strikes and other electrical problems. You might be surprised to know that most computerized gear can also be damaged by *low* voltage as well. Purchasing a power conditioner helps this immensely.

Better yet, many power conditioners have built-in batteries, so that if the power goes out, you have a few extra minutes to save your work and do an orderly power-down. Depending upon how "clean" your power is, you might even notice a decrease in audible noise in your system.

TIP
Though power conditioners and surge protectors are important safety devices indeed, there's only one sure way to protect your gear in a lightning storm—unplug it!

Good Monitor Health

You might not know this, but video monitors (including your TV) don't respond very well to magnets. A magnet in close proximity to a monitor can cause problems with color and even mess with the shapes of the images being shown. Before you get an idea to play around with this yourself, keep in mind that being real close to a monitor isn't that great for us, either.

Why do we talk about this in a music book? Because your monitor speakers have magnets (sometimes powerful ones) inside, and this can play havoc with your video monitor. That fact can be an issue sometimes, since it is often convenient to put your speakers to either side of the screen in your workstations. Many professional speakers are magnetically shielded for just such a reason, but many are not, so if you see discolorations on your screen (usually near the speakers), you should consider repositioning them to save your computer monitor (and your eyes).

Your Monitor Speakers

It might sound stupid for me to say it, but it's awful hard to do any good work with music if you can't tell what it sounds like. Of course, there are exceptions—for example, Beethoven was almost totally deaf when he wrote his famous Ninth Symphony. But for us mortals, we're going to need speakers to hear what we're doing. The good news is that computer speakers are cheap, but the bad news is you get what you pay for.

Although you can certainly do *some* work with just the powered computer speakers that came with your PC, you might soon feel the itch to upgrade to some studio monitor speakers. The type you're looking for is called "nearfield," which simply means that they're made to be used in close proximity to the listener, perfect for our compact workstation. There are many manufacturers of nearfield speakers, and they come powered or unpowered (in which case you'll need an amplifier), but they all strive to do the same thing, which is to give you the most accurate picture of how your music will sound in the real world.

Choosing and Using Nearfield Monitors

There's a trick with nearfield monitors and a pitfall. The temptation might be to spend extra and get speakers with kickin' bass, and when you play a CD through your system it sounds great. There's a problem, though. Those speakers are sometimes *too good* and don't give an accurate representation of what your mix really sounds like. I've seen many a student create songs using these kinds of speakers only to be disappointed when they played the fruits of their labor in their car CD player. "Where did the bass go?" they ask, but the truth is, that full bass sound never was in the mix—it was only in their expensive speakers.

The goal in choosing monitor speakers isn't so much to buy anything spectacular, but to get the most average sound possible. Beyond that, you should try to find the "flattest" speakers possible, meaning that they don't emphasize any specific frequencies. Of course, this sort of "averageness" is sometimes hard to find, so if you find yourself using regular stereo speakers, keep in mind that they may be boosting frequencies, and you might have to compensate accordingly.

The positioning of these speakers is a pretty simple matter, but an important one. The distance between you and the speakers isn't too critical (though they typically are set up to be a yard from the listener), but the side-to-side position is an issue. The ideal positioning of theses speakers is 30 degrees off dead center in either direction and angled toward you, as shown in Figure 9.1.

Figure 9.1

Speaker placement.

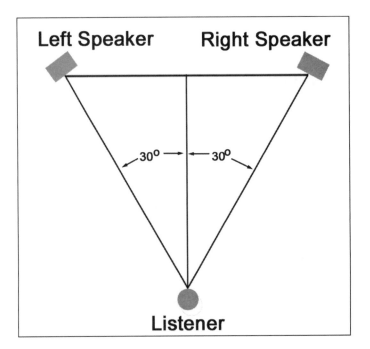

TIP

Sometimes, measuring angles can be a headache, so here's another trick for placing your speakers. Make sure that your speakers are as far from each other as they are from you. That will make for an equilateral triangle (each angle being 60 degrees), which will position each speaker 30 degrees off center (assuming that you're facing the speakers).

Mixing with Headphones

If you can't use speakers, then mixing with headphones might be your only option. (Your parents might appreciate you working a bit more quietly, and this way you can choose to unveil your work when it's done.) Headphones are indeed convenient, but in professional circles they're generally frowned upon when creating mixes. The tendency when using headphones for mixes is to create a final product that sounds fine in the headphones but sounds altogether different when played back through speakers (the stereo feeling is usually not as wide, and the bass is often unnaturally loud). Bottom line: If you are going to use headphones in the studio, you should prepare yourself to have to tweak the mix a little after listening to it on your living room speakers.

Recording Digital Audio

Once you've got the audio connections between your gear and your computer's audio inputs all set, there's simply the matter of just hitting "record" on the application you're using, and everything will be fine. Actually, there are a few things to think about before you start converting those sound waves to digital bits.

Making Smart Choices

In the next chapter, you'll begin to work with digital audio, including recording. Part of the great power of working with digital audio is that you can make certain decisions regarding the audio that you'll be recording. For the informed producer, this is a great thing, but it's your responsibility to make the right choices.

NOTE

If you want to learn more about the essence of digital audio and how it is fundamentally different from MIDI, check out Appendix C: The Basics of Digital Audio.

Sample Rates and Bit Depths

There are a few rules of thumb about the benefits of different bit depths and sample rates. Basically, it boils down to this:

* Higher sample rates will give you better audio quality and technically give you the possibility of capturing higher frequencies, but higher sample rates will devour more of your hard disk space.

* Lower sample rates will not only be less aggressive with your hard drive but will also be faster and easier for your computer to play back and process with effects and processes (things like reverbs and equalizations).

TIP

The upper end of the human audible range is roughly 20 kHz (kilohertz) That means that a sample rate of 44.1 kHz (CD quality) more than takes care of our hearing range. Be careful not to go to a lower sample rate than 44.1 because you will hear a loss of higher frequencies as you reduce the sample rate.

* Higher bit depths will give you greater dynamic range (a greater difference between the softest and loudest sounds) and a lower level of dynamic error due to the doubled resolution that each extra bit adds to each sample. Better yet, you'll get this benefit with a minimal investment in extra disk space and processing power.

Files and Folders

Before you record, your application will ask you what to name your audio files and where to stash them on your hard drive. You might be tempted, in your enthusiasm to get going, to just go with whatever default filename and location your software chooses, but over the long term that can add up to problems. Here are a few guidelines to consider when setting up your files:

* Name your file *descriptively*. Naming a file "audio 1" really doesn't give much of an idea of what's been recorded. You can get as descriptive as you want, and generally the more the better. Try this on for size: Name your files after the instrument you're recording. A file named "slap bass (take 2)" will give you a far better idea of what you'll hear when you play the file. Trust me, this will make hunting down that perfect part *much* quicker (even years after you originally recorded it).

* As you start doing more and more work, you'll start piling up filenames like "bass" or "Lead Vocal," so naming your files will only go so far down the road of good file organization. Deposit specific files into *folders* (also known as *subdirectories*) to further help you keep tabs on what is what. A folder named "New Folder" tells nothing about the music that might be contained within. You can set up your own logic for naming your folders, but I've found some success with naming my folders after the project title and the date that the folder was created. Saved in that folder are audio files named after their sonic role, and between the folder name and the filename you can get a very clear idea of what each individual file is all about. For example, a folder named "Wonders of the Universe soundtrack (November 12 2003)" tells me what I need to know about the data within, and a file named "String Orchestra" tells me what each individual file is doing in that project.

> ❄ **TIP**
>
> Some DAWs have their own way of organizing files, in which case it's best to let the program store the files in a way that works for that program. Naming your project and tracks descriptively will help you keep tabs on your work with these kinds of DAW applications.

❄ **Don't delete or overwrite files unless you have to!** Keep in mind that one of the biggest advantages of working with a computer is that it tends to be *nondestructive*, and you'll notice that when you do want to overwrite a file, your computer gives you some sort of "Are you sure you want to replace this file?" message. I've got my own version of "Murphy's Law" (which pessimistically states that anything that can go wrong *will* go wrong) that I've modified for digital audio production, which states that "as soon as I'm *positive* that I'll *never* need a specific file ever again and delete the file, *that's* when I'm going to need it again! The moral of the story: Don't delete or overwrite a file unless you have no other option (like for example, if you've run out of hard drive space). Instead, use the software's Save As function to name your altered file as some other filename (taking care to be descriptive about the file).

Digital Audio Recording Tips

When you've squared away your file-related issues, there's still the issue of getting the audio into your computer and digitized with the greatest amount of accuracy possible. The good news is that you already understand the concept behind good digital audio recording, so this should make sense.

The governing rule of recording audio digitally is to record as "hot" (loud) as possible *without clipping*. To learn what clipping is, and *why* it is, we need to take another look at the bit depth of your samples.

One of the advantages of greater bit depth, is a greater dynamic range, with each extra bit giving about 6 dB (decibels) of dynamic range. This dynamic range is measured *downward* from –0 dBFS (decibels full scale). So the dynamic range of CD-quality audio, for example, having 16 bits per sample, is measured from –0 dBFS down to –96 dBFS. Greater bit depths will give the ability to record *softer* sounds and will yield a greater overall dynamic range, as shown in Figure 9.2.

Figure 9.2

Bit-depth and dynamic range.

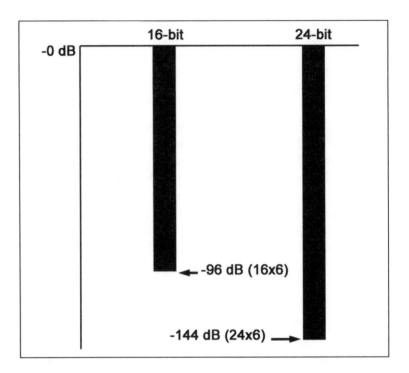

Digital audio cannot express a digital number above –0 dB. That means that if you try to record a signal whose amplitude goes above this maximum value, digital audio has no way to represent that loud signal and will do the best it can to reproduce it—a string of –0 dB values, which will wind up looking (and sounding) something like the example shown in Figure 9.3.

Figure 9.3

Digital clipping.

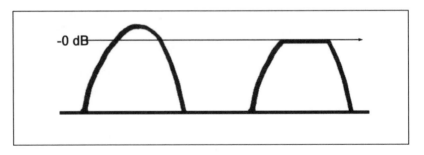

In addition to the recorded digital audio being radically different from the original audio, this series of –0 dB samples (called "clipping" "flat-tops," or "overs") sounds particularly nasty. The solution? When you're setting your levels, make sure that the meters on your software's input aren't pegging their red clip lights. If they are, then turn down your source device (synth module, microphone, guitar, and so on) until you're no longer clipping.

✳ **TIP**

If you're clipping when you're recording, you might be tempted to simply turn down the output of your software. Ironically, that won't fix the problem. The source of the clipping problem when recording is on the input end of the signal path, and turning down the output of your computer will only give you softer clipping!

If clipping is such a bad thing to do with digital audio, then why don't we just go ahead and record everything really soft, to minimize the possibility of clipping in the first place? That thinking isn't completely off base, but be careful about recording things at too low a volume. The reason for this is also related to the bit-depth of your samples.

Because digital audio is a numerical representation with a fixed resolution of a natural analog phenomenon (sound waves), at some point, some rounding off of numbers will have to happen. When numbers are rounded off, a degree of error will be introduced, making the recorded digital audio different from the original analog audio (see Figure 9.4).

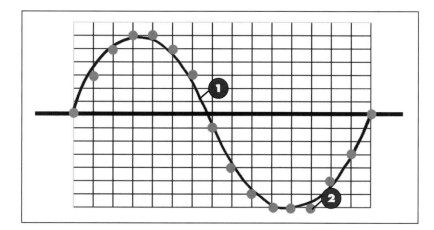

Figure 9.4

Digital recording of analog audio.

1. Original analog audio signal.

2. Each digital measurement of the analog signal will have to be rounded off to the nearest number, or quantization interval.

This distortion of the original audio is called *quantization error.* Make every effort to make the amount of rounding off as minimal as possible. Thankfully, there are ways to minimize the potentially destructive effects of quantization error.

By using one additional bit to a single sample, you *double* the different values that it can create. That means that with only one more bit of data to each sample, you double the number of quantization intervals and cut the amount of quantization error in half for any given recording level. This is yet another good reason to make it a standard practice of choosing the greatest bit depth of audio that your system will support when creating audio.

NOTE

If you're interested in learning the math behind these aspects of digital audio, refer to Appendix C.

Quantization error will *always* be present in digital audio, although to varying degrees, based upon the incoming volume of the analog signal. Lower volumes coming into your A/D (analog/digital) converters will be digitized into lower numbers. For example, an extremely soft analog signal being converted into 16-bit audio (CD quality) might be represented by a value like 0000000000000001. (Digital silence is represented by a string of zeros, like 0000000000000000.) Essentially, at this very low amplitude, you're really only using *one* of many bits of your sample. You're still going to have to round to the closest number, but in this extreme example it could give you 50% error, as shown in Figure 9.5.

Figure 9.5

Each sample must be rounded up or down to the nearest quantization interval, but at this low volume, it could really change the shape of your sound wave!

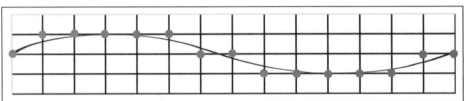

On the other hand, recording your audio at a higher level can *minimize* the negative effects of quantization error. Higher levels will be encoded as higher digital numbers, giving you a sample like 1111111111111110. Keep in mind that rounding off will still have to happen, so there will be quantization errors. Because this signal is using so many of the 1s and 0s of the sample, though, the *percentage* of destruction caused by quantization error will be much less, and more of the original shape of the original audio waveform will be preserved. Each sample will still be rounded to the nearest quantization interval, but at a high recording level, any amount of rounding off will be a smaller percentage of the overall wave. The bottom line when recording is that recording as loud a signal as possible *without clipping* will give you the greatest resolution without those annoying flat-tops.

Now let's dive into some digital audio.

10 Exercise 4: Digital Audio Workstations

Recording a single instrument digitally is certainly important, but digital audio production shines brightest when dealing with many different audio elements in one all-encompassing environment. That's what a DAW (digital audio workstation) does best, but it doesn't stop there. Do you want to cut out a wrong note, repeat a phat beat, or even fix a pitch? Not a problem for a DAW.

Before you get any deeper into the world of DAWs, you should take a moment to understand the general principals behind this powerful way of working. In this chapter, you'll learn:

- ❊ How to set up your DAW for digital audio.
- ❊ The power of DAWs and how to use it.
- ❊ How DAW files work with audio files.
- ❊ DAW signal flow.
- ❊ Editing in a DAW.

❊ **NOTE**

The exercises in this section, just like the MIDI exercises in the earlier section, will use the Cakewalk Home Studio and Quartz AudioMaster Freeware applications, but there's a little more preparation you'll need to do before you can work with this session.

Instead of opening the session file from the accompanying CD-ROM, please copy the Exercise/Ex_04 folder to a suitable hard drive (if you have a hard drive dedicated to digital audio, that one is best). After the folders are copied, you can open the tutorial files from your hard drive.

Setting Up Your DAW for Audio

You've already set up your system so that you can hear your virtual synthesizers, so most of the work in setting up is already done. There are a few things left to be done that refer specifically to recording and playing back digital audio.

> **NOTE**
>
> In this section, you'll be asked to choose a sample rate and bit depth for your applications. To learn more about these important aspects of digital audio, check out Appendix C.

Using Cakewalk Home Studio

After you've copied the exercise folder to your hard drive (see preceding note) and opened up the Exercise 4 file in the Cakewalk Home Studio folder, here's how you can customize your audio options (see Figure 10.1).

Figure 10.1

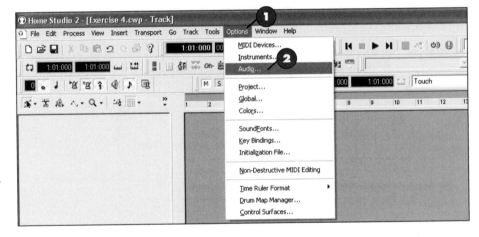

1. **Click** the **Options** drop-down menu.

2. **Click** the **Audio** menu item. The Audio Options window will appear (see Figure 10.2).

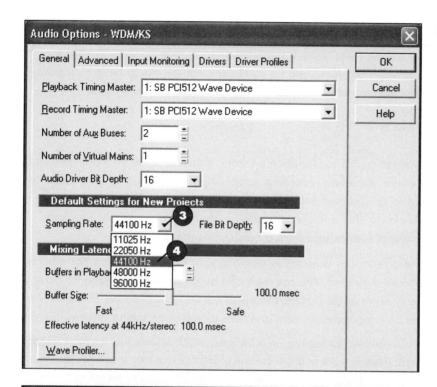

Figure 10.2

3. **Click the arrow button** to the right of the Sampling Rate display. A list of possible sample rates will appear.

4. **Click on the Sample Rate** you want to use in new sessions (see Figure 10.3).

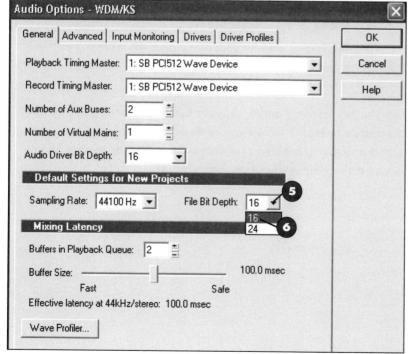

Figure 10.3

5. **Click** the **arrow button** to the right of the File Bit Depth. A list of possible bit depths (resolutions) will appear.

6. **Click** on the **Bit Depth** that you want to use in new sessions.

> **CAUTION**
>
> Though you may have a list of many different sample rates and bit depth resolutions, that doesn't necessarily mean that any of those choices will work for your particular system. You must be sure that your choices reflect the capabilities of your audio hardware (interface or sound card). Refer to your computer's documentation (or audio interface manual) to find out what sample rates and bit depths it supports. If you choose something that your hardware doesn't support, your audio won't play back properly (if at all).

This next bit is important, but it requires a little explanation up front. Your computer's CPU is involved with every aspect of your digital audio, including recording, processing, and mixing for playback. To do its job properly, it must be able to receive and send a steady stream of digital audio to and from your audio hardware. If your CPU *doesn't* have this steady stream, there can be audible problems, ranging from clicks and pops to gaps of silence and even a crash of your computer.

To ensure that the flow of digital audio data is as constant as possible, your DAW application has a buffer (and some applications even have more than one). You can think of a buffer as a holding area for data, between your application and your system's audio drivers. Nearly every DAW application allows for the user to set the size of this buffer, but beware, there are pros and cons to any given setting.

* A **low** buffer setting will give you the smallest holding area for data, which will result in the most responsive system. Among other things, this will result in a low amount of latency (the time it take for the system to play back data). A low buffer setting is generally recommended when you're recording audio, so that the you can monitor your input with the lowest possible difference in time. However, low buffer settings can lead to audio playback problems, or even system crashes.

* A **high** buffer setting will give you a larger holding area for your data, which will result in a more reliable performance (especially if your computer is on the slow side to begin with). Be aware, though, that a higher buffer setting will increase the playback latency of your system.

Here's a good rule of thumb: When you're recording audio, set your buffer as low as possible (the lowest setting that won't cause your system to crash). When you're done with recording, raise your buffer setting to prevent playback and processing problems (when you're editing or mixing, latency is not as big an issue). Here's how you make your settings (see Figure 10.4).

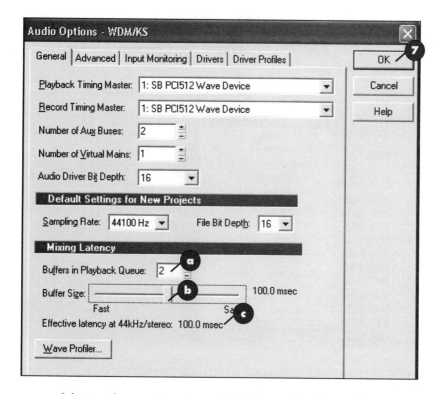

Figure 10.4

a. **Buffers in Playback Queue:** Type a number (or use the increment/decrement buttons to the right of the queue display) to change the number of buffers that the application can use. The more buffers you choose, the more "safe" your system will be, but it will increase playback latency.

b. **Buffer Size:** Drag the slider left or right to change the size of the buffer(s). As the slider's scale suggests, a lower buffer size will result in a "fast" (or at least faster) system, whereas larger buffer sizes will give you a "safer" system.

c. As you change the number of buffers or the buffer size, you'll see your latency change (measured in milliseconds). Larger and more buffers will result in greater latency

7. When you're done setting up your system, **click** the **OK** button. The window will close, and you're ready to move on!

❋ **NOTE**

With more advanced audio interfaces, you may need to re-run the Wave Profiler (at the bottom left corner of the Audio Options window). On still others, the buffer settings must be set on the interface itself. It's a good idea to check your gear's documentation to find out if there are any special setup considerations.

Using Quartz AudioMaster Freeware

The concepts behind setting up audio in Quartz AudioMaster are similar to Cakewalk's, but as always, you have to know where to look (see Figure 10.5).

Figure 10.5

1. **Click** the **Options** drop-down menu.

2. **Click** the **General** list item to open the Options (General) window (see Figure 10.6).

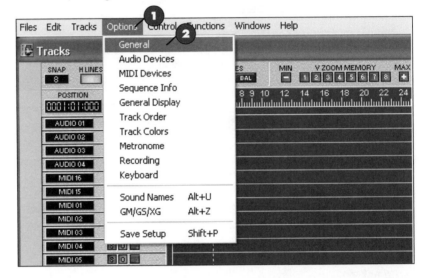

Figure 10.6

3. **Click** the **arrow button** to the right of the Output Sample Rate display. A drop-down list of options will appear.

4. **Click** the **desired sample rate** for Quartz Audio-Master.

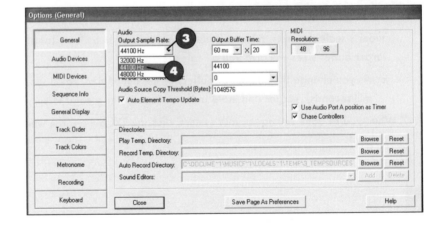

> ❋ **NOTE**
>
> Choosing a buffer time in Quartz AudioMaster is the same thing as choosing a buffer size in Cakewalk Home Studio.

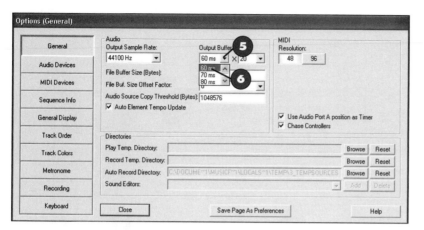

Figure 10.7

5. **Click** the **arrow button** to the right of the right Output Buffer Time display.

6. **Click** on the **buffer time** that you want to use.

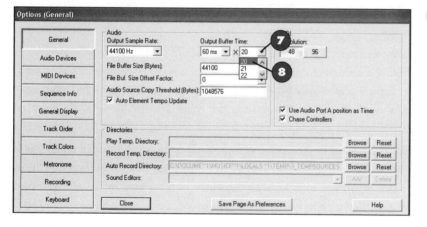

Figure 10.8

7. **Click** the **arrow button** to the right of the left Output Buffer Time display.

8. **Click** on the **number** of buffers you want to use.

❈ **NOTE**

This is the same as choosing the number of buffers in Cakewalk Home Studio. The total latency of your system can be found by multiplying the single buffer time by the number of buffers used. For example, in this case (60 milliseconds multiplied by 20 buffers), the latency would be 1200 milliseconds.

In Quartz AudioMaster Freeware, there are a couple of other options you should be aware of. Generally, the default settings work well here, but an understanding of these parameters will help you troubleshoot your system if the need arises.

Figure 10.9

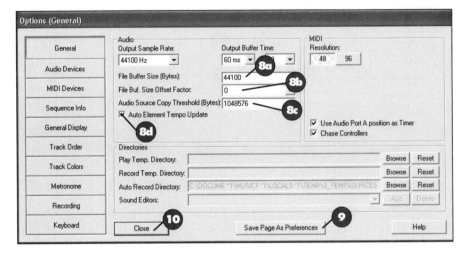

8a. **File Buffer Size:**
This is a buffer
(data holding
area) for audio
as it is transmit-
ted from your
hard drive. The
default value of
44,100 Bytes is
usually fine, but
if you hear
breaks in the
audio as you play back your song, you can increase that value.

8b. **File Buffer Offset Factor:** This allows your hard drive to access different audio files more efficiently by staggering the file reading from the surface of the drive. Generally, this is not necessary, and a value of 0 (no offset) is fine, but if you have a particularly slow or complex song, you may notice that your pro-gram begins to respond sluggishly. That's the time to increase that value. (Your audio will still be per-fectly in sync as it plays back.)

8c. **Audio Source Copy Threshold:** This value (by default it is a megabyte) is the point at which audio that is used by a specific sequence file is copied into a subdirectory called Sources. That means that any file in this song that's bigger than 1MB, regardless of its location anywhere on your hard drive, will be copied to this subfolder. It's a neat feature designed to help in file organization, but copying large audio files can eat up space on your hard drive. Set this value to zero if you don't want to copy files at all (or want to do it manually).

8d. **Audio Element Tempo Update:** When this box is checked, audio regions will change location to match any tempo changes you make. When the box is unchecked, the regions stay where you place them, regardless of tempo.

9. **Click** the **Save Page As Preferences** button if you want to use these settings in future sessions.

10. **Click Close.**

The Power of DAWs

The introduction (and evolution) of digital audio workstations has transformed the way that we create music, as you've already learned. Now it's time to dig deeper, to learn how these powerful work environments "think," so that you can use these wonderful tools more effectively.

DAWs as Pointer-Based Applications

In order to understand how to use a DAW to its greatest power, you'll have to understand how a DAW "thinks" about audio data. You've probably heard the term "pointer" before—it's common to refer to a cursor as a *pointer*, but when you're discussing pointer-based applications like DAWs, it's referring to the way the program deals with digital audio data.

In this case, the pointer-based structure can be broken down into interdependent elements, starting with DAW files and audio files. Here, the term "pointer" refers to the fact that a DAW file will access (or "point") to other files on your hard drive as your session plays. There's a reason for this. If the DAW file actually had all the audio that it needed to play, that file could get *huge* (you've seen by now how digital audio can really eat up disk space). No kidding, I've worked on projects that have involved *gigabytes* of audio—if all that information were wrapped up in one file, it wouldn't be able to even open, much less run!

Here's how it works. After you launch your DAW application, you will need to open or create a DAW file. These files might go by any number of names (like "project" or "session" files), but they all do the same thing. These DAW files typically contain the following kinds of data:

- ❋ The names, types, and arrangement of all tracks in your session.
- ❋ All MIDI data.
- ❋ Essential settings, such as inputs and outputs.
- ❋ All edits and mix data.

This file is at the top of your project's file hierarchy. This is the file created by you when you create a new session, and it's the file you open to return to a session you already created. Although this file is relatively small, it is the master of all your session elements. Most often, when you create this file, it is put in its own folder, like Figure 10.10.

Figure 10.10

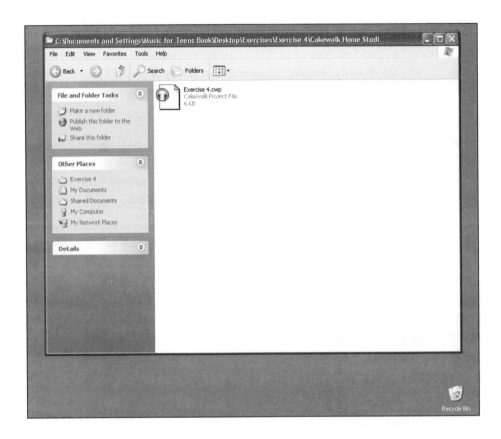

> ❋ **TIP**
>
> Although many DAW applications automatically create folders for their DAW files, some don't. In the cases where a folder *isn't* created to hold your DAW file, creating one manually (using Windows Explorer or in the Save File window) is a great way to manage all the files that you will create along the way.

It might sound like all you need is this DAW file, but that's not quite true (unless you only want to use MIDI, in which case this single file might be all you need). Although this file contains all the important aspects of the project listed, it doesn't contain any audio. Once you start working with digital audio, the DAW file is going to need to start using other files to get the job done. That's when your session file starts creating or accessing previously created audio files.

As soon as audio is recorded, it is stored as a digital audio file. This file is commonly stored in a subfolder of the session folder, like the Sources subfolder used in Quartz AudioMaster Freeware (see Figure 10.11).

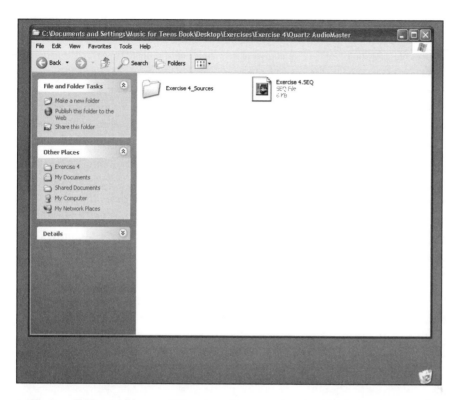

Figure 10.11

Different tracks and even different takes are stored as individual audio files. When you play a song, your DAW calls upon, or points to, these specific audio files at specific times.

> ✳ **TIP**
>
> If your application doesn't automatically create a subfolder within your project folder, creating a folder before you start recording is a great way to keep all your files organized. Just remember to create this file before you start recording because moving audio files around after the fact can cause confusion for your DAW.

> ✳ **TIP**
>
> When you record audio in your DAW environment, the name of the file created usually follows the name of the track that it is recorded upon. (This is a common default setting.) For example, if you record onto a mono (one-channel) audio track named *Bass*, the files created by your DAW application would be named *Bass*. If this is a part of the default operation of your program, remember to name your tracks *before* you start recording, or you'll wind up with a ton of files named something generic like "audio." If this *isn't* a default part of your DAW, and you're asked to name every file you record, it's usually best to have the audio file names follow the track name to some extent, to help you keep everything straight as your project gets more complex.

※ **CAUTION**

Often, people copy or e-mail DAW files, thinking that they've copied or sent their entire project. However, it's important to remember that this small file alone only refers (or points) to other important elements such as audio files—those audio elements aren't contained in the session file itself. When it's time to save (or move) your work, you'll have to include all the song's dependent files, in addition to the DAW file itself. For this reason, it's usually a good idea to keep all your project-related files grouped together in the file structures shown earlier, so files aren't accidentally lost.

Regions and Files

Given the fact that DAWs record audio to individual files on your hard drive, how does the user access these files? When audio is recorded to an audio track (or even MIDI data to a MIDI track), your DAW creates an object (often called a "region," "chunk," or "clip") in the DAW's Multitrack window. It is through these objects that your application refers (or points) to files on your hard drive, triggering them to sound as your session plays.

Let's take a look at a typical DAW's Track view. There's one audio track in this project (so far), and only one audio region on that track. That region is referring to a file named Drums (see Figure 10.12).

Figure 10.12

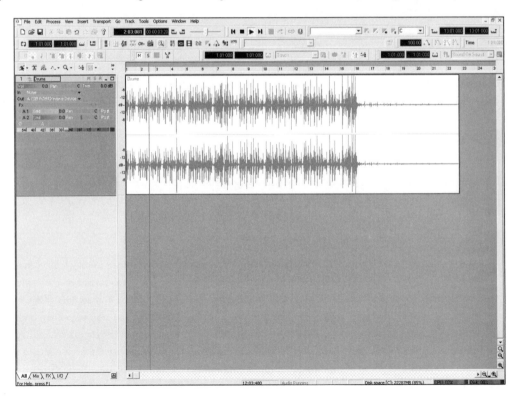

※ ※ ※

As the song plays, the Now line moves from left to right across the screen (you saw this when you worked with multitrack MIDI). When the line intersects the audio object, a command is sent from the DAW to play a specific audio file (in this case Drums) on your hard drive, like Figure 10.13.

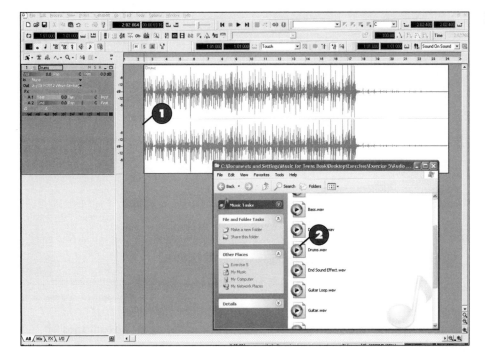

Figure 10.13

1. This...

2. Triggers this!

Once the play line reaches the end of the audio object, another command is sent from the DAW application to stop playback of the file (see Figure 10.14).

Figure 10.14

1. This...

2. Stops this!

So, aside from keeping your DAW files from getting enormous, what are the other advantages of using a pointer-based application?

Oooh, Nonlinear, Nondestructive!

Since the beginning of digital audio applications, there have been two buzz phrases that have been repeated over and over again. Even before I fully realized what these selling points really meant, I was hearing about this or that application featuring *nonlinear* editing and *nondestructive* processing. But what the heck does it mean?

Nonlinear

Working with audio regions has many advantages. One of the first that you'll discover is that you have the ability to move them earlier or later on your song's timeline, allowing you to position precisely the regions in time, like Figure 10.15.

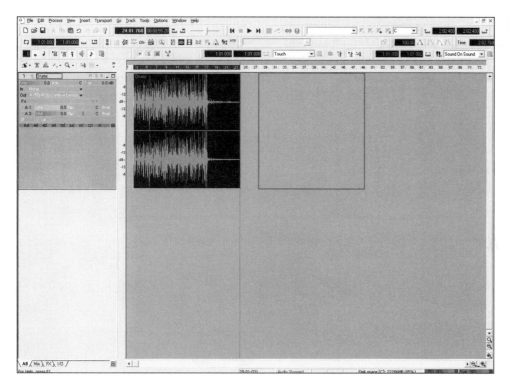

Figure 10.15

An environment in which you have the ability to manipulate elements independently on the timeline is commonly known as *nonlinear*. You can move any individual object later or earlier in time without affecting any other audio objects at all—try doing that with tape! In addition to moving regions to different locations in time, you have the option of moving them to other similar tracks. (In other words, you can move a region on a mono audio track to another mono audio track, and so on.)

The really cool thing about these nonlinear environments is that moving (or even duplicating) these audio objects doesn't change the audio files on your hard drive at all. They just sit there patiently, waiting for the word from the DAW to stream from the hard drive and leap into action.

Nondestructive

Computers by nature tend to be nondestructive. Take your average word processor application. Make a mistake? No problem—just choose Undo from the Edit menu. Want to save a new version of a letter, but leave the original alone? Simple, just choose the Save As option in the File menu. Heck, that alone would make audio production on a computer worth the investment! Great news, though—the advantages of nondestructive editing go far beyond.

There's something about pointer-based applications that I haven't told you yet: You don't have to play entire audio files. Any given audio region can trigger the playback of only a section of a file if you so choose. In this example, the region named Drums is playing an audio file of the same name. What if you don't want to use the whole song in your session? No problem. You can just adjust the start or end boundary of that region, effectively taking the unwanted bit of audio out of your session (see Figure 10.16).

Figure 10.16

1. As you change the left boundary of the audio region, you change the point in the audio file where playback will start.

2. The right boundary will change where the file will stop playback, and you can change that too.

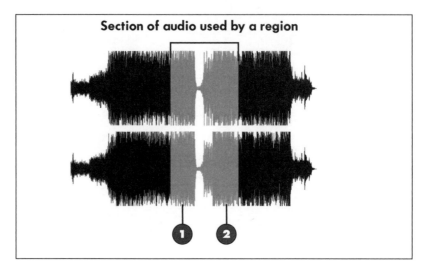

Section of audio used by a region

Does this mean that you've changed the file on your hard drive? No. You've only changed the audio region that is pointing to that file, so only a portion of that file will be heard in the session. This is where the nondestructive part comes in. Because you haven't changed the audio file (only the region that is pointing to it), you can always drag the region boundaries back out if you change your mind later and hear more of the file.

In addition to being able to trim data, there are other situations in which nondestructive editing can aid you in your production work, and you'll discover them as this book proceeds. The bottom line is that a nonlinear pointer-based environment coupled with nondestructive recording and editing gives an educated DAW user a huge amount of flexibility and power *and* the ability to undo changes and operations when needed!

Importing Audio

Getting audio into either of these typical DAWs is super easy. Here's how to import that phat drum loop or smokin' lead line (see Figure 10.17).

Using Cakewalk Home Studio

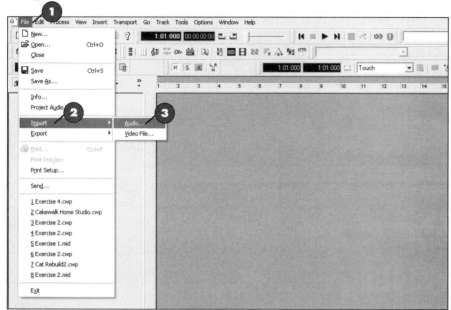

Figure 10.17

1. **Click** the **File** drop-down menu.

2. **Click** the **Import** menu item. A second drop-down menu will appear.

3. **Click** the **Audio** menu item. The Import Audio window will appear (see Figure 10.18).

Figure 10.18

4. **Navigate** to the **location** of the desired audio file(s). In this case, I've navigated to the Ex_04 folder, which you've copied to your hard drive.

5. **Open** the **subfolder** that contains your specific audio file(s). In this case, there are some audio tracks in the Ex_04 Audio Files folder (see Figure 10.19).

Figure 10.19

6. **Click** the **file** that you want to import. **Hold** the **Shift** key to select multiple files.

6a. **Copy Audio to Project Folder:** When this option is checked, these files will be copied to Cakewalk Home Studio's global Audio Data folder.

6b. **Stereo Split:** When this option is checked, if you're importing a stereo file, it will be split to two mono audio tracks.

6c. **Play:** Clicking this button will allow you to listen to a file before importing it. Note: This option doesn't work if you have multiple files selected.

7. **Click Open**. The files will be imported to your session, and tracks will automatically be created. When you're done, your screen should look like Figure 10.20.

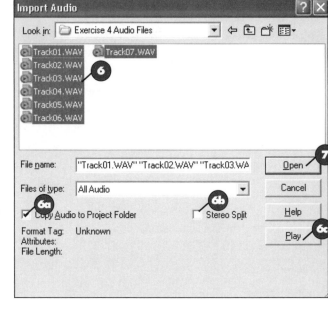

Figure 10.20

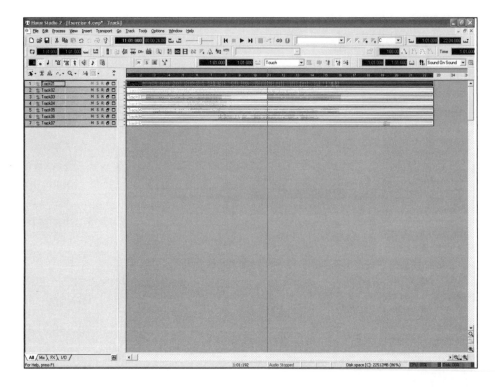

254
❀ ❀ ❀

❋ **TIP**

So what do you do if you already have a track, and you just want to import some audio to it? Just select the track and import audio just as you did here. The new audio region will be imported to the selected track at the Now line position.

Using Quartz AudioMaster Freeware

There are two limitations with Quartz AudioMaster Freeware that you need to know. First, you can only import files one at a time. Second, there is a limit of four audio tracks in the freeware version of this program. However, you can still get the job done—it will just take a little longer. (See Figure 10.21.)

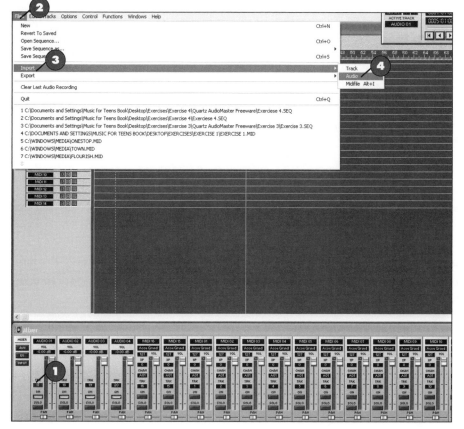

Figure 10.21

1. **Click** the **track number** of the audio track to which you want to import an audio file.

2. **Click** the **File** drop-down menu.

3. **Click** the **Import** menu item. A secondary drop-down menu will appear.

4. **Click** the **Audio** menu item. The Import Audio window will appear (see Figure 10.22).

Figure 10.22

5. **Select** the **Audio file** you want to import.

6. **Click** the **Open** button. The audio file will be imported to your sequence at the current play line position.

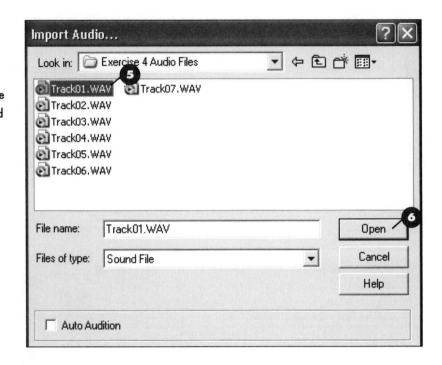

 NOTE
As with Cakewalk Home Studio, multiple files can be imported to a single audio track.

Repeat Steps 1–6, importing the first four audio files to the four audio tracks in your session. If your play line happens to be in a position other than the beginning of the track, use the Move tool to drag it to the beginning of each track, so that your window ends up looking like Figure 10.23.

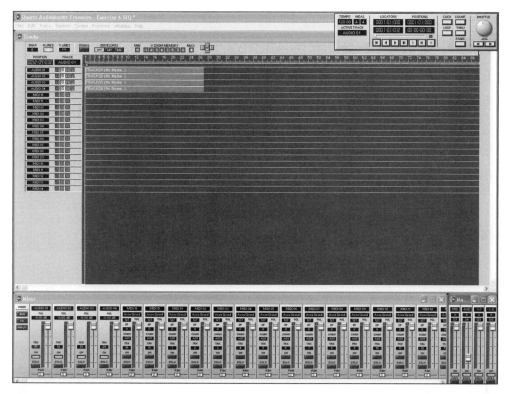

Figure 10.23

❄ **TIP**

There's an obvious problem here. There are seven files, presumably representing seven different tracks, but the Quartz AudioMaster Freeware doesn't support more than four audio tracks. In Chapter 12, you'll figure out a workaround to this limitation.

Naming Tracks and Regions

Audio files are all too commonly named nondescriptively (like track 01, track 02, and so on as shown in this example). On top of that, tracks are usually created with some sort of generic name (audio 1, audio 2, and so on). Now would be a good time to go over how to name tracks and regions (this works for MIDI tracks and regions as well as audio) in your project.

❄ **TIP**

Good naming practices, though easy to do, are among the most important habits that you can start, and there's no time like the present. Make it a point to always name your tracks, regions, and even files as descriptively as possible. It'll really come in handy when you're looking for specific tracks and songs.

Using Cakewalk Home Studio

Let's start off by naming your new tracks (see Figure 10.24).

Figure 10.24

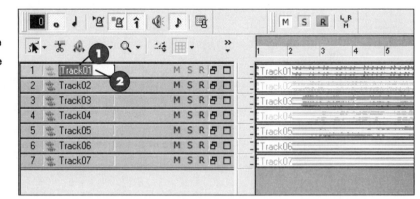

1. **Double-click** the **track name** area of the track to rename it. The name will become highlighted.

2. **Type** a **descriptive name** for your track (in this case, it's a drum track).

3. **Press** the **Enter** key to apply your new name.

> ❈ **TIP**
>
> Try soloing individual tracks to find out what they sound like alone. That will help you determine the best name for that track.

Naming tracks is one thing, but it doesn't change the name of your audio regions. Here's how to name them (see Figure 10.25).

Figure 10.25

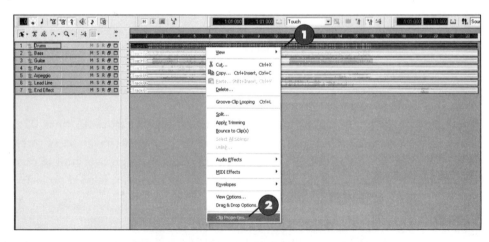

1. **Right-click** the **region** that you want to rename. The region will become highlighted, and a drop-down menu will appear. You'll notice that many of the items in the Edit drop-down menu are also shown here.

2. **Click** the **Clip Properties** menu item. The Clip Properties window will appear (see Figure 10.26).

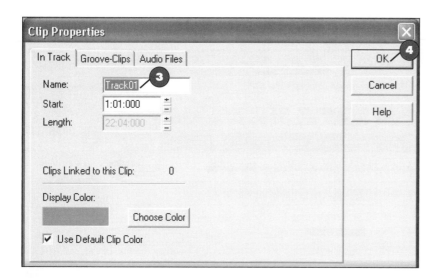

Figure 10.26

3. The Clip Properties window opens with the
   Name field already highlighted, so all you have to
   do is **type** a **descriptive
   name**.

4. **Click OK**.

> ❊ **NOTE**
>
> Though your audio region names will commonly follow the name of your track to some degree, there's no rule say-
> ing that you have to name your audio blocks (Cakewalk calls them "clips") that way. In fact, when you have multiple
> clips on a track, you'll have to decide on different names for different blocks of audio data. The only golden rule of
> naming is to be descriptive, but beyond that, whatever works for you is fine.

Using Quartz AudioMaster Freeware

Just for some review, here's how you name a track (see Figure 10.27).

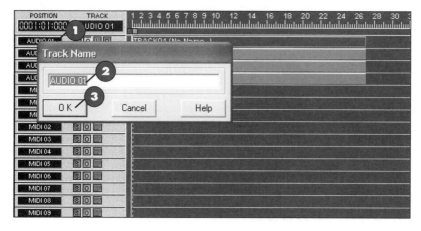

Figure 10.27

1. **Double-click** the **track
   name** that you want to
   change. The Track Name
   window will appear.

2. **Type** a **descriptive name**
   in the name field. (The
   window opens with the
   name field already highlighted, so all you have to
   do is enter a name.)

3. **Click** the **OK** button.

Naming individual regions is a little bit different than Cakewalk (see Figure 10.28).

Figure 10.28

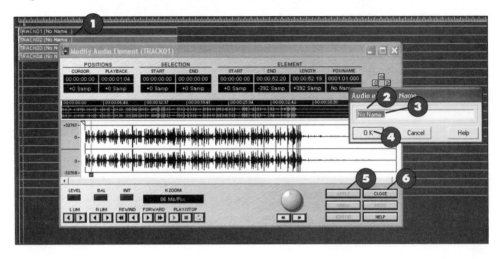

1. Using the Arrow tool, **double-click** the **audio region** that you want to rename. The Modify Audio Element window will appear.

2. **Click** the **name display**. The Audio Element Name window will appear.

3. **Type** a **descriptive name** for this region (or "element," as AudioMaster calls it).

4. When you're done, just **click OK.**

5. In the Modify Audio Element window **click** the **Apply** button. The name will be changed.

6. **Click** the **Close** button.

❄ **CAUTION**

When working in the Modify Audio Element window, try to keep your cursor out of the light-colored waveform area of the window. We'll get to that later, but for now changing settings in that area can only cause problems.

Getting the Big Picture

You've seen some of the basic windows of a DAW during our earlier discussion of MIDI. Some of these windows have similar audio and MIDI functions, but others are completely different. Let's dive in.

The (Multi)track Window

Many DAWs (the vast majority these days) allow you to work on MIDI and digital audio in one unified environment. Back in the old days, this wasn't the case. The fact that you can now work on MIDI and audio side by side is absolutely fantastic, just so long as you remember that *MIDI isn't digital audio,* as you learned earlier.

You've already seen the Track window. Virtually every DAW has a multitrack window like this, but now that you've added audio into the mix (literally), there's a little more to look at. Here are the primary features for audio tracks that every DAW has (see Figure 10.29).

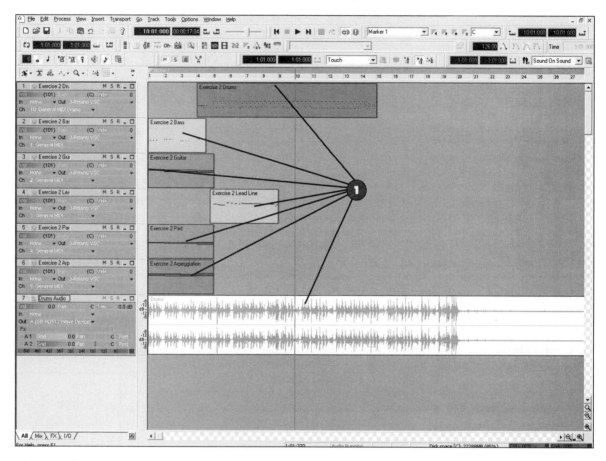

Figure 10.29

1. Look, MIDI regions and audio regions playing simultaneously! The one on the bottom, with the waveform within, is the audio region.

How is the signal coming and going to a specific track? The Track view tells you at a glance (see Figure 10.30).

Figure 10.30

1. When recording audio, where is the signal coming from? This area will show you and allow you to make changes to which audio input (on your sound card or audio interface) will be captured to a given audio track.

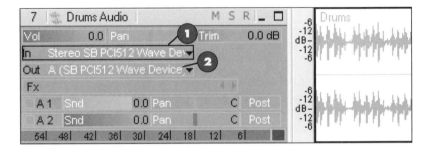

2. Where is the audio *going*? That's what you'll choose here, when you set the track's output. For example, if you wanted to hear this track through your monitor speakers, you'd choose the output of your sound card (or audio interface) that is connected to them.

> ❄ **NOTE**
>
> Most applications allow audio effects to be applied to audio regions in real time as they're played. In this application, that is accomplished in the FX and sends (in this case, they're named "A1" and "A2") areas. You'll learn about these features when we discuss the art of mixing in Chapter 11.

There are a couple of ways to look at volume levels on your track (see Figure 10.31).

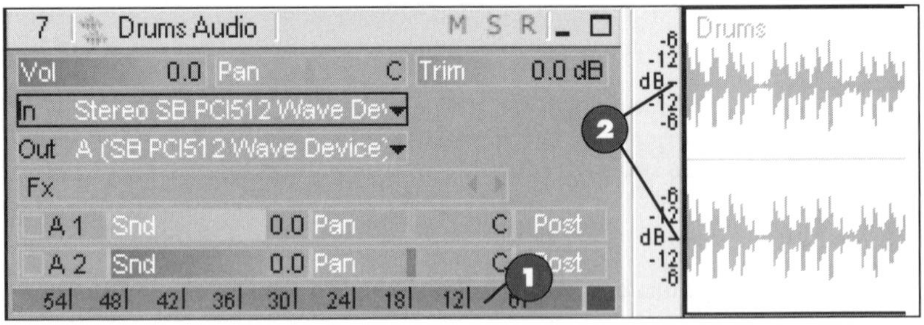

Figure 10.31

1. First, the level meter will show the fluctuating amplitude levels as soon as you start playing, or...

2. The amplitude markers on the track show how loud your regions are. Just follow the markings from left to right to find out how strong your audio region is.

> ❄ **NOTE**
>
> Changing the playback volume of a given track will not change the appearance of the audio objects on that track. The only thing that will change is the loudness of the audio that is output to your monitor speakers, leaving the audio region (and the file on your hard drive) alone. Just another benefit of a pointer-based application.

Editing Audio

Okay, life is about to get a *lot* better. The great news is that all the tools that you learned while editing MIDI regions work exactly the same when working with audio regions. On top of that, working in Grid mode is every bit as useful when moving audio blocks as it was when you were working with only MIDI.

Cut, Copy, and Paste

Because you've already learned to do this with MIDI, this'll just be a quick review of basic editing tools.

Using Cakewalk Home Studio
To move a region (see Figure 10.32).

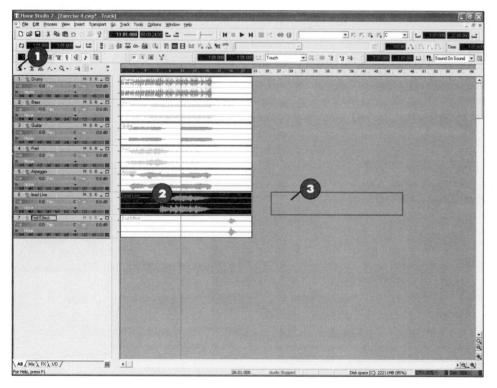

Figure 10.32

1. In the Track window, **click** the **Select** tool.

2. **Click** and **hold** on the **region** you want to move.

3. Still holding down the mouse, **drag** the **region** to the right or left. You'll notice as you drag that a hollow square lets you know where the region will be moved once the mouse is released.

4. When you release your mouse, you'll be presented with a familiar looking window, allowing you to copy or replace the region.

To delete a region:

1. Still using the Select tool, **click** the **region** you want to delete. The region will become highlighted.

2. **Press** the **Delete** key on your computer keyboard. The region will disappear.

To cut a region (see Figure 10.33).

Figure 10.33

1. Using the Select tool, **click** the **region** that you want to cut.

2. **Click** the **Edit** drop-down menu.

3. **Click** the **Cut** menu item. The region will be cut.

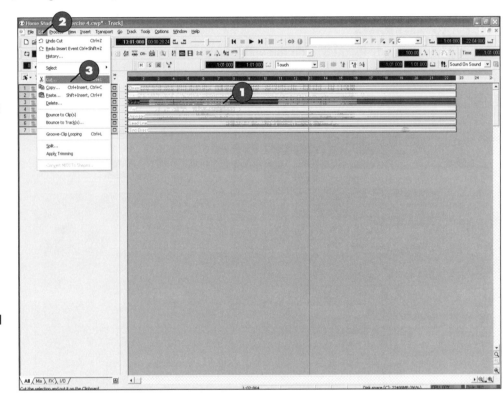

To copy a region:

1. Still using the Select tool, **click** on the **region** you want to copy.

2. **Click** the **Edit** drop-down menu.

3. **Click** the **Copy** menu item. The Copy window will appear (see Figure 10.34).

Figure 10.34

4. The different check boxes refer to different kinds of data that may be on your track, and you can choose what to copy by checking the appropriate boxes. Once that's done, just **click** the **OK** button, and your region will be copied and ready for pasting.

To paste:

1. **Click** the **Edit** drop-down menu again.

2. This time, **click** the **Paste** menu item. The Paste window will appear (see Figure 10.35).

Figure 10.35

3. **Type** the **desired point** at which the pasted region will start.

4. **Type** the **number** of **times** you want to repeat this pasted selection.

5. **Type** the **number** of the **track** you want to paste to (or select it from the drop-down list of tracks by clicking the arrow button to the right of the track number).

5a. Checking the **Link to Original Clip(s)** option will apply any changes made to the contents of the original region to the copied regions and vice versa.

6. Once you're done, **click OK**. The region will be pasted.

To create a new region on a pre-existing track (see Figure 10.36).

Figure 10.36

1. **Move** the **Now line** to the point in your song that you want to insert the new region.

2. **Click** the **track number** of the track that you want to use for this new region.

3. From the Edit menu, **choose**

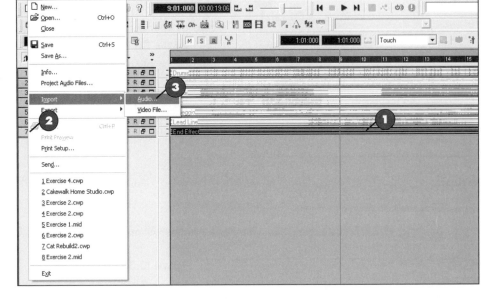

Import, then **Audio**, and go through the same procedure for importing audio that you used earlier in this chapter.

To cut one region in two (see Figure 10.37).

Figure 10.37

1. **Click** the **Split** tool.

2. **Click** at the **point** that you want to chop the region. The region will be split at that point into two smaller regions.

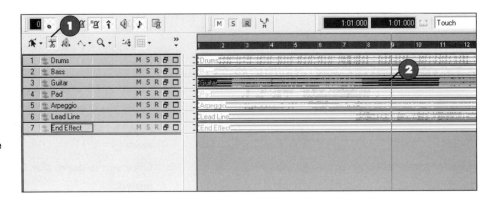

Using Quartz AudioMaster Freeware

To move a region (see Figure 10.38).

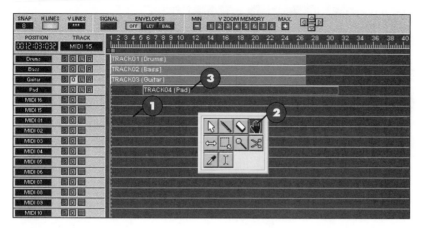

Figure 10.38

1. **Right-click** in the **Track window**. The toolbox will appear.

2. **Click** on the **Move** tool. Your cursor will turn into a hand.

3. **Click** and **drag** the **desired region** to the desired position.

4. **Release** the **mouse,** and the region will be moved to its new location.

To delete a region (see Figure 10.39).

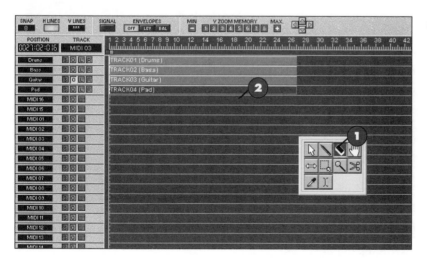

Figure 10.39

1. **Right-click** on **anywhere** in the Track window and the toolbox will appear again. This time, **choose** the **Eraser** tool.

2. **Click** on the **region** that you want to delete.

To copy a region (see Figure 10.40; remember, the locators determine what will be copied).

Figure 10.40

1. **Click** in the **respective locator box** (top is left, bottom is right); then **type** in the **value** (in measures, beats, and ticks). See Figure 10.41.

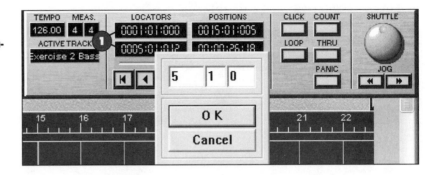

Figure 10.41

2. **Click** the **Edit** drop-down menu.
3. **Click** the **Copy** menu item. The Copy window will appear (see Figure 10.42).

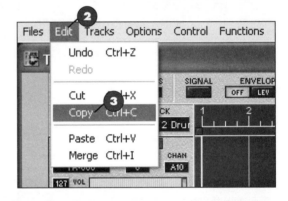

Figure 10.42

4. Now you must choose the track(s) you want to copy. **Click** the **Track** button. The Track Select window will appear (see Figure 10.43).

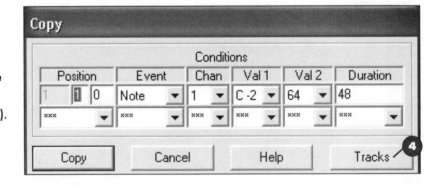

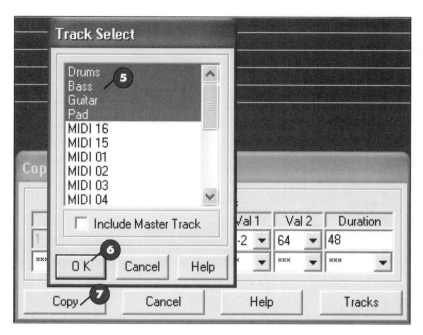

Figure 10.43

5. **Choose** the **track(s)** you want to copy. Remember that on all the chosen tracks, audio that lies between the locators will be copied.

6. **Click OK.**

7. **Click Copy.**

To paste: The left locator determines the location of your pasted regions (see Figure 10.44).

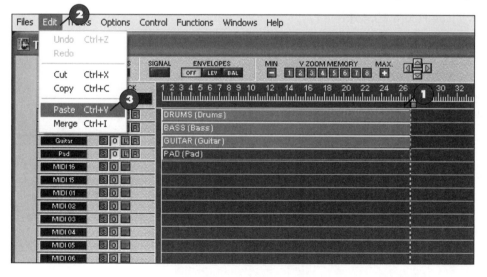

Figure 10.44

1. **Set** the **Left locator** to the position where you want your pasting to start.

2. **Click** the **Edit** drop-down menu.

3. **Click** the **Paste** menu item. A dialog box will appear, asking you to confirm that you want to paste.

4. **Click** the **OK** button of the dialog box. The regions will be pasted.

To create a new region on a pre-existing track (see Figure 10.45).

Figure 10.45

1. **Right-click** in the **Track window** to view the toolbox.

2. **Click** the **Pen** tool.

3. **Click anywhere** on an audio track to reveal the Import Audio window.

4. **Choose** the **file** you want to import. A region will be created where you clicked the Pen tool.

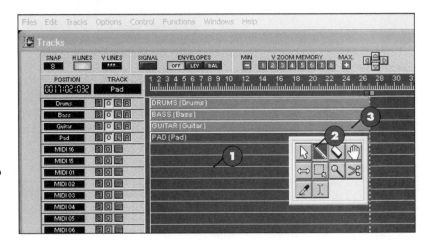

※ NOTE

You can create new MIDI regions using the Pen tool.

To cut one region in two (see Figure 10.46).

Figure 10.46

1. **Right-click** in the **Track window,** and you'll see the toolbox.

2. **Click** on the **Scissors** tool. Your cursor will turn into scissors.

3. **Click** on the **region** you want to separate at the point you want the separation to occur. The region will be separated.

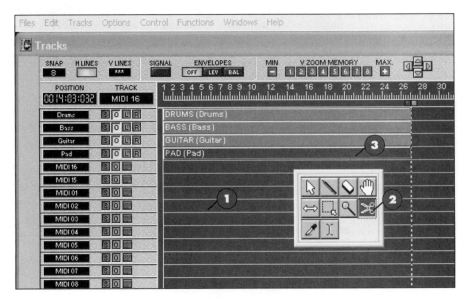

Trim

You've already used the Trim tool in Cakewalk Home Studio and the Size tool in Quartz AudioMaster Freeware to change the boundaries of MIDI regions. While it certainly is a useful tool for removing excess MIDI notes, using these tools on blocks of audio opens up a whole new world of usefulness.

You'll see that the tools work just the same with audio regions as they did with MIDI regions, but what they are doing is fundamentally different. The trick is to remember that these applications don't contain any audio, but rather refer to separate audio files that are stored somewhere on your hard drive. By adjusting the boundaries of your audio block, you're in essence telling your application which portion of a specific audio file that you want to use.

So when do you use this tool with audio? Try this one on for size: You record a *perfect* vocal track, but just at the end of the recording, after you're done with the vocal line, you cough. If you look at the waveform of your take, you'll see your vocal line, and at the very end of the block (towards the right end), you'll see a huge spike, which is your coughing. By changing the boundary of this region, in this case moving the rightmost boundary to the left, you can take that unwanted audio out of your session. The thing to remember is that the audio itself still exists in a portion of an audio file that resides on your hard drive, so nothing has been destroyed. In fact, if you wanted to bring that cough back, all you have to do is move that end boundary to the right.

Virtually every DAW has a version of this trimming tool. Here's how it's done in the two applications we've been using (see Figure 10.47).

Using Cakewalk Home Studio

Figure 10.47

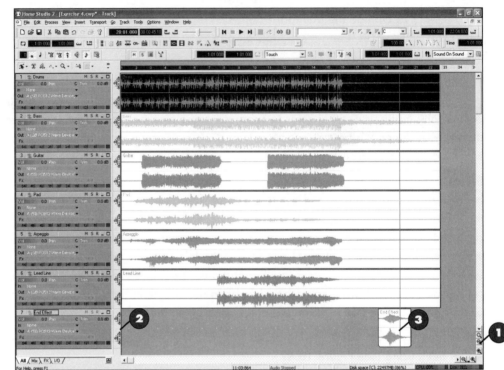

1. This feature is easier to use if the tracks are a little taller. **Click** the **Zoom In Vertical** button to change your view of the regions.

2 **Move** your **cursor** close to the right or left end of the region you want to trim. The cursor will turn into a small rectangle.

3. **Click** and **drag** your **cursor** to the right or left to adjust the boundary of your region.

4. **Release** the **mouse**, and the region boundary will be changed.

Using Quartz AudioMaster Freeware

There are two ways to trim an audio event in AudioMaster (see Figure 10.48).

Figure 10.48

1. **Right-click** in the **Track window,** and the toolbox will appear.

2. **Click** the **Size** tool. Your cursor will become a double arrow (see Figure 10.49).

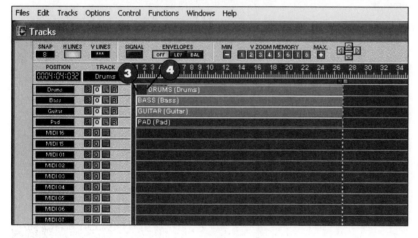

Figure 10.49

3. **Move** your **cursor** to the right or left end of the desired audio region.

4. **Click** and **hold** your **mouse,** and **drag** the **region boundary** to the left or right.

5. **Release** the **mouse,** and the region will be changed.

Here's another way:

1. Using the Arrow tool, **double-click** the **region** you want to adjust. The Modify Audio Element window will appear (see Figure 10.50).

Figure 10.50

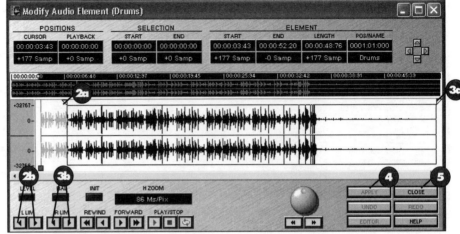

2a. **Click** and **drag** the **flag** at the top left of the waveform area of the window to adjust the left boundary flag. Release the mouse at the desired trim point, or

2b. **Click** the **L Lim** buttons to nudge the left boundary in small increments.

3a. Similarly, **click** and **drag** the **right flag** to change the end boundary flag of the region, or

3b. **Click** the **R Lim** buttons to nudge the right boundary.

4. **Click** the **Apply** button. Your region will change in the Track window.

5. **Click** the **Close** button.

Recording Audio

Recording audio into your DAW is also a pretty straightforward process, but one that you should take a moment to run through.

 NOTE

Don't have an instrument handy? No prob—I've included an audio track on the accompanying CD-ROM. Just put the disk into a regular CD player, attach the line out of the player to the line in your sound card or audio interface, and you can record it just as you would a real instrument.

If you're using your sound card to get audio into and out of your computer, you'll have to set up the correct input (see Figure 10.51).

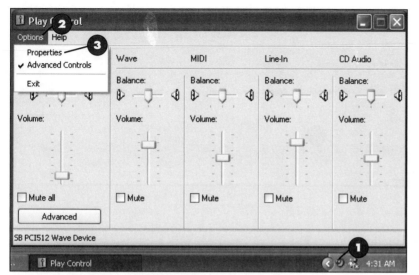

Figure 10.51

1. **Double-click** the **speaker icon** in your windows taskbar. The Play Control window will appear.

2. **Click** the **Options** drop-down menu.

3. **Click** the **Properties** menu item. The Properties window will appear (see Figure 10.52).

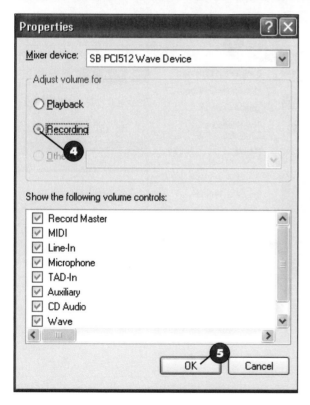

Figure 10.52

4. **Click** the **Recording** radio button.

5. **Click** the **OK** button. The Record Control window will appear (see Figure 10.53).

Figure 10.53

6. **Click** the **Select** box that matches your input source. For example, in this case, I'll be recording from a portable CD player that is attached to the Line In input of my sound card.

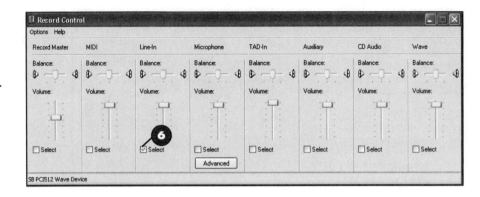

Now you're ready to set up your application.

Using Cakewalk Home Studio
First things first—you need to create a new audio track (see Figure 10.54).

Figure 10.54

1. **Click** the **Insert** drop-down menu.

2. **Click** the **Audio Track** option. A new audio track will be created (see Figure 10.55).

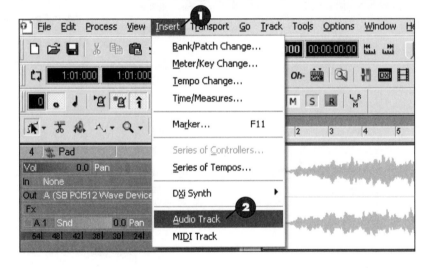

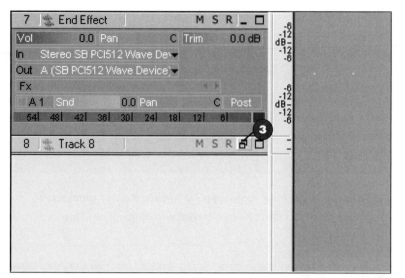

Figure 10.55

3. **Click** the **Restore Strip Size** button to reveal more of the track's settings.

Now it's time to set up the track for recording (see Figure 10.56).

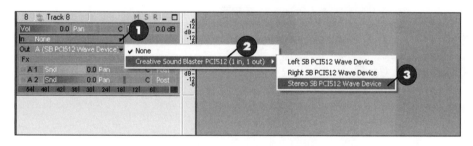

Figure 10.56

1. **Click** the **arrow button** to the right of the In display (which by default reads "none"). A drop-down menu will appear.

2. **Click** the **hardware device** that is receiving audio signal into your computer. In this case, I'm using a SoundBlaster sound card. Another drop-down menu will appear.

3. **Choose** whether you want this to be a **mono** or **stereo track**. Keep in mind that if you have a mono track, you can still pan it to any position between your left and right speakers. If you do choose mono, you'll have to choose between the left and right channel of your sound card to be your source. (Make sure that it matches the connection of your instrument, microphone, and so on.) If you choose the stereo option, input will be recorded on both channels to a single stereo track. Since I'm recording a stereo CD player, I'll click the stereo option (see Figure 10.57).

Figure 10.57

4. **Click** the **Arrow button** to the right of the Out display. A drop-down menu will appear.

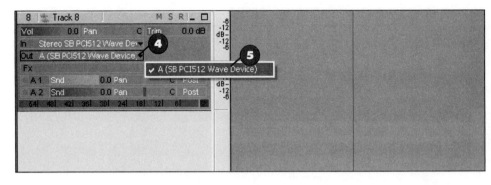

5. **Click** the **hardware device** that is sending audio signal from your computer to your monitor speakers. In this case, I've only got a SoundBlaster sound card, so I don't have a choice of output options (see Figure 10.58).

Figure 10.58

6. **Click** the track's **Record button**. The button will turn red, letting you know that the track is ready for recording.

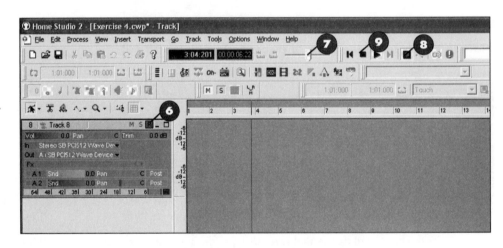

7. **Place** the **Now line** at the point at which you want to begin recording.

8. **Click** the **Record** button. The session will begin recording.

9. **Click** the **Stop** button. A new audio region will appear, like Figure 10.59.

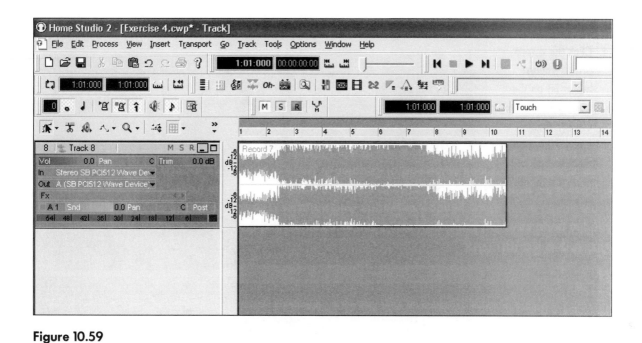

Figure 10.59

Using Quartz AudioMaster Freeware

> ❋ **NOTE**
>
> At this point, you've put audio on all four of your available audio tracks, so there's not a completely open track to record to. Either set your play line after the end of the last region in your session and begin recording there or delete a region from one of your tracks (I recommend clearing track 4) to make room for the new audio.

Since Quartz AudioMaster Freeware only supports one audio input and output device, you don't need to worry about choosing your inputs and outputs (see Figure 10.60).

Figure 10.60

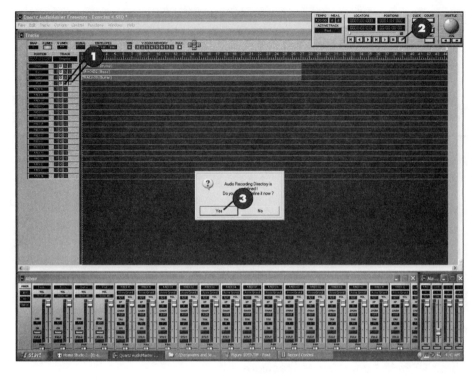

1. **Click** the appropriate **Record** button(s) on the track you want to use for recording. Clicking only the **L** button will record only the left input; only the **R** records only the right side. Since I'm recording a stereo source (my CD player), I'll click both buttons, which will light up red, showing that that track is "armed" for recording.

2. On the Control window, **click** the **Record** button. A message will appear.

3. This **message box** is telling you that you haven't chosen a location on your hard drive for this song's audio files. **Click** the **Yes** button to define a location (see Figure 10.61).

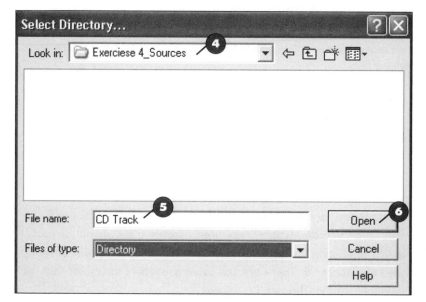

Figure 10.61

4. **Navigate** to the **folder** you want to use for storing recorded audio files for this song. Quartz AudioMaster automatically creates a sources subdirectory, which is a convenient choice for me.

5. **Type** a **descriptive name** for this file.

6. **Click** the **Open** button. The Navigation window will close and recording will begin (see Figure 10.62).

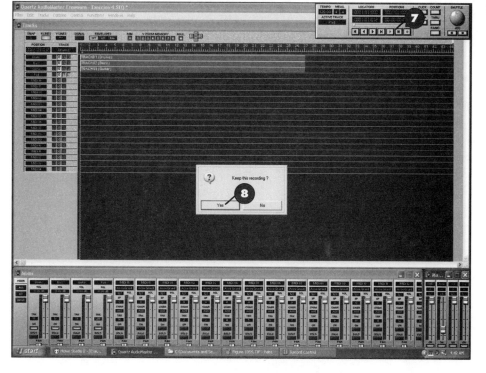

Figure 10.62

7. **Click** the **Stop** button. Another message window will appear.

8. This window is asking if you want to keep this recording. If it was a good take, **click Yes** (if not, click **No**). A new audio region will be created.

> ❈ **NOTE**
>
> Recording will also stop when the right locator is reached. To ensure that recording doesn't stop before you hit the Stop button, just drag the right locator out of the way.

> ❈ **NOTE**
>
> You'll only have to define a location for your files once. Subsequent recordings will go to the same folder on your hard drive.

Making a Rough Mix

And the good news just keeps on comin'! You've already used the Console window in Cakewalk Home Studio or the Mixer window in Quartz AudioMaster Freeware to create a rough mix of your MIDI, and the exact same logic applies to making a rough mix of audio tracks. For a layout of the Mixer window, take a look at the end of Chapter 8. There are still some aspects of the mixer that we haven't touched on yet, but we'll dive into that in Chapter 12.

> ❈ **NOTE**
>
> If you recorded the CD audio track from the CD-ROM, you have a rough mix already finished for you. Use this as a reference to give you some ideas on how to approach the balance of your instruments. Of course, this isn't the only way to blend instruments, but it should give you a good starting-off point.

> ❈ **NOTE**
>
> Because of the audio track limitations of the Quartz AudioMaster Freeware, you have to make a choice. You can either keep the semi-mixed file that you've recorded and use that file as a guide, or you can clear that track, import the track 4 audio file to audio track 4, and mix the four tracks that you have available to you. Don't worry too much because there's a workaround to this track limitation that you'll learn in Chapter 12.

> **❋ NOTE**
>
> Now that you've done some work, you probably want to save your song file, as you learned Chapter 4. Generally speaking, the same default method of saving that you used then will work here. However, now that you've got audio involved, some of the different saving options will take on new meaning.
>
> Cakewalk Bundle (Cakewalk Home Studio): Instead of pointing to audio files, digital audio is incorporated into the Cakewalk file. The good news is that you'll only have one file to worry about—the bad news is that the single file could be *huge* if you've got a lot of digital audio in your session. This type of file is only for backup purposes and will extract itself to a regular Cakewalk file when opened.
>
> Compiled Sequence (Quartz AudioMaster Freeware): Saving as this sort of file will save MIDI and digital audio into a single file (much like Home Studio does with bundle files). You even have the option of documenting your session with a title and other information and selectively choosing which MIDI and audio tracks will be included in the file.
>
> Compressed Compiled Sequence (Quartz AudioMaster Freeware): Same as a compiled sequence but with lossy data reduction to help keep the file size small (though keep in mind that sonic quality may well suffer).

11

Bringin' It Home: Mixing with a DAW

The great news just keeps on comin'! You've already learned a great deal about the general workings of a typical DAW application (a couple of different ones, actually), and that experience will work to your advantage as you add digital audio into the mix (literally). Now, instead of just MIDI regions that you can edit and move, you'll have audio regions. What's more, you'll have an expanded toolbox of audio effects that you can apply to your work! In this chapter, you'll learn:

❊ How to route signals within your DAW to get cool audio effects.

❊ How to mix your music and even change the mix in real time.

❊ How to tweak your final mix and prepare it for an audio CD.

Signal Flow, Signal Flow, Signal Flow

There's a term you've probably run across as you've talked to people in the profession or while browsing through the trade magazines—*signal flow*. Invariably, a great deal of importance is attached to this particular concept, but what exactly does it mean? Simply put, signal flow refers to the path that some sort of information takes from a source to a destination. That seems pretty straightforward, but the importance of understanding signal flow can't be emphasized enough. It is at the very core of everything we do as computer musicians.

MIDI data has its own signal path certainly, from the MIDI controller to the computer-based DAW, and then from the DAW to a MIDI instrument, which then responds by making sound. Once the MIDI slave device makes its noise, the job of MIDI is done, and now it's time to deal with audio signal flow issues. As discussed previously, the audio outputs of your external MIDI devices (or any other instrument that you want to record) must be connected to the appropriate input of your sound card (or audio interface). Once connected, the signal may be digitized and used by your DAW application. To hear the audio that you've recorded, all you need to do is attach the outputs of your sound card (or interface) to an amplifier that powers your monitor speakers.

There's a lot that can happen inside the computer, however. Digital audio can be internally routed from one track to another with perfect digital clarity. It's a powerful way to work, but it can be hard to understand because it's virtual, and there are no physical cables to show us how the audio is traveling.

Inserts, Sends, and Buses

When talking about signal flow in a digital audio workstation, it's important to remember that most of the terms and concepts have been handed down by our predecessors, the analog mixing boards and effects. Of course, with the power of a virtual computer environment, we're able to bend the laws of physics that are limiting factors for more "real" analog devices.

Inserts

An insert is pretty much what the name would suggest—it is an insertion or interruption into the signal flow. If you examine a typical track's signal flow, including an insert, it might look something like Figure 11.1.

Figure 11.1

A track's signal flow, with an insert.

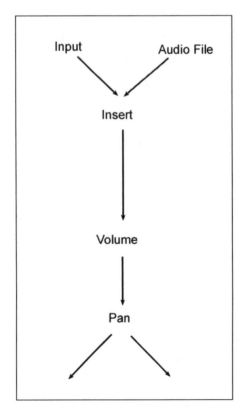

❄ ❄ ❄

- ❋ **Input:** This is a live audio source—for example, a guitar connected to your sound card and being heard through your DAW.

- ❋ **Audio File:** Your track doesn't always need a live signal. If you're using an audio file from your hard drive on this track, the file itself is the beginning of the signal path.

- ❋ **Insert:** The very next thing your signal will hit is any active inserts. Most DAWs support multiple inserts, as well as the option *not* to use any inserts if you don't need them. After the insert stage, the signal goes to the track's volume control.

- ❋ **Volume:** This is the track's individual volume control, usually adjusted with a fader in the program's Mixer window.

- ❋ **Pan:** After the volume's been tweaked, you can use the Pan control (usually a knob or slider in the Mixer window) to adjust the signal's position between the left and right speakers.

So, what do you use an insert *for*? You'll use a track's insert any time you want to process the entire signal in some way, which is the most common way to apply dynamic-based effects and equalization. For example, if you want to change the track's sound with a graphic equalizer (to boost or cut specific frequencies in the audio), you can use an insert to divert the signal to the EQ and then route the signal back to the track to be further affected by volume and pan controls.

Sends

While inserts are a great way to apply processes and effects to individual audio tracks, they're not the only way to route audio. In fact, routing the audio another way might have added advantages in some situations. That's where *sends* (sometimes called *auxiliary sends*) come into play.

Whereas an insert is essentially an interruption in the signal path, a send is essentially a signal copier. A send *sends* a copy of the track's audio to another location, and it allows the original signal to pass right on to the next stage in the track's signal flow. There are two kinds of sends: pre-fader sends and post-fader sends. Here's a modified signal flow diagram, taking into account the different kinds of sends in Figure 11.2.

Figure 11.2

Track signal flow with sends.

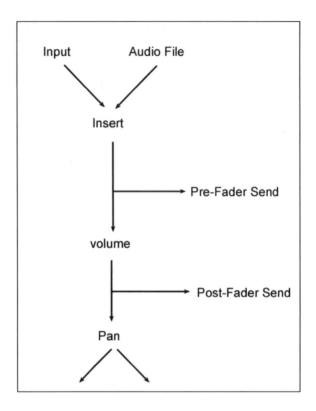

* **Input**

* **AudioFile**

* **Insert:** Since an insert completely interrupts the stream of audio, this is the ideal place for certain kinds of effects, like graphic equalizations, that typically are used on 100% of a track's signal.

* **Pre-Fader Send:** If a pre-fader send is used in a track (it's optional), a copy of the audio signal will be routed to another location prior to the track's volume fader. Changes in the track's volume and panning will have no effect on the level of the copy being sent.

* **Volume**

* **Post-Fader Send:** If a post-fader send is used (again, it's up to you whether to use them or not), a copy will be routed to another location *after* any changes in volume that are made with the track's volume fader. That means that if you change the level of the track's fader, you'll also affect the level of the audio that's being sent.

* **Pan:** Pan adjustments don't affect either pre- or post-fader sends.

Sends have multiple uses. The most common use for sends is in the use of combining an affected signal with an unaffected signal (the affected signal is commonly referred to as "wet," and the "dry" signal is the unaffected original). The send will route a copy to another location in your project, in which will reside the effect for the wet output. By sending a copy, you'll have control over the dry signal by changing the track's volume fader, and you'll have separate control over the wet signal by adjusting the level elsewhere in the session. Where is this other location where the wet signal is adjusted? That's what buses are for, and we'll get to that soon.

Another practical use of sends lies in their ability to use effects efficiently. Consider this: You've got a song with 10 tracks in it, and you want to apply a reverb to six of those tracks. With sends, it is no problem—just activate a send on the six tracks that you want to reverb and send them all to a single location in your session where the reverb resides. You can even control the level of each of the tracks' signal going to the reverb, since sends have adjustable levels. The signal flow in this situation would look something like the diagram in Figure 11.3.

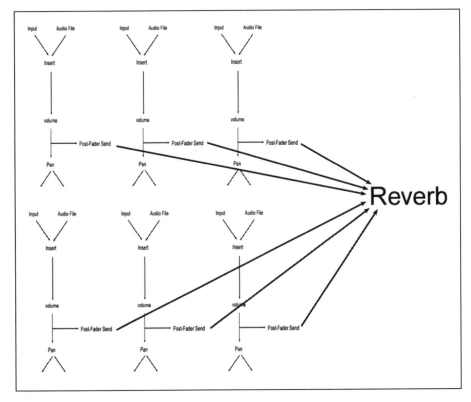

Figure 11.3

Routing multiple tracks to a single reverb.

And how does this audio data get routed from one place to another? Buses, that's how.

Buses

The term "bus" isn't exclusively a digital audio term. Its roots can be found in the early days of ana-log mixing techniques, referring to the routing of a signal within a system (commonly a *mixing board*). In the digital realm, the function is much the same, but the possibilities are enhanced by the power of the virtual digital environment.

Think of a bus as a virtual audio cable that can be used to carry a signal from one point to another within the DAW environment. Because it is virtual, you can do things with a bus that you can't do with a physical cable. For starters, you can have multiple sources for a single bus, which allows you to route many signals to a single destination. Through buses you can route copies of several tracks' worth of audio signal to a single effect within the DAW environment, as you saw earlier in Figure 11.3.

The advantages of buses go beyond that. Because they're completely virtual, buses don't have any of the physical limitations of an audio cable. First, there is no cable length to worry about, and for anybody who has had to wire up a studio, that's a *huge* advantage! Also, routing audio within an application with a bus is noiseless, which is usually not the case with real cables.

If there's one down side to buses, it's that they're often virtual, invisible, and working behind the scenes. The challenge to the digital audio producer is to be able to use these powerful tools without the benefit of being able to see them. Next, you'll learn how to put them to use in your DAW.

Plug-Ins

When the computer workstation revolution brought recording into the virtual world, tape decks weren't the only devices that were "digitized." Soon after basic audio workstations arrived on the scene, plug-ins marched in to add to the power of this new digital environment.

By definition, a plug-in is a bit of software that is designed not to run on its own, but rather work *within* a host application. You've probably used plug-ins before in a variety of applications. In a graphic application, for example, a plug-in might be used to apply some special visual effect to the file. In an audio application, a plug-in generally applies an effect as well. In fact, plug-ins have become a driving force in the audio and music industries, replacing racks full of audio processing gear.

Like buses, plug-ins have advantages that are impossible to achieve with more tangible devices. Need a reverb effect in your session? Not a problem—just launch a reverb plug-in within your DAW application. Need *five* reverbs? Still not a problem—launch the plug-in five times! If you've tweaked your effect, you can choose to save your settings as a preset that you can recall later in a later proj-ect. And because they're virtual, the noise (and headache) of connecting an external device and set-ting it up simply doesn't exist. In many ways, plug-ins combine the best qualities of outboard effects and computer programs.

Of course, there's always a catch. Plug-ins require processing power to perform their job. Every plug-in that is running as your song plays takes up valuable CPU resources. In extreme cases, too many plug-ins can overwhelm your CPU's processing horsepower, resulting in an interruption in playback or even a system-wide crash. The bottom line: Get the most powerful CPU you can (a more powerful CPU can support more simultaneous plug-ins), and only use the plug-ins that you need. Even with these limitations, you'll find that plug-ins are a powerful production tool.

Processing Your Audio (Part 1: Dynamic–Based Effects)

We've talked about all the ways you can transform your MIDI, but what about digital audio? Let's take a look at some common audio processes. We'll start off by exploring some standard dynamic-based effects. Dynamic-based effects, including processes like equalization (EQ) and compression, all share some common traits:

1. Dynamic-based effects affect the amplitude (or "dynamics") of a waveform.

2. Traditionally, 100% of the audio is processed as it plays. Basically, this means that you don't typically blend a processed and an unprocessed version of a track together (don't worry, this'll make more sense in Chapter 12).

Equalization

Equalization (also called "EQ") is an indispensable aid in fine-tuning sound. Not only can proper equalization change the character of a sound, but it can also allow multiple tracks to fit together soni-cally, like the pieces of a puzzle. Equalization works by boosting or reducing the amplitude of specific ranges of frequencies (or "bands") within audio. Ever use a radio with "bass," "mid," and "treble" knobs? That's essentially what you do with EQ in your DAW environment, only you use this effect on individual audio elements and with greater precision. Here's an example of a basic EQ, capable of adjusting many frequency ranges at once (see Figure 11.4).

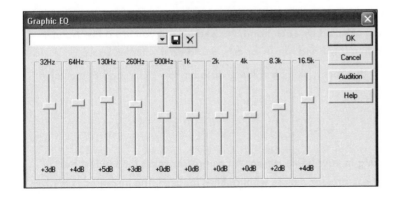

Figure 11.4

A graphic equalizer plug-in.

This might look real familiar. You might have a device that looks like this in your living room, tailoring the sound of your stereo to the contours of your room. Either way, virtual or physical, these gizmos work the same. The individual faders will boost or cut specific frequencies. Note that each frequency assigned to each fader can't be changed—it's a fixed value. This kind of device is also known as a *graphic equalizer.*

There's another way to work with an EQ. The following is an example of a parametric EQ. This kind of effect operates on the same principles of any equalizer but offers a different way of working. With a parametric EQ, you can adjust a number of bands (in this case, four) that *aren't* fixed vales. That means that in addition to boosting or cutting loudness, you can move the frequencies of these bands. Take a look at a basic parametric EQ in Figure 11.5.

Figure 11.5

A parametric EQ plug-in.

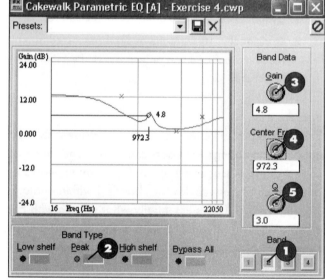

1. Select which band you want to adjust by clicking any one of these numbered buttons.

2. There are three types of bands that you can use for each of the four bands. In this case, you can choose a low shelf (boosting or cutting the low frequencies like a bass knob), a peak (also called a *band EQ*, boosting or cutting a specific range like a midrange knob), or a high shelf (acting like a treble knob).

3. The volume of each band, whichever its type, can be adjusted using the Gain knob.

4. The Center Frequency knob allows the user to change the frequencies that are being affected by each band. For example, if you use a low band and want to change the frequency at which that low band boosts or cuts, you'd do it with this knob.

5. The Q knob changes the width of your adjustments. A high value gives a narrow peak, and a low value gives a broader one.

Compression/Limiting

This is one audio process you won't find lurking in your home stereo. A compressor takes the loudest part of audio and reduces its volume. How does the compressor decide what defines loudest? The threshold is the key. This is a user-definable volume level, and the compressor only affects those portions of the audio that are above that level. How much will it reduce audio that exceeds this threshold? Again, this is a parameter that you set, called a *ratio*, which directs the compressor to bring the level down by a certain percentage. For example, if you had a compressor with a threshold of −12 dB and a ratio of 2:1 (two to one), the compressor would decrease the level of any audio that exceeded −12 dB by 50%. The lower the threshold, the more your signal will be affected. The higher the ratio (3:1 is a higher ratio than 2:1), the more aggressively that audio will be mashed down.

Here are the basic features of a compressor (see Figure 11.6).

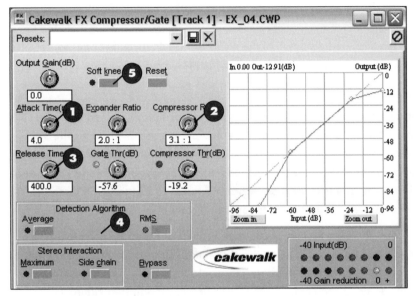

Figure 11.6

Basic compressor features.

1. **Attack Time:** This refers to the amount of time it takes the compressor to respond to increases in signal level. Typically, attack times are set pretty short, so that the compressor kicks in quickly after the threshold is reached. Attack times that are too long can often let quick peaks go by without compressing them.

2. **Compression Ratio:** Here's where you control how much the audio (that goes above the threshold) will be reduced in volume.

3. **Release Time:** This refers to the amount of time it takes a compressor to stop compressing after the level has dipped back below the threshold. Traditionally, release times are a bit longer than attack times, but be careful of setting them too long, as the compressor might keep compressing softer audio.

4. **Compression Threshold:** Here's where you change the level at which the compressor springs into action.

5. **Detection Algorithm:** Any compressor, whether software or hardware in nature, must somehow monitor audio as it plays. Monitoring the audio in different ways will cause the compressor to respond in different ways. Cakewalk recommends that the Average setting is typically used for instrumental tracks, whereas RMS is more commonly chosen for vocals (both sung and spoken).

6. **Soft Knee:** With this button enabled, the compressor will ease in as it approaches the threshold (the compression curve to the right of the screen will show a curving around the threshold point). If you don't select the Soft Knee option, the compressor will begin compressing right at the threshold level (called a "hard knee").

Compressors are commonly used to add "punch" to individual tracks (particularly bass and drums). The way it treats audio makes it the obvious choice if you want to minimize fluctuations in volume and get a smoother and fuller sound in the bargain. Compressors can even be used on entire songs to give them extra power (see Chapter 12).

Again, the greater the ratio, the more the audio will be compressed. At a certain point—a ratio of 10:1 or higher—a compressor stops audio loudness like a brick wall. At that point, the compressor becomes a limiter. Think of a limiter as an extreme compressor, whose primary job is to prevent audio from exceeding the threshold.

The operation of a limiter is pretty straightforward, and so are its uses. Very often, sudden spikes can cause an otherwise fine track to clip the output of your mix. No problem—a touch of limiting on the offending track is just what the doctor ordered. Only one thing to watch out for with limiters, though. If you set the threshold too low, the limiter can effectively be "on" all the time, and distortion of the audio can result. If you hear this sort of change in the tonal color of your audio, simply raise the threshold until the problem disappears.

Expansion/Gate

Perhaps the best way to think of an expander is to think of it as the mirror image of a compressor. It does roughly the same thing, but in the opposite direction. Whereas a compressor reduces the volume of everything *above* a certain level, an expander reduces the level of sounds *below* a certain level. The sonic effect is opposite as a result. A compressor tends to reduce dynamic range (by reducing the difference between loud and soft sounds), and an expander tends to increase the dynamic range (by increasing the difference between loud and soft sounds). Pretty cool, huh?

Though they do radically different jobs, there's still a lot of common ground between compressors and expanders. The level at which the effect kicks in is still called the *threshold*. The amount of reduction performed by the expander is still called the *ratio*. Even the effect window looks similar. The parameters you see here all look familiar—they're the same as the compressor's—with one exception (see Figure 11. 7).

Figure 11.7

An expander plug-in window.

1. **Expansion Threshold:** Audio levels below this point will be reduced by the ratio amount.

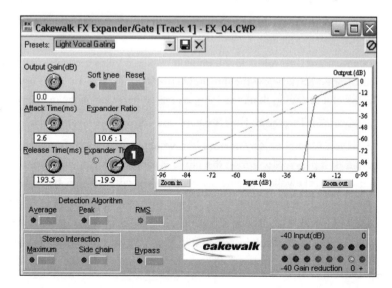

Though the attack and release time parameters do the same thing in both compressors and expanders, they're used a bit differently. Compressors and limiters typically attack quickly (low values) and release gradually (higher values), while expanders commonly attack slowly and then release quickly. Of course, as with any effect, the best teacher is experimentation, but as a general rule, quick attacks can be unpleasantly abrupt.

You know that an extreme compressor becomes a limiter, effectively barring audio from getting any louder than the threshold. An extreme expander becomes something else, too, which is a gate (also called a *noise gate*). When the expansion ratio is high, an expander effectively eliminates all portions of the audio signal that fall below the threshold. Basically, noise gates are used to get rid of unwanted low-level signal—in other words, noise.

When will you use a noise gate? When you use compressors, for one. Compressors often have the net effect of raising background noise (like room tone, air conditioning, etc.), and a noise gate is the perfect tool for counteracting this problem. This is such a common thing to do that many compressors (hardware and software versions) have compressors and gates built into one device. By using compression and noise gating together, you can boost the audio's overall level without boosting the noise (just make sure that you don't set your noise gate threshold too high, or you run the risk of cutting out important audio material).

NOTE

Compressors aren't the only kinds of effects that can generate or aggravate a pesky noise situation. Many kinds of effects can have such problems, which only makes noise gates even more useful and valuable. Be careful how you use them, though, so they don't get in the way of the effect. You'll learn more about using multiple effects together in Chapter 12.

Normalization

All the audio effects we've talked about so far are tried and true staples of any recording studio, analog or digital. Normalization, on the other hand, is a cool little trick that specifically takes advantage of digital audio. Think of normalization as a "smart" volume change, which automatically maximizes the volume of your digital audio. Here's how it works (see Figure 11.8).

Figure 11.8

Before normalization.

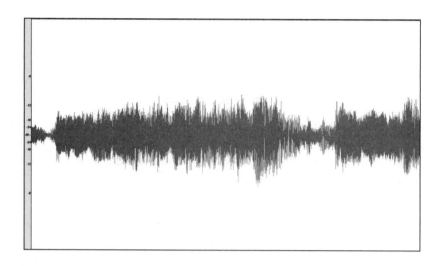

❋ Like most audio that you'll record into your system, the levels won't go all the way up to -0 dB (the maximum level for all digital audio). The loudest peak is here, at a level of about -7 dB.

Selecting the audio and choosing the normalize operation (most commonly found in the Edit or Process menu, depending on the software) will change the volume (or "gain") of that audio so that the loudest peak is -0 dB, similar to Figure 11.9.

Figure 11.9

After normalization.

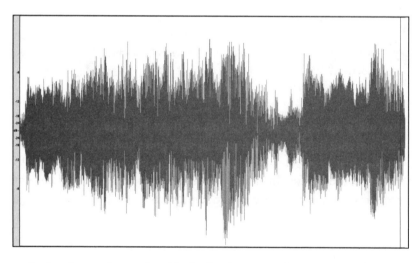

Note that the level of the entire audio has been changed, with the loudest point being maxxed out without clipping.

Normalization can be a useful tool when used correctly, but is easily misused. The thing to remember is that normalization treats the symptom of recording too softly without curing the disease. Normalizing quiet audio will not gain any greater resolution to the audio (though the normalized audio may respond better to further processing). The original quantization error that occurred when the audio was originally recorded will still be there, just at a different volume level. Another important thing to keep in mind is that as you normalize the audio, any background noise will also be raised.

The news gets worse: Mathematically speaking, the process of normalization can sometimes introduce new problems into audio and often make a bad situation worse. Still, when you absolutely need to get soft audio louder, sometimes normalization is your only recourse, but always remember one thing. The best thing to do is to record your audio as loudly as possible (without clipping) so that you don't *need* to normalize any more than absolutely necessary.

Processing Your Audio (Part 2: Time-Based Effects)

Traditional effects, even plug-in effects, fall into one of two categories: dynamic-based effects and time-based effects. You've already learned that dynamic-based effects change the volume (or amplitude) of the audio being effected. Time-based effects, on the other hand, modify the audio's duration in some way. The most common time-based effects are reverb and delay, which we'll discuss later in this section.

Because of their different effects on audio, their traditional application is different as well. You've learned that dynamic-based effects are traditionally applied on a track's insert, affecting the entire signal of the track. Time-based effects, on the other hand, are typically used more sparingly. With a reverb effect, for example, you'll want to combine a dry signal and a wet signal. Of course, this is easy to achieve using a send, as you learned previously. Here's a closer look at the most common of the time-based effects.

Reverb

Reverb is probably the most common of the time-based effects. This nifty little effect adds a sense of spaciousness to an otherwise dry signal. Through the use of reverb, you can take a dry vocal, for example, and add to it the ambience of a huge cathedral, a small room, or anything in between. Here are a few of the basic controls on a typical reverb (see Figure 11.10).

Figure 11.10

A reverb plug-in window.

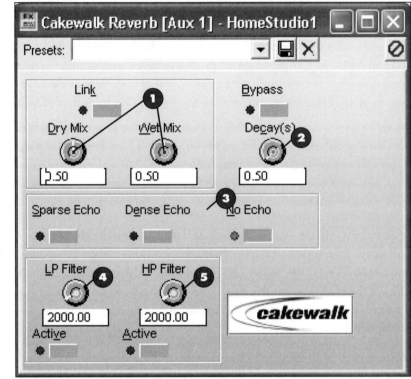

1. **Mix:** This section allows you to mix a wet and dry signal together. Clicking the Link button will cause the dry level to decrease as you increase the wet level, and vice versa.

2. **Decay:** This parameter determines the length of the ambience. Put simply, a longer decay time gives the impression of a larger space.

3. **Echo:** In addition to basic reverb, an echo effect can be added. Adding echo (either sparse or dense) repeats the audio signal in addition to applying reverb. Adding an echo to a reverb adds the sensation of walls to your sonic space.

4. **High Pass Filter:** When you activate this filter, you can control what frequencies will be affected. The high pass filter only allows frequencies *above* a certain threshold to be processed by the reverb.

5. **Low Pass Filter:** This feature works very much like the high pass filter, but from the other direction. Enable this feature, and you'll be able to set a limit to allow lower frequencies to be processed, but no frequencies above the threshold.

TIP

When using a send to route a dry signal to a reverb plug-in, the reverb is typically set to 100% wet.

NOTE

As with all plug-ins, the Bypass button, when clicked, will allow the signal to pass through the plug-in unaffected.

Delay

A delay does exactly what its name suggests—it causes the signal to be heard later than the original audio. The effect on its own is not that exciting, but when mixed with the dry signal, it gives an echo effect. Here's a rundown of the different ways you can tweak this effect (see Figure 11.11).

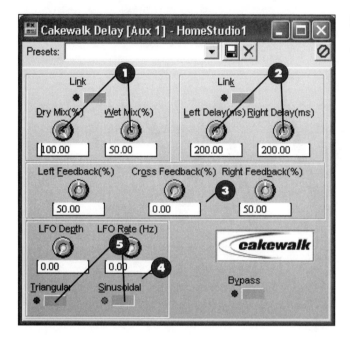

Figure 11.11

A typical delay plug-in window.

1. **Mix:** This section allows you to mix a wet and dry signal together. Clicking the Link button will cause the dry level to decrease as you increase the wet level, and vice versa.

2. **Delay:** Obviously, the most critical parameter, this allows you to specify the amount of time that the signal will be offset. Larger values will result in a bigger difference between the time you hear the dry signal and the time that you hear the wet signal. Clicking the Link button will allow you to have the same delay times for both the left and right speakers.

3. **Feedback:** Feedback allows for some of the delayed signal to be rerouted back to the delay's input. In the case of delay plug-ins, adding feedback will result in multiple echoes. Higher feedback levels will result in more (and stronger) repetitions of the original signal. In some cases (as shown here), you can have independent control over the feedback in each channel of a stereo track and can even route signal from left to right and right to left, using the Cross Feedback feature.

4. **LFO:** The LFO (or *Low Frequency Oscillator*) has an interesting role in an effect like delay. The job of the LFO is to create a very slow wave. An LFO itself isn't audible (the oscillations are *way* below the range of human hearing), but when it's used to affect audio, its influence can be heard. In the case of a delay effect, the LFO affects the pitch-delayed signal, adding a tremolo effect. The rate changes the speed of the tremolo, and the depth determines its strength.

5. **LFO Waveform:** Some flangers will allow you to change the shape of the LFO's wave. The two most popular choices for LFO wave shapes are triangle waves, as shown in Figure 11.12.

TIP

As with reverb, when using a send to route a dry signal to a delay plug-in, the delay is usually set to 100% wet.

TIP

Longer delay times will give the impression of a larger space, whereas a short delay will sound like a smaller room.

Figure 11.12

A triangle wave.

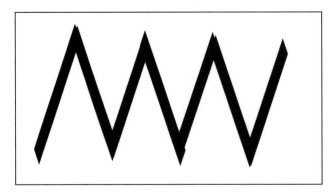

If you don't like the sound that triangle LFOs give you, you can use a smoother sinusoidal (sine) wave like Figure 11.13.

Figure 11.13

A sine wave.

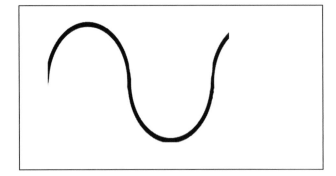

Processing Your Audio (Part 3: Special Effects)

There are still other effects that don't fall neatly into the traditional families of effects. Take a look at some other ways to spice up your sounds.

Reverse

This is a cool trick, too, and made all the easier through the power of digital audio. Technically speaking, we've been able to reverse audio all the way back in the analog-only age, but to do it we had to actually play tape or records backwards. Usually, that meant that the whole song would get played backwards, and we had to go to great lengths to make reversed audio and regular audio play nicely together. Digital audio changed all that!

Reverse does just what you think it does—it takes an audio region and flips it back to front. For example, you could start out with a wave that looked like Figure 11.14.

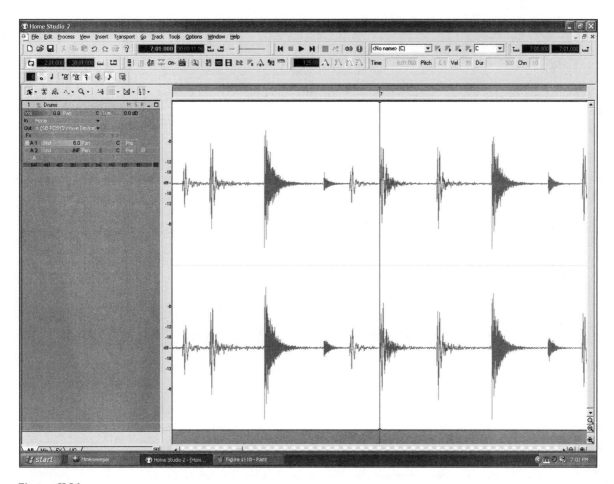

Figure 11.14

Before reversing.

Then you could apply Reverse (like Normalize, this is usually found in the Edit or Process menu, depending on the software), and you'd end up with Figure 11.15.

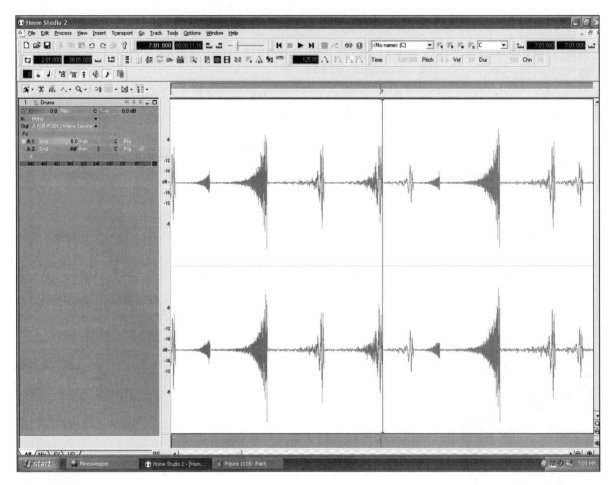

Figure 11.15

After reversing.

❄ **NOTE**

Fortunately, unlike normalization, you won't hear any negative sonic fallout by reversing audio, nor is it going to alter your audio other than the fact that the order of the audio has been reversed. In fact, this is a great effect to use in conjunction with other effects, which you'll explore in Chapter 12.

Flange/Chorus

Just as compression and expansion are related effects, so are flange and chorus. Also like compression and expansion, you can apply these effects as you would a dynamic effect. The problem with these two is that these effects aren't as easy to put into words as the other effects that we've discussed. When it comes to flange, for example, words like "ethereal," "spacey," or "whooshy" come to mind. (Heck, those same words have been used to describe *me* from time to time!) Obviously, you'll have to hear these effects for yourself to get a sense of what they *really* do to your sound.

Basically, flanging involves combining a signal with a very slightly delayed copy of itself. Though this is easily accomplished in the digital realm, this effect actually has analog roots. Back in the early days of analog, multiple reel-to-reel tape decks were used to create delay effects. As the story goes, during a Beatles session, someone touched the rim of the reel that was being used for the delay, which changed the timing and pitch slightly on that deck. After some experimentation, the technique of "flanging" (named after the rim of a tape reel, which is called the flange) found its place in engineers' bag of tricks.

Although flanging technically involves using a delayed signal, the amount of delay on the sound isn't perceived by the human ear as an echo or other traditional delay. Instead, the sound is so minutely adjusted that it interacts with the original signal. Not to get unnecessarily technical on the subject, but the delayed audio has a certain altering effect on the original audio. This interference between the delayed audio and the original generates a filtering effect. This filtering sweeps up and down as the delay is subtly adjusted over time, giving the classic flanging sound—like I said, you've gotta hear it to really appreciate it!

Here's an example of a basic flanger in Figure 11.16.

Figure 11.16

A flange plug-in effect.

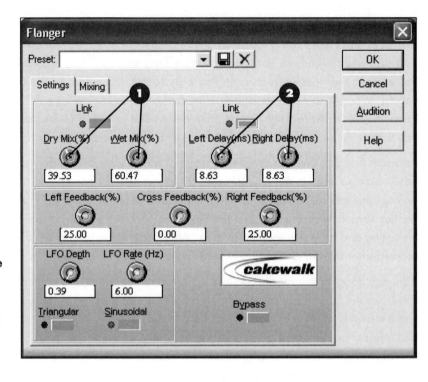

1. **Mix:** Generally speaking, when talking about effects we refer to the unprocessed audio as being "dry" and the processed audio as being "wet." Many effects, like reverb, require a mixing together of the wet and dry parts to give the desired result. Flangers are the same way—a more "wet" mix will result in a more pronounced flanging effect, and a mix more to the dry side will be more subtle. Often, the wet/dry mix is a single knob or slider (wet on one side, dry on another). In this case, you have independent control over the wet and dry with a Link button above them to make sure that the wet/dry combination never goes above 100 percent (as the dry is increased, the wet goes down, and vice versa).

2. **Delay:** This determines the minimum delay that will be used by the flanger (the maximum delay depends on the depth of the flanging). Lower values generally yield more subtle results. In this case, you've got independent control over the left and right side's delay and the option to link them. (Linking in this case will make sure that the values are the same in both the left and right sides of your stereo track.)

> ❋ **NOTE**
> Some people use the term "mix" interchangeably with "depth." Technically, this can be misleading, as there is another parameter called "depth," which we'll get to in just a second.

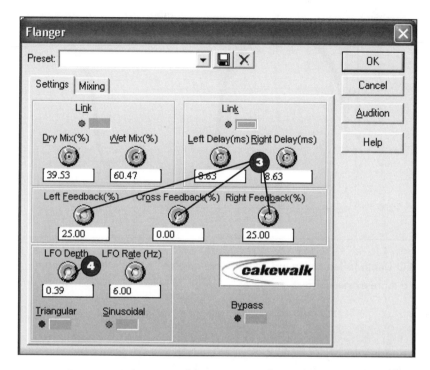

Figure 11.17

Controlling feedback and LFO on a flanger.

3. **Feedback:** This feature (shown in Figure 11.17) is available in some (but not all) flangers and allows for some of the flanged signal to be rerouted back to the flanger's input. The use of feedback can result in an edgy or metallic kind of sound, but be careful. Too much feedback can get out of hand and possibly result in distortion or clipping. In some cases (as shown in Figure 11.14), you can have independent control over the feedback in each channel of a stereo track and can even route signal from left to right and right to left, using the Cross Feedback feature. (This often deepens the sense of stereo in a track.)

4. **LFO Depth:** Perhaps the most defining characteristic of the flange effect is its slow sweeping sound. The component of the flanger that delivers this sweep is called a *Low Frequency Oscillator* or *LFO*. The job of the LFO is to create a very slow wave. An LFO in and of itself isn't audible (the oscillations are *way* below the range of human hearing), but when it's used to affect audio, its influence is certainly recognizable. In a flanger, the LFO changes the amount of change in the delay, based upon the delay value that you set in the Delay parameter. Graphically, it looks something like Figure 11.18.

❄ **NOTE**

You've probably heard the term "feedback" before, and not in a very flattering light. If you haven't heard the term, you've almost certainly heard the phenomenon. Ever hear somebody talking into a microphone, then a soft ringing starts, growing louder and more unpleasant until someone fixes the problem (or the speakers blow!)—that's feedback. The cause of this kind of feedback is that the sound of a speaker's output is being picked up by a microphone, and goes back out of the speakers, is picked up by the microphone *again*, and so on. The result is an endless and ever-growing loop of signal (which is why professionals often refer to feedback as a "feedback loop"). The same principle that is at work in this unfortunate situation is what we use in a more controlled way in a flanger's feedback feature.

Figure 11.18

What an LFO does in a flanger.

4a. The lowest point of the LFO's sweep represents the lowest total flange delay, which you determine when you set the delay value.

4b. The amplitude of the wave (the difference between the peaks and troughs) is determined by

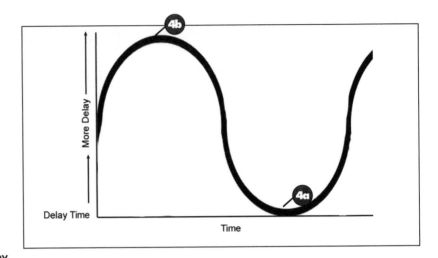

the value you choose for the LFO Depth (often called just "depth") parameter. Higher values will result in a greater flange sweep and a more extreme effect.

> ❋ **NOTE**
> The low point of the overall flanging is always determined by the delay value, and changing this value will change the position of the trough of the LFO. The shape of the LFO's wave, however, will be unchanged (it is just proportionally shifted up or down as the delay is changed) until you change the depth value.

You have a good bit of control over the behavior of the LFO, as you can see in Figure 11.19:

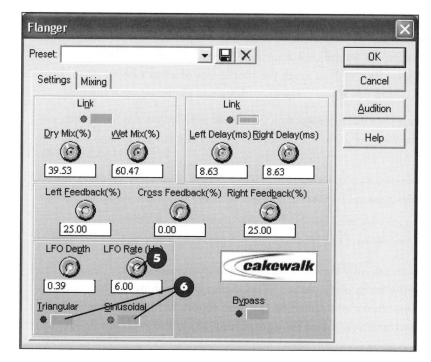

Figure 11.19

Setting up the LFO.

5. **LFO Rate:** This parameter controls the frequency of the LFO, which in turn determines the speed of the flanger's sweeping sound. Note that the LFO rate (often simply called "rate") is measured in Hertz (Hz), which is the same way we measure pitch when we're talking about audible sound, although these values are below our ability to hear them. Higher rate values will result in more peaks and troughs per second, and the flanging effect will sound faster.

6. **LFO Wave:** Just as you saw before in the delay plug-in, you have your choice of two popular LFO wave shapes—triangle or sinusoidal.

Changes to the LFO waveform will change the way the flange sweeps (in other words, how the delay in timing between the combined signals changes over time).

Whew, that's a lot to think about for just one effect! Don't worry. It's a really cool effect, and understanding how it works will help you use it better. (It's a really easy effect to waste time with if you don't understand it.) Also, if you understand flange, you'll understand another really neat effect, which is chorus.

Applying chorus to a bit of audio makes it sound as if there is more than one instrument (or voice) playing in unison. Keep in mind that even unison musical parts will differ slightly in timing and in pitch, and chorus gets the job done by mixing a slightly delayed and slightly detuned copy of the audio with the original.

Sounds a lot like what flange does, doesn't it? Well then, it won't come as a shock to learn that a Chorus Effect window often looks just like a Flanger window. In fact, the parameters for flange and chorus in this application (Cakewalk Home Studio) are *exactly* the same. The main difference between a chorus effect and a flange effect isn't so much the mechanics of what's being done, but rather the way the process is used. There are a few differences between chorusing and flanging:

1. Typically, delay values in choruses are much greater than those used with flanges. Common delay values for choruses might fall in the range of 20 to 30 milliseconds, whereas a flanger's range is closer to 1 to 10 milliseconds.

2. The LFO speed is slower (a lower value) with a chorus than with a flanger. Generally speaking, the LFO rate is set to be 3 Hz or less. This gives the lushness of a chorus without the obvious sweep of a flanger.

3. Chorus effects generally use no (or very little) feedback. The characteristic sound of a chorus is one of smoothness and lushness, and the edginess that feedback creates generally works against that goal.

Using a chorus effect, you can create not only the illusion of multiple instruments where once there was only one, but you can also create completely unique tones. Being a bassist myself, I've come to be quite fond of a little chorus to smooth out and fatten up my bass sound. In fact, the chorused electric bass sound has long been a tried and true sound for ages, especially in the jazz world (sounds *great* on a bass).

Get on the Bus—Internal Mixing

Often, when we talk about "mixing," we're referring to the process of blending individual tracks of multitrack projects so they work together well as a whole song. It includes (but is certainly not limited to) adjusting the volume and panning of tracks so that no track is too loud or soft, and that each instrument has its own "location" in the stereo environment. The term has a deeper meaning, however, which pertains more to how the application itself deals with the combining of multiple digital audio tracks.

DAW applications all must deal with the issue of internal mixing, or the combination of many signals in the session to a more manageable output for the producer and artists to listen to. For example, take a session with 10 tracks. On the Track window, you actually see (and can manipulate) these 10 individual audio streams, but certainly your sound card can't play back 10 different outputs. The DAW application must internally combine these signals, along with your volume and pan settings, to match the format you are using for monitoring (such as stereo in this case).

You've learned that the term "bus" is commonly used to describe a signal being routed within a DAW, and this sort of signal flow is no exception. This bus is fundamental to the operation of the software and different in nature than other kinds of buses, so it has a special name, which is *mix bus*. Here's a rough diagram of the management of a multitrack DAW's many components using the mix bus (see Figure 11.20).

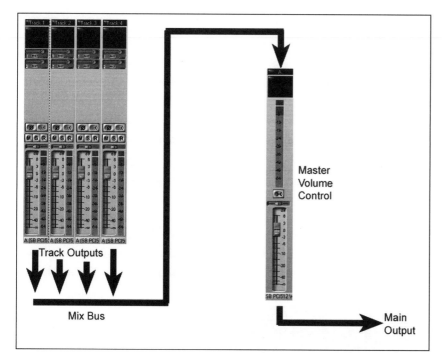

Figure 11.20

How the mix bus works.

The signal that travels along this mix bus to the output of the system is a combination of all your audio tracks, effects, and other sound-creating processes. This mix bus is a critical element of your DAW application and goes a long way toward defining the overall quality of your audio. To keep the quality of this mixed audio high, many DAW applications use super high-resolution audio, higher in fact than the ability of the hardware to play back.

This is a nifty little feature called *internal resolution*. For example, some applications use 32-bit internal resolution, which means that the mixed audio traveling along the mix bus is 32-bit audio, preserving the quality of the mixed audio as levels are changed. Of course, there's no audio interface that can play back 32-bit audio, so the mixed audio must be downgraded back to a playable form. While it may seem that reducing the resolution upon playback eliminates the benefit of the higher internal resolution, the data reduction is done in such a way as to deliver the highest audio quality possible. In fact, the internal resolution of your DAW application can make a big difference in the quality of your final product (the higher the better).

Mixing Basics

The word "mix" has come to have many meanings these days. For example, you might have a radio "mix" of a song, a club "mix," and so on. The use of the word "mix" in this case is really referring to a different arrangement or version of a song. There's another meaning to the word "mix"—a more traditional meaning—that you'll be learning about in this section.

The traditional meaning of the word "mix" in the production world refers to the blending of different audio elements to create a unified final result. At its simplest level, we're talking about changing the faders of individual tracks so that all the instruments and voices can be heard clearly, but that's only the tip of the iceberg. The art of mixing (and it *is* an art, taking a lifetime to perfect) involves creating a complete sonic environment, from volume levels to panning, to complex routing and use of effects.

You've already worked with volume faders and pan sliders in Chapter 8, so you're solid with the basics. Here are a few tools to make the process of mixing even more efficient and creative.

Groups

Simply put, a group is a user-defined collection of controls in your Mixer window that move together. That isn't to say that the controls are all at the same volume, but rather that they maintain a consistent relationship to each other. For example, you might have a number of drum tracks, as shown here in Figure 11.21.

Figure 11.21

Four drum tracks.

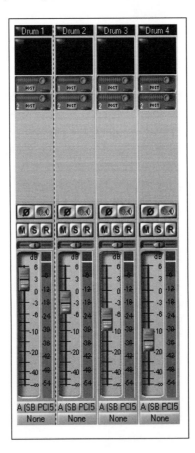

Let's assume that this is a perfect sounding set of drum tracks, but what if you want to change the volume of the entire group? Without setting up a fader group, you'd have to manually change all of the tracks individually, but with a fader group, it's easy. Setting up a fader group can vary, depending upon the application, but the result is the same. The grouped faders will now move as a unit, similar to Figure 11.22.

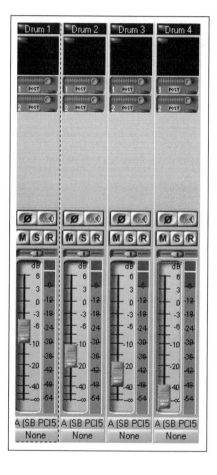

Figure 11.22

Four *grouped* drum tracks.

Using fader groups can really simplify your music, while still giving you control over individual tracks. For example, let's say that you decided as your mix progressed that these drum tracks *weren't* perfectly blended, and you wanted to change their overall relationship with each other. It's easy to just deactivate the group, make your changes, and then group your faders again. The movements of the group will reflect this new proportion.

Nearly every application will allow you to group faders. Many applications, like Cakewalk Home Studio, allow other controls to be grouped together as well. You can even have many different groups in a single song, allowing you to control a great many tracks with just a few faders. You'll find that by grouping tracks, you can make a complex project more easy to manage.

Automation

Using groups to move multiple controls at a time is all well and good, but there's much more mixing power at your disposal. The next stage in mixing is to automate it. Precisely, what is mix automation? It's one of the coolest parts of a computer-based DAW, allowing you to record the motion of faders and other controllers over time, and then have the controls move accordingly during playback.

Automation used to be exclusive to high-priced professional mixing boards, but the computer revolution changed all that. By automating controls, you can have a dynamic mix that evolves over the course of time. Suppose that you want a sound to move from the left speaker to the right speaker over the first few seconds of a song. The specific steps vary slightly, but the process is as follows:

1. Select the parameter (in this case a Pan control) that you want to automate.

2. Enable that parameter for automation.

3. Configure the software to record the parameter's movements.

4. Begin playback.

5. Move the parameter as desired over time.

6. Stop playback and move the playback cursor back to the beginning of the song.

7. Begin playback, and watch your control move.

Once you're done, you'll notice that there is a graphic representation of the automation that looks something like Figure 11.23.

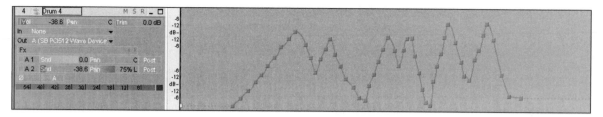

Figure 11.23

Mix automation.

What you're looking at is the automation for a Pan control as it moves from side to side. Why make a visual record of something like this? Because after you've recorded the motions of a given control, you'll be able to fine-tune those motions by graphically editing this line.

 NOTE

You'll be creating and editing mix automation in Chapter 12.

Fades

One mark of a quality DAW is its ability to do the same kind of thing in a number of different ways. Take fades, for example. Fades are gradual changes in volume. For example, at the beginning of a song, the volume of the song (or even certain elements *in* the song) commonly starts off very quietly and then gradually builds over the first few seconds. That's called a *fade-in*. Even more common is the *fade-out*, which is a gradual decrease in volume, the preferred ending to many songs.

One of the ways to achieve this volume change is by automating your track's volume fader, but it's not the only way. Most DAW applications process individual audio blocks. The process varies from application to application, of course, but the basic procedure involves using a specific Fade tool and then clicking and dragging with your mouse to create the desired fade curve within a single region. What you'll wind up with will look something like Figure 11.24.

Figure 11.24

Creating a fade.

The curved line within the region represents the decrease in volume as the region fades out. Using this tool, you can also create fade-ins on specific regions. What are the advantages? How about the ability to move regions without having to re-record fader automation to get your fades? One of the big advantages to this method of creating a fade is that the fade travels with the audio block itself. Also, the precision and editing capability of the fade is often more precise. It's very easy to change the duration and even the shape of the fade using the Fade tool, which is something you'll learn about in the next chapter.

12

Exercise 5: Mixing

The home stretch! You've got a solid foundation, and now it's time to start getting a bit more specific. This exercise is essentially a series of individual tasks, designed to make the most of your mixes. In this chapter, you'll learn how to:

❋ Use a dynamic-based effect like a compressor or EQ to add punch to your mix.

❋ Use time-based effects like reverb to give a sense of spaciousness to audio.

❋ Automate your mix and use control groupings to your advantage.

❋ Make a final mix of your song, ready to be burned onto an audio CD.

> ❋ **NOTE**
>
> For these exercises, you'll need to open the Exercise 5 files. First, copy the Exercise\Ex_05 folder from the accompanying CD-ROM to a location on your hard drive.
>
> After that's done, for Cakewalk Home Studio, simply open the file named Ex_05 in the Ex_05\Cakewalk folder that you've copied to your hard drive. For Quartz AudioMaster Freeware, open the file named Ex_05 in the Ex_05\Quartz folder.

> ❋ **NOTE**
>
> Depending on where you copy the Cakewalk files, you may need to relink the audio files with the audio files in the 05_Audio folder. Basically, it means that Cakewalk Home Studio, a pointer-based application, has lost track of what files to point *to*.
>
> It's not too difficult to fix—if you're prompted to find needed audio files, just navigate to the 05_Audio folder that you've copied to your hard drive and find the appropriate file. You'll notice that there's a parenthetical number in the file that Cakewalk's looking for, but don't worry about that—just pick the file that shares the same instrument name (for example, when Cakewalk prompts you to find Drums (3).wav, just navigate to the 05_Audio folder and select Drums.wav. When you're done, just remember to save the Cakewalk project file, and you're good to go.

> ❄ **NOTE**
>
> Like Cakewalk, Quartz AudioMaster Freeware might get confused as to the location of needed audio files. Again, it's not terribly difficult to remedy—just navigate to the Sources subfolder in the Exercise\Ex_05\Quartz folder and click on the file that matches the name of the region that AudioMaster is trying to find. When that's done, save your work, and you're all set to proceed.

Using Dynamic Effects

Using a dynamic effect plug-in is as simple as can be as long as you keep in mind how this effect will be used. Remember, dynamic effects (like EQ, compressors, and expanders) are traditionally used to process an *entire* signal. This can happen in the form of applying a compressor to a bass track to add a sense of "punch" to the sound, or using EQ to brighten the sound of a vocal.

Because of the way this sort of plug-in is used, a track's insert is the ideal place to use a dynamic-based effect. Let's take a look at the way these effects are used in our two applications.

Using Cakewalk Home Studio

One good place to set up a dynamic plug-in is Cakewalk Home Studio's Console window. Here's how to get to it (see Figure 12.1).

Figure 12.1

1. **Click** the **View** drop-down menu.

2. **Click** the **Console** menu item. The Console window will appear (see Figure 12.2).

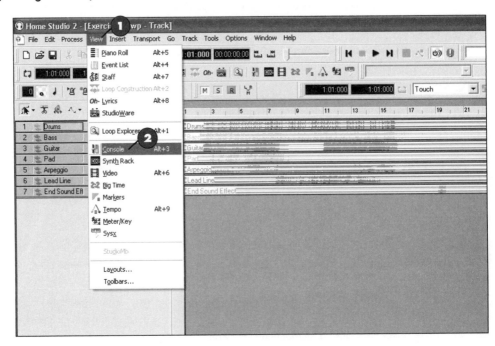

Let's add a little guitar-type distortion to liven up the bass part.

Figure 12.2

1. **Click** the **Solo** button on the bass track so that you can listen to the bass part on its own.

2. **Right-click** on the **effect** area below the track name. A drop-down menu will appear.

3. **Click** the **Audio Effects** menu item. A second drop-down menu will appear.

4. **Click** the **Cakewalk** menu item. Another drop-down menu will appear.

5. **Click** the **Amp Sim Lite** menu item. The Amp Sim Lite plug-in window will appear (see Figure 12.3).

Figure 12.3

6. **Start off** with a **preset sound** and work from there. **Click** the **arrow button** to the right of the Presets field. A drop-down menu will appear.

7. **Click** the **American Lead** preset. The parameters of the plug-in will change slightly (see Figure 12.4).

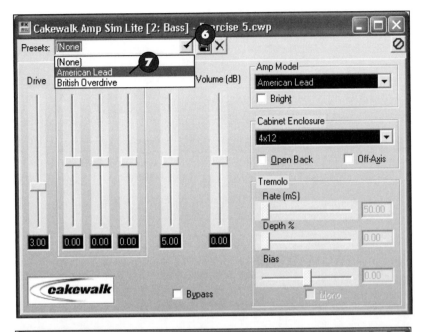

Figure 12.4

8. **Adjust** the **parameters** to make the part jump out of the mix a bit. **Click** and drag the **Treb** fader to bring up the treble of the bass part. (I've found that a value of 1.00 works well.)

9. To add a bit more life to the bass, **ring up** the **Presence** fader. (I've set mine to 8.00.)

10. **Boost** the **volume** of this virtual guitar amp a bit. (Again, I've set this one to 8.00.)

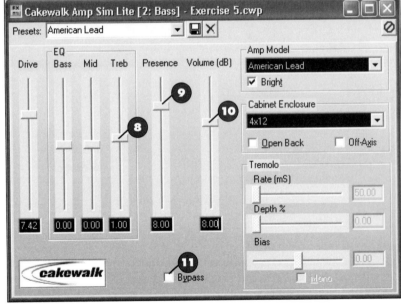

11. **Click** the **Bypass** box to hear the original track without the effect. Quite a difference, isn't it? Just click the box again to un-bypass the effect.

That's it, and using this method, you can use any plug-in on a track. Remember that this effect area is an insert on a track, so 100 percent of the track's signal will pass through any plug-in(s) you have on the track (which is the ideal way to use dynamic effects). To hear the change in your mix, just un-solo the track and hear how you've added interest to the bass part.

Using Quartz AudioMaster Freeware

AudioMaster Freeware is a little bit simpler than Cakewalk Home Studio, but there is still a usable EQ you can use on a track. Remember, this EQ is inserted on the individual track and will alter 100 percent of the entire signal (which is the traditional way to apply an EQ). Other than that, it's very simple to use and operates just like the tone controls on a home stereo system. Here's how to get to it (see Figure 12.5).

Figure 12.5

1. In the Mixer window, **click** the **EQ** button to reveal the equalization row of the mixer.

2. On each of the four audio tracks, you'll see separate Hi, Mid, and Low tone controls. Adjusting the Hi control will boost or cut higher frequencies. The Mid control will change the mid-range frequencies, and the Low knob will boost or cut the bottom frequencies.

3. At any time, you can hear the track unaffected by the EQ by **clicking** the **BP** (for **Bypass**) button. The button will light up when the EQ is bypassed.

Using Time-Based Effects

Time-based plug-in effects may look like dynamic plug-ins, but they're traditionally used in a much different way. The secret to using a time-based effect (like a reverb or delay) is to create a dry signal/wet signal kind of setup. The dry signal (unprocessed by an effect) is a no-brainer—simply don't put any effect on the track's insert. The plug-in effect will be in another place instead, an auxiliary (or simply "aux") section of the Mix window. A *copy* of the dry signal will be routed to this aux section using a *send*, and the blending of the wet and dry sound can be accomplished by adjusting the levels of the track's fader (for the dry sound) and the aux level (for the wet sound).

You'll find that sends and auxes can be powerful tools. Here's how to use them.

Using Cakewalk Home Studio

Let's add a little reverb ambience to the lead line (see Figure 12.6).

Figure 12.6

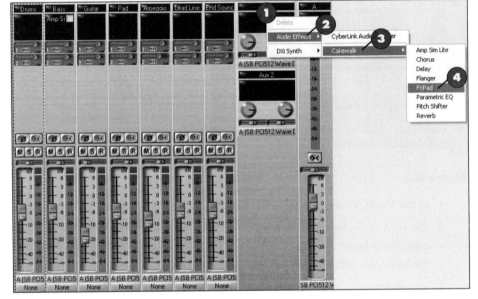

1. **Right-click** on the **effect** area below the Aux 1 heading. A drop-down menu will appear.

2. **Click** the **Audio Effects** menu item. A second drop-down menu will appear.

3. **Click** the **Cakewalk** menu item. Another drop-down menu will appear.

4. **Click** the **FXPad** menu item. The FXPad plug-in window will appear (see Figure 12.7).

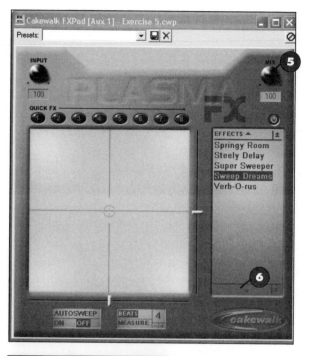

Figure 12.7

5. Turn the **Mix** knob to 100%. Does that mean that the plug-in will sound super-reverbed? Actually, yes, but you'll be controlling the wet/dry mix elsewhere.

6. Click the **down arrow** in the Effects area to choose the desired effect. In this case, I've chosen Sweep Dreams—try it, I think you'll like it!

The process is not quite complete—now you have to use a *send* to route a copy of the dry signal to the reverb. It's simple if you know where to look and can follow the signal path (see Figure 12.8).

Figure 12.8

7. On the track you want to affect (in this case, the lead line track), **click** the **Aux 1 send enable** button. The button will turn green.

8. To hear the affected track alone, **click** the **Solo** button on the track.

Now let's follow the signal path (see Figure 12.9).

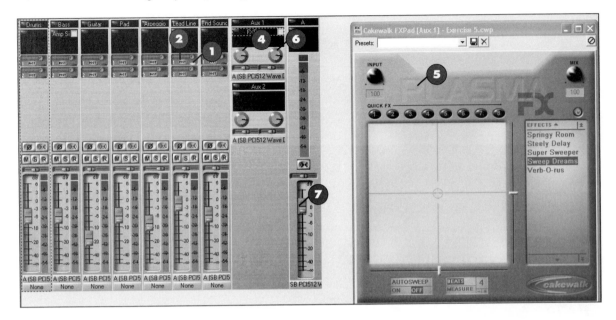

Figure 12.9

1. A copy of the dry signal is routed by activating a given track's send.

2. The volume level of the copied audio can be controlled by adjusting the Send Level slider.

3. The copied audio is routed internally to the Aux section.

4. The overall level of the bus going to the time-based effect can be further adjusted by changing the aux bus Send Level knob in the Aux section of the mixer (panning may also be changed using the slider below the knob). This controls the audio going to the effects in the Aux section.

5. Time-based effect(s), which processes the audio. The output of the plug-in(s) is controlled by the aux bus Return Level knob.

6. Aux bus Return Level knob, which adjusts the volume of the plug-in's output. (There is also Pan Control under the knob.) This controls the overall output of all the plug-ins in the Aux section. This is mixed with all the other individual tracks and controlled by the main volume fader.

7. Main Volume fader, which controls the entire output level of your song.

This can get pretty complex, but with this complexity comes flexibility. For example, you can also apply the same reverb to the Arpeggio track but have a completely different control over the wet/dry mix (see Figure 12.10).

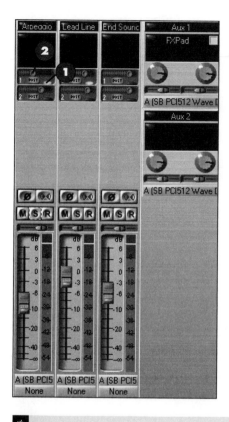

Figure 12.10

1. **Click** the **Aux 1 Send Enable** button on the Arpeggio track. Now a copy of the Arpeggio track, in addition to the Lead Line track, is being sent through a bus to the Aux 1 section of your mixer.

2. **Click** and **drag** the **slider** in the Aux 1 send area of the Arpeggio track to control the wet/dry mix. You will probably find that the Arpeggio track should have less effect than the lead line. No problem—just drag the slider to the left to send less signal to the FXPad plug-in, resulting in a dryer overall sound.

❄ **TIP**

You'll notice that the tracks that you've set up to use sends now sound a bit louder than they did before. That's natural, as their signal is now effectively doubled—one dry signal coming out of the track and a wet signal through the aux. You'll probably want to bring down these reverbed tracks a bit to compensate.

That's it! Just a couple more things to note (see Figure 12.11).

Figure 12.11

In each send, you'll see a small button that reads *Post*. That means that this send is a post-fader send. You can also click on the button and change it to read Pre, which stands for a pre-fader send.

1. A post-fader send is a send whose levels are determined not only by the level of the send itself but also by the overall level of the track. In other words, raising and lowering the level of the track will raise and lower the level of the audio going out of the send.

2. A pre-fader send's level is completely independent of the level of the track's fader. This means that the send level is the only volume control for audio going out of the send. You can move the track volume up or down, and you won't change the level of the send at all.

Generally speaking, post-fader sends are most commonly used. All you have to do is set a nice blend between the wet and dry signal using the send's level control; then as you change the volume of the dry track, the level going to the reverb will change accordingly, maintaining a constant wet/dry relationship.

You can have multiple plug-ins on a single aux, and you have seen that you have two auxes. That alone will give you a lot of creative options. Do you need more auxes? Here's how to get 'em! See Figure 12.12.

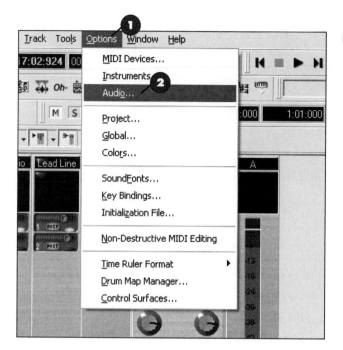

Figure 12.12

1. **Click** the **Options** drop-down menu.

2. **Click** the **Audio** menu item. The Audio Options window will appear (see Figure 12.13).

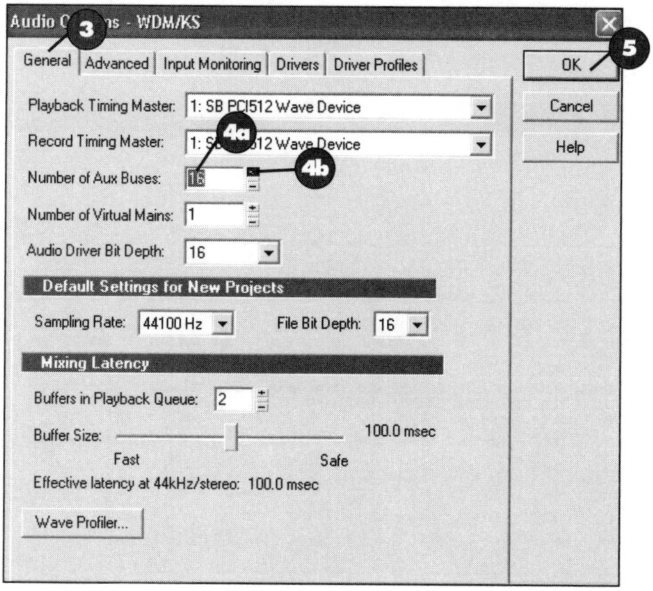

Figure 12.13

3. **Click** the **General** tab.

4a. **Type** the **Number of Aux Buses** you need, up to a maximum of 16, or

4b. **Click** the **increment keys** to the right of the Number of Aux Buses display to change the number.

5. **Click** the **OK** button.

Next time you open Cakewalk Home Studio, the Mixer window will change to reflect your choices. Take care, though, as having too many aux buses can make the Mixer window a little cumbersome, like this mixer showing 16 auxes (see Figure 12.14).

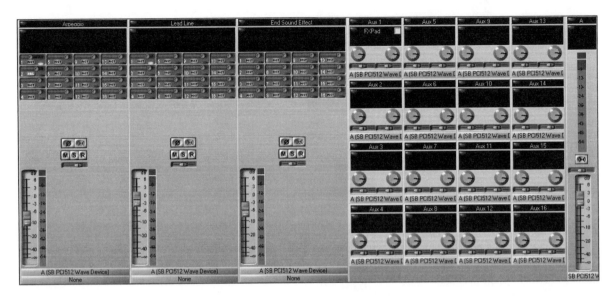

Figure 12.14

Using Quartz AudioMaster Freeware
Quartz AudioMaster Freeware has two auxes with a decent assortment of common effects (see Figure 12.15).

Figure 12.15

1. In the Mixer window, **click** the **Aux** button. The Aux section of the mixer will appear.

2. On any track, **click** the **DSP** button. The Signal Processing window will appear (see Figure 12.16).

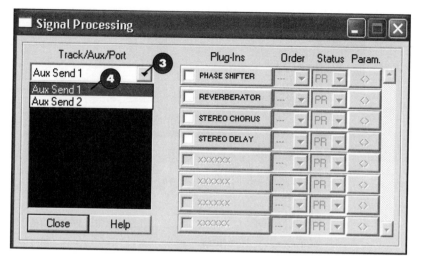

Figure 12.16

3. **Click** the **arrow button** to the right of the Track/Aux/Port display.

4. **Click** to choose the **Aux Send** that you want to configure (see Figure 12.17).

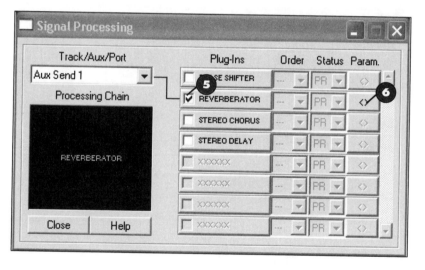

Figure 12.17

5. **Click** the **check box** by the plug-in you want to use.

6. **Click** the **Param** (for Parameters) button. The plug-in window will open (see Figure 12.18).

Figure 12.18

7. **Click** the **Load** button to view a list of preset parameters. A confirmation window will appear.

8. **Click** the **Yes** button. The Presets window will appear (see Figure 12.19).

Figure 12.19

9. **Click** the **desired preset.**

10. **Click** the **Load** button to load the preset values into the plug-in.

11. **Click** the **Close** button. The parameter window will disappear.

12. When you're done, **close** the **Plug-in window** and **click** the **Close** button in the Signal Processing window.

Now let's set up the individual tracks to use that reverb (see Figure 12.20).

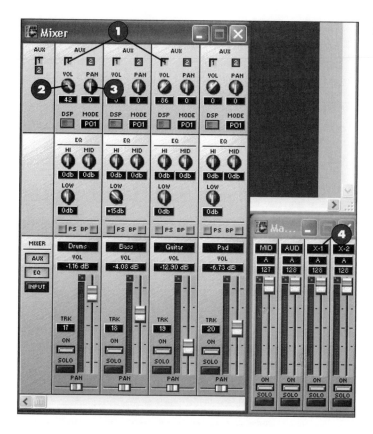

Figure 12.20

1. **Click** the **desired Aux** button. In this case, I've set up a reverb on Aux 1, and I want to add that reverb to the drum and guitar tracks, so I'll make sure that they're both set to 1.

2. The Vol (for **Vol**ume) knob on each track controls the send level to the plug-in.

3. The Pan knob controls the panning of the signal being sent to the plug-in.

4. The X-1 fader in the Master Mixer window controls the overall output of the Aux 1 (the X-2 fader controls aux 2).

Quartz AudioMaster Freeware gives you up to two auxes and up to one plug-in per aux. Even with this limited setup, a fairly complex mix can be created.

One additional tidbit: If your song has MIDI tracks along with audio tracks, you can add a little bit of MIDI reverb (which is actually part of your synthesizer's sound engine, rather than an AudioMaster process) to them by using continuous controller data. An easy way to get to this is through the Control section of a MIDI track, which shares the same row as EQ for audio tracks. Configuring reverb on MIDI tracks is pretty straightforward:

Figure 12.21

1. On the MIDI track where you want to add reverb, **click** the **Settings** button. The Real Time MIDI Controllers window will appear.

2. **Click** the **arrow button** to the right of the Controller 4 area. A drop-down menu will appear.

3. **Click** the **Reverb** menu item. Knob #4 in the Control section of that MIDI track will now control the amount of MIDI reverb added to the track.

4. **Click OK.**

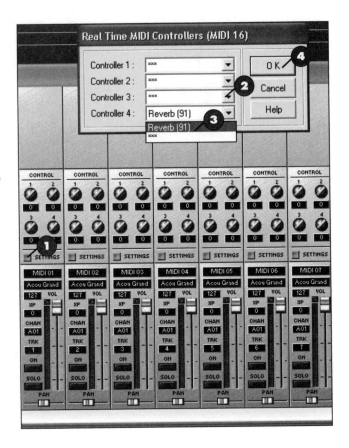

Creating a Fader Group

Different DAW applications will allow different kinds of controls to be "grouped" or set up to move as a unit. Most commonly, the controls that are grouped are track faders (some applications allow other controls to be grouped, but nearly *all* DAW will at least allow faders to be linked in this way). Let's create a fader group that joins our drum, bass, and guitar tracks together.

> **NOTE**
>
> Groups are not offered in the freeware version of AudioMaster, although upgrading to any of the other versions of the program will give you up to eight different groups. The description of groups that follows will only apply for Cakewalk Home Studio.

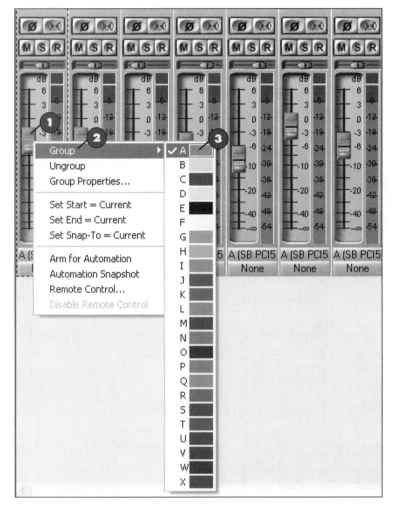

Figure 12.22

1. **Right-click** the **first control** that you want to group. A drop-down menu will appear.

2. **Click** the **Group** menu item. A second drop-down menu will appear.

3. **Click** the **group letter** (and corresponding color) that you want to associate with this control. The control will be highlighted in the group color.

4. Repeat Steps 1 through 3 for the other track(s) you want to add to this group. All the grouped tracks must share the same group letter in order to move together.

The grouped faders will now move together, making mixing a *lot* easier. Cakewalk Home Studio can even group other kinds of controls as well, including send levels and panning of all kinds.

Automating Your Mix

Now that you know how to make different controls move, the next step is to "record" these control movements. When I say "record," I'm using the term loosely—you don't record this kind of control data in the same way that you record MIDI or audio data. Instead, you use Mix automation. With Mix automation, you can create a much more interesting mix than a simple "static mix" (a mix with no fader or pan changes over time).

As with groups, the most common controls to be automated are track faders, with panning a close second. Let's start creating a more interesting mix through the power of automation, starting with the Arpeggio track.

NOTE

Again, this feature isn't offered with AudioMaster Freeware. We'll go through the process with Cakewalk Home Studio only.

Figure 12.23

1. **Right-click** the **control** that you want to automate. (In this case, I've chosen the Pan control on the Arpeggio track.) A drop-down menu will appear.

2. **Click** the **Arm for Automation** menu item.

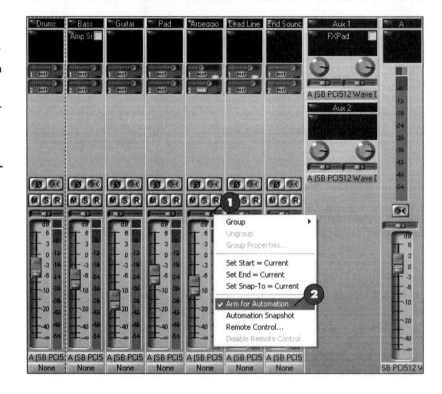

Figure 12.24

3. **Move** the **Now line** to the point at which you want to start recording your control's movements.

4. **Click** the **Record Automation** button. Your song will begin playback.

5. **Move** the **control** that you're automating as the session plays. Your motions will be captured. I've recorded very slow side-to-side panning, which works well with this Arpeggio track.

6. When you're done, **stop playback**.

Not only have you captured your control's motion, but also you can edit it. Let's take a look at the track in the Track window:

Figure 12.25

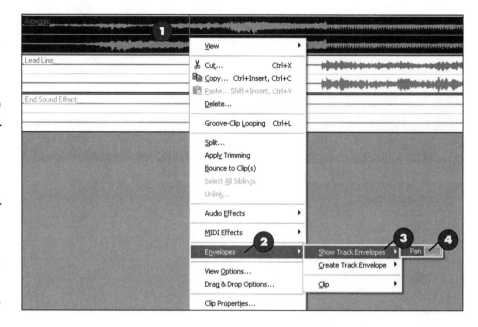

1. **Right-click** on **any track** that has an automated control. A drop-down menu will appear.

2. **Click** the **Envelopes** menu item. Another menu will appear.

3. **Click** the **Show Track Envelopes**. Yet another menu appears.

4. **Click** the **parameter** that you want to view. In this case, I want to take a look at a graphic representation of my Pan control movements.

The line in the following illustration shows panning movement from right (bottom) to left (top). This line is defined by a series of blocks, which Cakewalk Home Studio calls "nodes." Not only can you look at this data, but you can edit it as well:

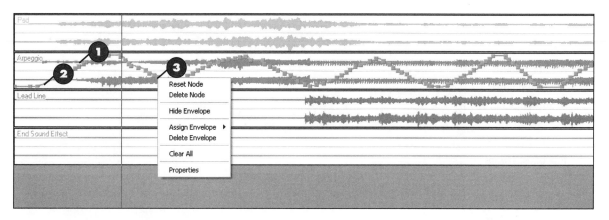

Figure 12.26

1. **Click** and **drag** on any **node** that you want to change. You can drag it higher or lower, or even earlier or later in time (until it reaches the next node).

2. **Double-click** on the **line** to create a new node.

3. **Right-click** on the **line** to reveal a drop-down menu of other automation-related functions. For example, you can **right click** on a **node** and **choose Delete Node** to remove the node.

As with grouping, a wide variety of controls can be automated, allowing you not only to create a complex mix, but one that changes over time. Better still, you can automate multiple controls on a single track.

Creating Fades

You know by now that you can use Mix automation to create a fade-in or fade-out on a track, but that's not the only way. You can easily create a fade-in or a fade-out on a single region, or even a crossfade between two audio regions (where an earlier region fades out while an overlapping later region fades in).

Although this kind of fade isn't supported with Quartz AudioMaster Freeware, it *is* included in Cakewalk Home Studio and most other DAW applications. The function of this kind of tool is very similar from application to application, so dive in and create a fade-in and fade-out on the Bass track.

Figure 12.27

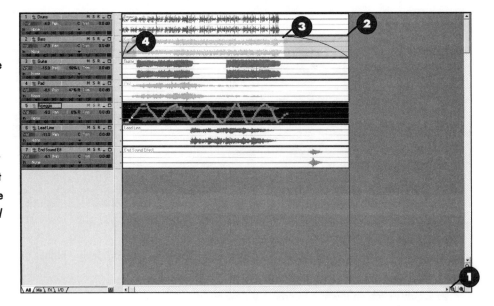

1. **Zoom out** so that you can see the beginnings or the ends of the region you want to fade. In this case, I want to do a fade-out at the end of the bass region *and* a fade-in at the beginning, so it's convenient for me to see the entire region.

2. **Move** your **cursor** to the upper right-hand corner of the region you want to fade out. The cursor will turn into a triangle. This is the Fade tool.

3. **Click** and **drag** to the left. A dark area of the track, along with a diagonal line (which may be curved), will appear. This is the region's fade-out.

4. Doing the opposite at the other end of the region will give you a fade-in. Just **position** your **cursor** in the upper left-hand corner until you see the fade icon; then drag to the right to make your fade.

The farther you drag, the longer your fade will be, but don't worry, you can edit that fade even after you've let go of the mouse.

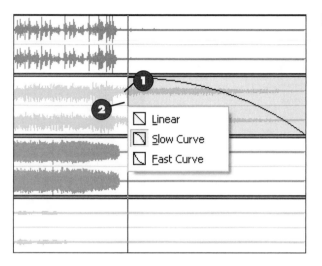

Figure 12.28

1. Position your cursor at the beginning of your fade-out or the end of a fade-in. Your cursor will turn into the Fade tool. Just click and drag to change the duration of your fade.

2. Position your cursor at the beginning of your fade-out or the end of a fade-in. Your cursor will turn into the Fade tool. Right-click to view a menu of different fade curves. Click to choose the desired fade curve. The diagonal line in your region will change to reflect your choice.

A crossfade is a fade-out of one overlapping region into another overlapping region. You can set up Cakewalk to automatically create a crossfade whenever regions overlap:

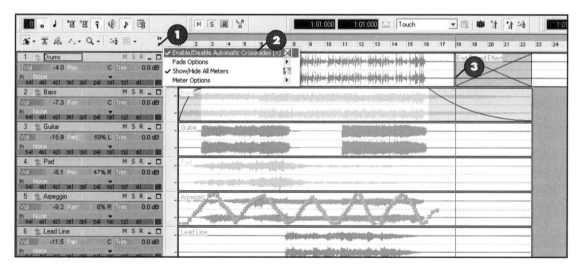

Figure 12.29

1. **Click** the **small arrow** button to the right of the Snap to Grid button. A drop-down menu will appear.

2. **Click** the **Enable/Disable Automatic Crossfades** menu item to enable it. The menu item will be marked with a check.

3. **Move** a **region** and drop it so that it overlaps another region. A crossfade will be created in the overlapping portion.

Figure 12.30

4. **Right-click** in the **crossfaded area** to view all the different fade-in/fade-out options.

5. **Click** the **desired crossfade** option. The diagonal lines of the crossfaded area will change accordingly.

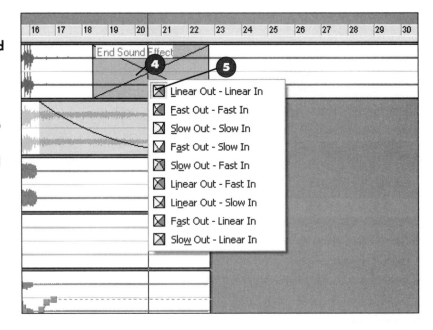

❄ **NOTE**

The next section will involve a different tutorial exercise, so now would be a great time to save your work. When you get to the section on mixdown and mastering, you can open these files again and finish your work.

Using Groove Clips

Before discussing Cakewalk Home Studio's cool Groove Clip feature, we need to clarify a couple of things. First, MIDI tempo and audio tempo are very different things. In other words, if you change the tempo of a song, the MIDI regions in your song will change their speed accordingly, but the audio regions won't change at all. Keep in mind that MIDI tempo can affect MIDI data only, and by its own nature, digital audio is not affected by MIDI changes. The second thing to remember is that an audio region doesn't "know" what its tempo is (or its pitch for that matter). It's up to us to listen to audio and decide for ourselves the speed (and pitch) of any given section of audio.

Many applications support loop-based features, which by all appearances break both of these rules. By "looping," we're talking about taking a small slice of audio (like a one-measure drum beat) and setting it up to repeat over and over (until you program the loop to stop). What makes these special loop-based features (like Cakewalk Home Studio's *Groove Clips*) so cool is that you can essentially "tell" the application about the tempo and pitch of an audio region. Once that's done, when you make tempo changes in your song, the Groove Clips you set up will change their speed as well. Here's a basic Loop Creation window (see Figure 12.31).

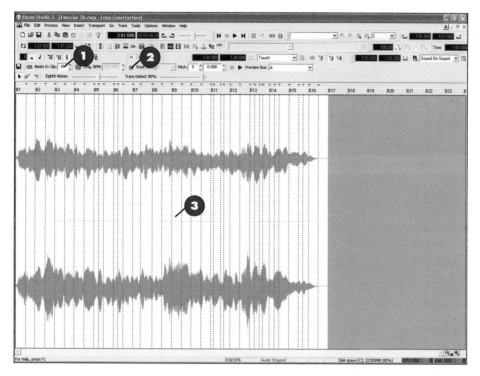

Figure 12.31

1. You can tell your DAW how many beats are in your loop, and the DAW will respond by stretching or compressing it in time to fit the tempo of your MIDI data. Right now, the loop is 16 beats (4 measures), but you could easily make it play twice as fast by changing it to an 8-beat loop.

2. Often, loops follow not only the timing of a project, but the pitch as well. This means that if you change the key of a song, your audio loop can follow such a change. In this application (Cakewalk Home Studio), this is a feature that can be enabled and disabled by clicking this button.

3. Markers are created at points of interest in the audio. This program allows markers to be placed at different beats and also at *transients* (points at which the audio's amplitude sharply rises, like when a drum is hit). Through the creation of these markers, the sonic quality of the loop can be maintained even when the timing and pitch of the song are changed.

Let's set up a song using the Groove Clips feature (see Figure 12.32).

> **❊ TIP**
>
> For this particular exercise, please open the file named Ex_05b in the Ex_05\Cakewalk folder that you've copied from the CD-ROM to your hard drive. If you had to manually locate files for the Exercise 5 file, you'll have to manually find these, too. They're in the same 05_Audio Folder.

Figure 12.32

This song is comprised of short regions. If you listened to them, they would sound like four measures. If you look closely, you can see that this doesn't agree with the measures in the time ruler. By setting up Groove Clips, you'll not only be able to match the

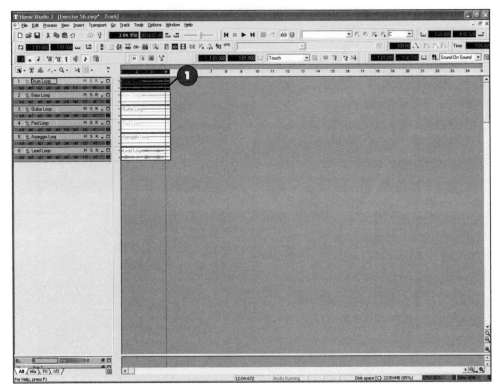

audio tempo with the MIDI tempo of the ruler, but you'll have new control over their looping. It's easy!

1. **Double-click** the **region** on the Drum track. The Loop Construction window will appear (see Figure 12.33).

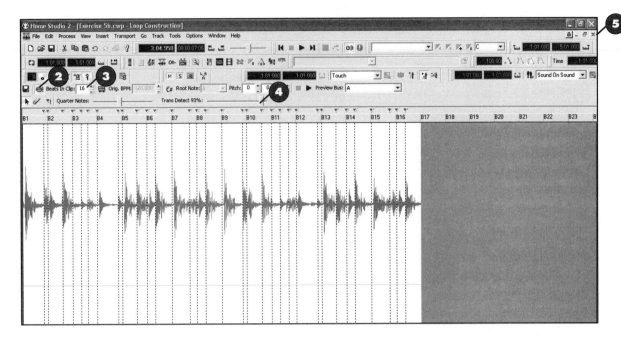

Figure 12.33

2. **Click** the **Enable Looping** button. You'll notice that dotted lines have appeared at every peak of your audio.

3. **Type** the **number** of **beats** in the section. Since this region is a four-bar section, 16 works well here (4 measures times 4 beats per measure).

4. **Adjust** the **Trans Detect** slider until the loud attacks have dotted lines. (This is a subjective call, and different audio files will have different types of peaks.)

5. **Close** the **window**. Your Track window will look a little different (see Figure 12.34).

Figure 12.34

6. Next, **click** the **region** on the bass track.

7. Setting up this region is pretty similar. You'll still **click** the **Enable Looping button**, **set** the number of beats in the selection, and **adjust** the **trans detect**.

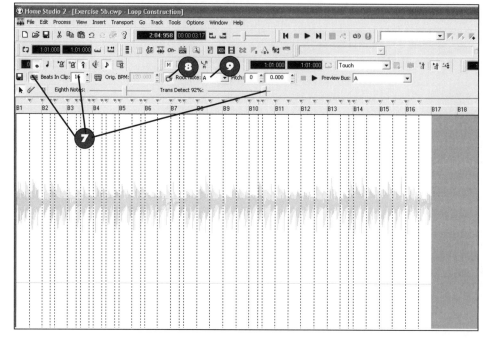

8. **Click** the **Follow Project Pitch** button.

9. **Choose** a **root pitch** for the region. The note letter you choose won't change the pitch of the audio. The actual audio is in the key of A, so go ahead and choose that.

10. **Close** the **window** when you're done.

Set up the rest of the tracks in the same way that you set up the Bass track. Your Track window should look like this when you're done (see Figure 12.35).

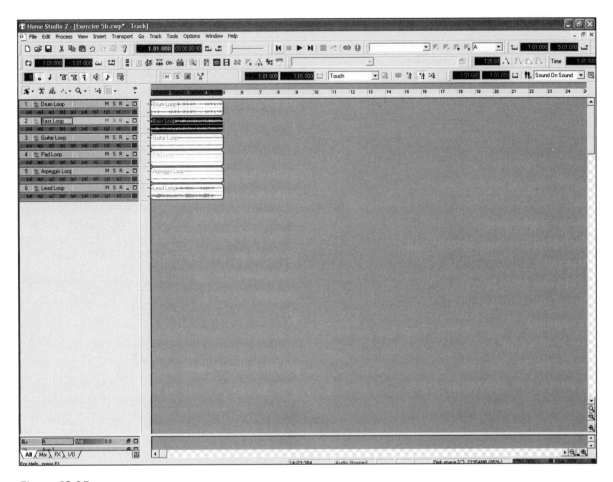

Figure 12.35

You now have a new degree of control over these regions. Let's start with tempo (see Figure 12.36).

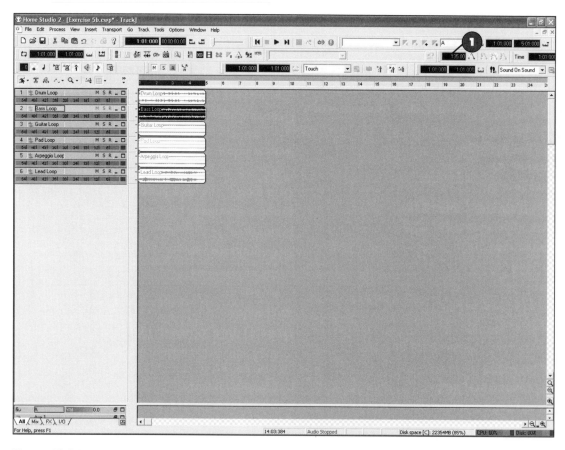

Figure 12.36

1. As you change the tempo of Cakewalk, the speed of your audio will now follow. Notice that changing tempo from slow to fast will now cause the tempo to change. This is a particularly nifty feature, especially when working with MIDI and audio tracks together—now *all* regions will follow the tempo you set.

But wait, there's more (see Figure 12.37).

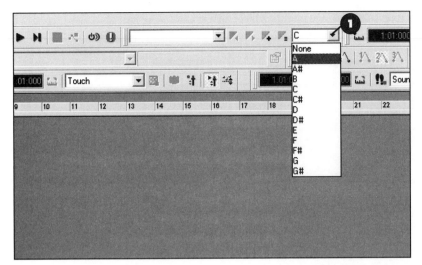

Figure 12.37

1. **Click** the **arrow key** next to the Default Groove Clip Pitch display, and you'll see a drop-down list of available root pitches for your groove clips. In this example, I selected A as the pitch for my groove clips, and when I chose A from this list, the clips played back at their normal pitch. Any other letter and the clips will change their pitches.

✳ **TIP**

I didn't set a pitch for the drum clip, and for a reason. Drums don't have pitches in the same sense as the other instruments in this song, so they don't need to be changed to match the pitches of the other clips. In fact, changing the pitch of the drums can sound pretty bad. Rule of thumb, don't transpose drum track pitches.

Last, but certainly not least, is Figure 12.38.

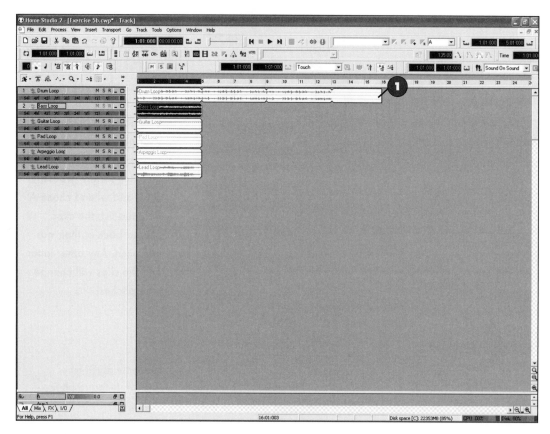

Figure 12.38

1. Do you want more than just one loop? Easy—just move your cursor to either end of a Groove Clip and then click and drag the clip boundary, just as if you were extending the end of a regular audio region. With a Groove Clip, this will make consecutive loops. Try to make a song out of the loops that you've created in this file—you'll find that Groove Clips are a very fun feature to work with and can open new creative avenues for you.

When You're Done (for Now): Mixdown

The last step in the process is to take your multitrack song and create a single audio file from it. This process is called the *mixdown* phase of production. Once you've mixed your tracks down to a single stereo (or mono) file, you can take that file and create an audio CD, using your favorite burning software, or e-mail the tune to friends. (Beware, though, as those audio files can get pretty big.) It's a straightforward process, but an important step to do correctly.

❋ **NOTE**

Can you mix your song down directly to an audio CD? Unfortunately not. A CD drive, fast though it may be, is not the kind of storage medium that your DAW needs in order to render your multitrack song down to a single final product. You'll have to burn your CD *after* you mix down your song to a file on your hard drive.

Using Cakewalk Home Studio

❋ **NOTE**

You can mix down either Ex_05 or Ex_05b, or even both of them. The process for mixing down will be exactly the same. For the purposes of illustration, the figures in this section will show Ex_05.

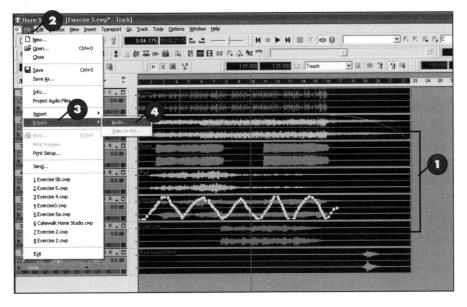

Figure 12.39

1. Holding the Shift key, **click** all the **regions** that you want to include in your mixdown.

2. **Click** the **File** drop-down menu.

3. **Click** the **Export** menu item. A second drop-down menu will appear.

4. **Click** the **Audio** option. The Export Audio window will appear.

❋ **TIP**

If you want to select everything, just hold down the Control key on your computer keyboard and then press the A key.

TIP

If your song has reverb, especially at the end, you'll want to select a few seconds *beyond* the end of the last audio clip, so that the reverb's decay will be mixed down.

Figure 12.40

5. **Navigate** to the **desired storage drive** or folder for your mixed-down audio.

6. **Type** a **descriptive name** for your final mix.

7. **Click** the **arrow** button to the right of the Files of Type display to reveal a list of file formats. Click the desired file type for your final mix.

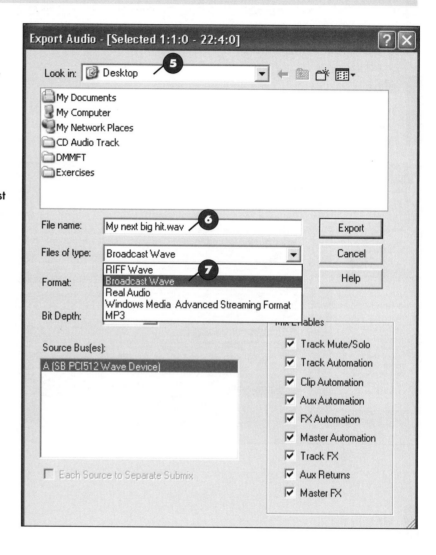

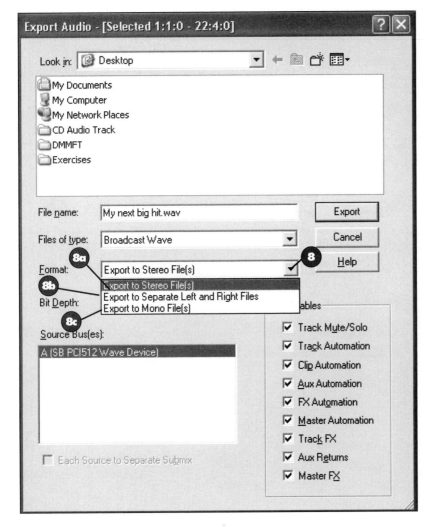

Figure 12.41

8. **Click** the **arrow** button to the right of the **Format** display to reveal a list of output formats:

8a. **Export to Stereo File(s)** will create a single stereo file of your mix. This is the most common format for mixdowns, particularly if you're going to burn the file to an audio CD.

8b. **Export to Separate Left and Right Files** will create one left file and one right file. This is a common option if you're going to use the audio in a future DAW project, as this format is more compatible with certain DAW programs.

8c. **Export to Mono File(s)** will give you a single mono mix of your song. All panning information will be lost. This is a popular format for e-mailing, as this file is smaller than stereo.

Figure 12.42

8d. The Mix Enables section includes or excludes certain aspects of your song into your mix. If you want to mix down everything in your session, your best bet is to leave all the boxes checked.

9. When you're done, **Click Export**. Your song will be rendered to the specified location, type, and format.

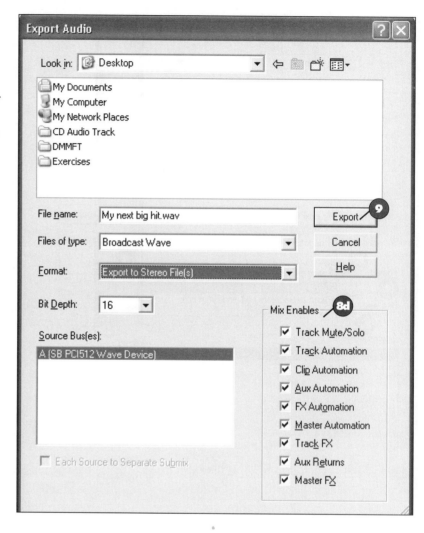

Using Quartz AudioMaster Freeware

This is very similar to Cakewalk and just as easy. You can even use this process to get more usefulness out of AudioMaster (see Figure 12.44).

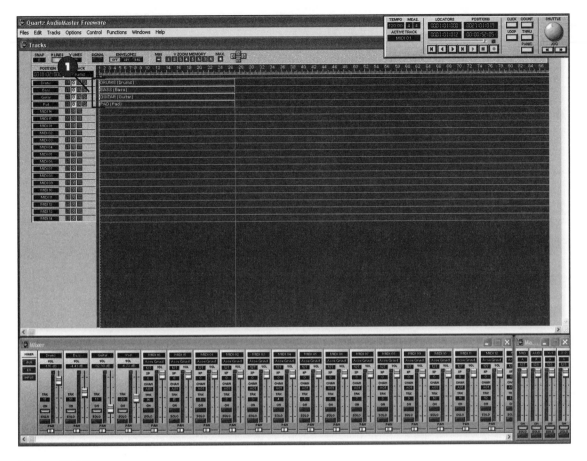

Figure 12.43

1. Holding the Shift key, **click all** the **regions** that you want to include in your mixdown.

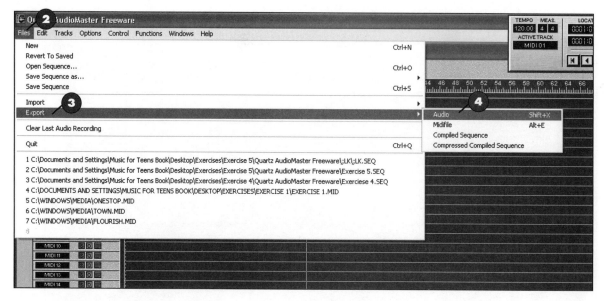

Figure 12.44

2. **Click** the **Files** drop-down menu.

3. **Click** the **Export** menu item. A second drop-down menu will appear.

4. **Click** the **Audio** option. The Export Audio as window will appear (see Figure 12.45).

Figure 12.45

5. **Navigate** to the **desired storage drive** or folder for your mixed-down audio.

6. **Type** a **descriptive name** for your final mix.

7. **Click** the **arrow button** to the right of the Save as Type display to reveal a list of file formats. **Click** on the **desired file type** for your final mix (see Figure 12.46).

Figure 12.46

8. Holding the Shift key, **click** on **all** the **aspects** of your mix that you'd like to include in your mixdown. If you want to mix down everything you're hearing, select all items on the list.

9. **Click Save**. A new file will be rendered in the specified location.

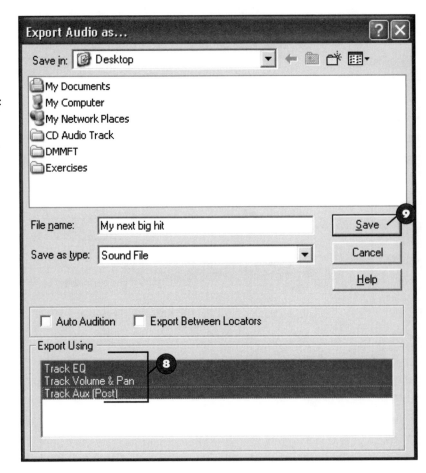

> ❄ **TIP**
>
> You can use the Export feature to squeeze more performance out of the Quartz AudioMaster Freeware. Just export four audio tracks and then create a new sequence and import that exported file. Now you've got three more tracks to add. After you've added those, you can export your mix again (and so on).
>
> For practice, try exporting the four tracks you've been working with so far. Then create a new session, import your mixdown, and add the Arpeggio, Lead, and Ending effect tracks. When you're done with that, export again to another file, and you'll have a complete piece!

The Last Day of Class

Well, you made it!

I hope that this book has been not only a source of information, but also a source of inspiration. You've taken the all-important first steps into the larger world of musical creation, a stage that is usually the most difficult, but also the most exciting. It's kind of like climbing a mountain—you've worked hard to get to the first plateau, only to see how much more there is to learn!

So, if you've done all this work, just to set yourself up to work even more, where does it all end? Here's the good news—it never does! Trust me, I've been at this for decades, and every time I master this or that application or concept, I am struck by the sense that I've only started on another journey to the next stage of growth. This is the nature of music (probably the essence of all art)—that learning and growing never end. To me that's one of the most amazing things about making music, the idea that one can always improve without any limit to the music that can be created!

That being said, this book only scratches the surface of what you'll be able to do. Even with these entry-level applications, there are buttons that haven't been pushed and options that haven't been checked. I hope that you'll take some time to explore these programs further and use them to create your own music. When it's time, you'll move on to the next level of application and so on. You'll find that the concepts you've learned here will serve you well as you evolve ever upward.

One last thing: Don't think for a second that being a computer musician is nothing but learning technical stuff. Yes, you'll learn new features, tools, and tricks, but they're only a means to an end. The goal will always be to create music. Just as learning the basics here makes that sort of creation possible, learning new ways to work and using new tools will make creation easier, allowing you to focus on the task of being creative, and that's what it's all about.

Music, whether you make it a hobby or your life's work, can enrich you in ways you can't imagine. Take me, as just one example out of many. It's no exaggeration to say that music has made my life what it is. Because of music, I've been able to work beside truly fantastic people, work on cool projects, and even travel around the world. All along the way, I've been excited and challenged by the prospect of creating something new, which is a great way to greet every day. Will you have exactly the same experiences that I've had? Probably not (you'll have your own story to tell), but I promise you that music can be as enriching to you as it's been to me. When all is said and done, that is my fondest wish for you.

Welcome to the party!

Setting Up Your Studio

Setting Up Your Audio

Once you've squared away the issues of processing and memory, you're ready to tackle the next level of hardware—your audio setup. Let's take a look at how audio will get in and out of your newly created DAW.

> ❄ **NOTE**
>
> If you're like me, you like to browse through all the catalogues and trade magazines you can lay your hands on. You've probably noticed that professional studios spend a *lot* of money on audio hardware for their DAWs. The big bucks they invest are well spent, providing studio owners with tons of channels of input and output and the highest sonic quality. That's good news for us—we won't have to spend nearly so much to begin working on a basic level. In fact, most of what you need to get started is probably already in your computer.

Sound Cards

Virtually every computer has a sound card. In fact, if you can connect your computer to speakers in some way, then you certainly have a sound card. In typical systems, sound cards are used for everything from e-mail (to let us know that we've got mail) to audio support for computer games and video. For average computer users, all they need to do is connect that sound card to some speakers, and they're set to go. For us, the situation is a little different than for an audio computer, but the basics remain the same.

Before the advent of sound cards, computers were limited to simple beeps and bloops coming out of a small speaker inside the computer chassis. These simple sounds were good for essential signals, like a successful startup or perhaps an error warning, but it was hardly up to the multimedia demands that started springing up in the late 1980s. To get more useful sound, a more advanced sound creation engine had to be introduced into the equation.

Some sound cards are actual computer cards (usually PCI, but sometimes ISA in older systems), while other sound "cards" are built right into your motherboard. Both do pretty much the same thing. A basic sound card must have the following:

❊ **Digital-to-Analog Converters (DAC):** These converters are needed to play back digital audio from your computer. Remember, *all* audio that you hear is analog, but audio is stored in a computer's memory in a digital form. Your computer must read the digital audio data (in the form of samples) and translate that data to an analog form (frequencies and amplitude). Here's where those concepts of the nature of audio will come into practice.

❊ **Analog-to-Digital Converters (ADC):** As the name suggests, this does the opposite of the digital-to-analog converters. These components of your sound card take sound from the "real" world—analog sound waves—and digitize them. This digitization process creates the samples that comprise audio files on your computer's hard drive. You'll need an ADC to record audio into your computer.

❊ **Physical connections for input and output devices**: Among these will be Line Out connectors (also called "jacks") that you might attach to an amplifier. Line In jacks can be used to record audio from devices like CD players.

Beyond the basic sound card, there may be other components:

❊ **Digital Signal Processor (DSP):** This chip on the sound card can be used for a variety of tasks. Very commonly found in sound cards, a DSP can be used as a way to generate sounds—the essence of synthesis. Also, a DSP can be used to process audio files coming out of your computer (for example, adding an echo effect to a file you're playing from your hard drive). Very often, a sound card will have on-board ROM containing data for the DSP chip, providing information on creating different kinds of sound effects, musical instruments, and more.

❊ **MIDI (Musical Instrument Digital Interface) Connector**: You've learned about MIDI in depth. You've got a keyboard (the music kind, not the computer kind), and you want to be able to play your computer like a synthesizer. MIDI will let you do that.

❊ **A Joystick Connector:** (Hey, even hard-core producers have to take a break sometime!)

❊ **Additional Audio Inputs and Outputs**: Includes microphone inputs, headphone outputs, or even surround speaker outputs.

❊ **NOTE**

Commonly, a sound card's game port can do double duty, functioning as a MIDI port in addition to a joystick connector. There's a catch because you'll usually have to buy a special cable that connects to the game port and splits out to a joystick and MIDI connector.

NOTE

When choosing a sound card for a music system, it's important to choose one that is *full-duplex*. What that means is that the card can play audio at the same time that audio is being recorded. Of course, this is absolutely necessary for a music production computer. The good news is that most cards these days are full-duplex, but it's a good idea to make sure before you make any purchases.

Getting Connected

If you can connect a CD player to your home stereo, you're not going to have much trouble understanding the routing of audio to and from your computer.

Hearing Things

Before you can get anything at all to happen, you're going to have to make your computer audible. Fortunately, setting things up is really easy. The Line Out of your sound card can go to the Line In input of an amplifier, which is then connected to conventional speakers. If you have self-powered speakers (most computer speakers fall into this category), you'll be able to connect the Line Out of your sound card directly to the speakers.

NOTE

Each 1/8" Line Out plug from your sound card typically carries two channels, which are left and right. In some rare cases other types of plugs, each carrying only one channel of the stereo pair, are used.

If you have a headphone output on your sound card (many cards do), then you can connect headphones directly to your system. First, avoid connecting the headphone output to regular speakers. The headphone output is more powerful than a regular line-level signal, and it won't sound as clear coming out of powered speakers or an amplifier. Second, be aware that, as a general rule, mixing using headphones is not recommended—what might sound great in your 'phones often sounds radically different through speakers!

TIP

You can easily test your audio connections by playing an audio CD and making sure that you can hear the output.

Recording

Setting up your inputs isn't hard, but it's not quite as straightforward as the outputs. Here's the trick—there are two kinds of inputs that your sound card might have, and it's important what to connect to what. On the one hand, you've got Line In inputs, and this plug is used to take in line-level signals. Everything uses line-level signals—including CD players, tape decks, and even some portable audio devices (though take special care, as a headphone output is not a line-level output). Beyond that, most professional audio gear includes line-level outputs—synthesizers, effects modules, and mixing boards.

Sounds like *everything* uses line-level signals and would be plugged into the Line In, right? Not so fast! For one thing, there are microphones. Microphones ("mics") use a different level signal and require a little extra amplification before they can be used. There are two ways to get this little bit of amplification. If your sound card happens to have a Mic In input, then you can plug your microphone in there, and the circuitry connected to that plug will provide the extra power needed. If you don't have a microphone input on your sound card, you're going to have to somehow amplify the signal *before* it gets to the Line In input of the sound card—a process call *preamplification*. You can find many inexpensive microphone preamplifiers (more commonly called *mic preamps*) on the market, and all you have to do is plug your microphone into the mic preamp and then plug the preamp into the line-level input of your sound card.

NOTE

Most mixing boards include a number of mic preamps. Read more on how to add a mixer to your system in the section entitled "When You're Ready: The Next Step in Hardware."

Microphones aren't the only devices that cause headaches when it comes to getting audio into your DAW. Guitars and basses don't use line-level signals, and they need to be helped out a bit. That's when a neat little device called a *Direct Inject* (DI) box, comes in. Also called a "direct box," this device changes the signal coming from a guitar or bass to a more manageable type of signal (it can usually output a mic or line-level signal) that you can bring into your DAW.

NOTE

Many mixing boards also include built-in direct inject inputs.

TIP

Because of the way a DI box works, it can often eliminate hum problems that can crop up, especially in live performance situations.

Here's a basic setup using only line-level signals in Figure A.1.

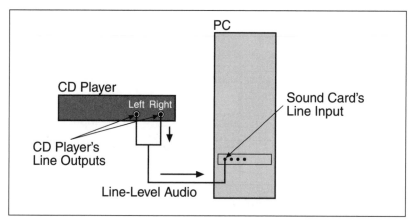

Figure A.1

Getting line-level signals into your computer.

The line-level outputs of the CD player have been connected (usually by way of an 1/8" stereo cable) to the Line Inputs of your computer's sound card. From there, you can record the CD into your DAW application. Now, instead of using a line-level device, how about freestylin' with a mic (see Figure A.2)?

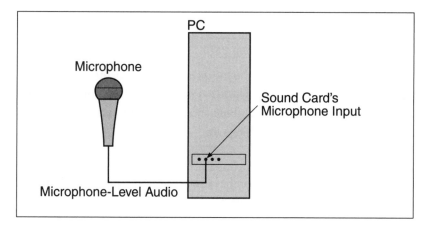

Figure A.2

Getting microphone-level signals into your computer.

This is really very similar to the previous example, except for in this case, you'll connect the microphone to the mic-level inputs of your sound card (if your sound card has them). Finally, here's how you might bring a guitar to the party (see Figure A.3).

Figure A.3

Using a direct box to record a guitar or bass.

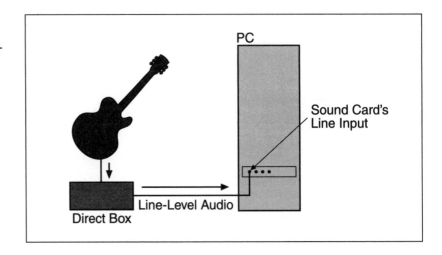

In this case, you'll need to use your DI box, which will take the signal from the guitar and change it into a regular line-level signal. From there, you connect the output of the DI box to the line-level input of your sound card, and you're set to go.

Setting Up Your MIDI

MIDI (Musical Instrument Digital Interface) is a great tool for the creative digital musician. Imagine playing a keyboard and not recording audio, but rather laying down some control data that will control a synthesizer! The flexibility that MIDI gives you is an invaluable tool in creating music in the computer. Before you can tap into that power, you'll have to set things up.

MIDI Interfaces

MIDI information is generally transmitted in and out of your computer workstation by way of a *MIDI plug* (also known in more technical circles as a *5-pin DIN connector*). To get MIDI into and out of your computer, you're going to need to add these plugs to your computer system, and that means getting a MIDI interface. Even though a MIDI interface is something you'll have to purchase, the good news is that it needn't be an expensive one, and you'll find that adding the power of MIDI is well worth the price.

For a computer-based music system, a MIDI interface needs to have the following:

1. **MIDI In port**: This port records MIDI data into your computer. This port will be connected to the MIDI Out port of your MIDI gear.

2. **MIDI Out port**: This port, on the other hand, sends MIDI data from your computer to an external device. This plug will be connected to the MIDI In port of a MIDI device that you want to have as a MIDI slave.

3. **Connection with the host computer**: Any MIDI interface that you use will have to communicate with your computer through some sort of physical connection. Many inexpensive MIDI interfaces send and receive MIDI data to your computer through a USB connection.

4. **Activity indicators**: There are three kinds of indicators to look for on a MIDI interface. First, there's MIDI Out, which will light up anytime you are sending MIDI out of your computer to an external MIDI device. Next, there's MIDI In, which will illuminate when MIDI is coming from an external device *to* the computer. Last, there's an activity indicator, which indicates that your connection to the computer is active and transferring data. These indicators are not absolutely necessary, but having one or more of these can make working with MIDI much easier.

There are many brands and models of MIDI interfaces, tailored to different types of studios. Whereas a beginners-level (though still powerfully useful) interface commonly had only one MIDI In and one MIDI Out, other interfaces might have more ins and outs. There are also a variety of ways to connect MIDI interfaces to your computer—USB, serial, parallel, or even FireWire.

> ✳ **NOTE**
>
> Here's a possible variation that you might run across: Some MIDI keyboards essentially have built-in MIDI interfaces (usually USB). In other words, instead of buying a keyboard *and* a MIDI interface, you can buy one of these all-in-one keyboards and simply attach it to your USB port, which will be the way that MIDI gets sent to the computer.

MIDI Hardware

You'll eventually need some sort of hardware to play and create MIDI data to be transmitted to the computer. Most often, a MIDI controller comes in the form of a keyboard like this one in Figure A.4.

Figure A.4

A basic MIDI keyboard.

However, a MIDI controller doesn't *have* to be a keyboard. Percussion-based controllers are great for creating realistic-sounding drum parts. Some controllers can even get a bit strange and allow the musician to create music in different ways, like by moving his hand in the air, or even playing a trumpet or saxophone type of instrument and triggering any kind of sound.

The good news is that even though MIDI controllers come in a wide variety of capabilities and features (and of course, price tags), you can begin creating MIDI data without breaking the bank. Take the keyboard shown earlier, which is a great example of an entry-level MIDI controller. For starters, it has a limited number of keys (instead of the full 88 keys of a piano), and even the keys that it does have are slightly scaled down in size. In addition to this, there aren't any sounds in the keyboard itself. It makes sounds through the power of MIDI and can transmit MIDI data, with or without a computer, to a MIDI slave device, like the one shown in Figure A.5.

Figure A.5

A MIDI sound module.

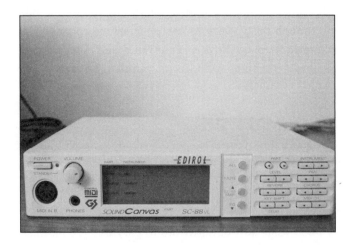

This is a good example of a basic MIDI sound module. This is the perfect partner to a keyboard that has no sounds—it's a box of sounds that has no keyboard! Simply put, this device takes in MIDI data and responds by making sounds.

> **NOTE**
>
> Do you *need* to buy a sound module just to get sound happening? Nowadays, the answer is a resounding *no*! There's a new breed of synthesizers called *software synthesizers* (or *soft synths* for short) that have shed their need for dedicated hardware. They'll run on your computer as software, and have all the power of professional hardware modules.

The Ins, Outs, and Thrus of MIDI

You've got the interface, and you've got the MIDI controller, so what's next? Making connections, of course, and the logic behind making those connections is pretty simple and easy to set up. Basically, the MIDI data travels out of a MIDI Out port and into a MIDI In port. Simple! So here's a basic setup with a single MIDI controller in Figure A.6.

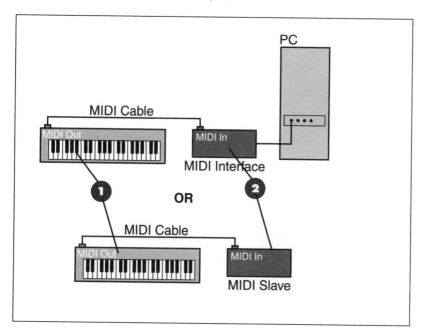

Figure A.6

Two simple setups.

1. MIDI data is sent from the controller keyboard via the keyboard's MIDI Out port through a MIDI cable to a MIDI interface or MIDI slave device.

2. MIDI data is received by the computer (or MIDI slave device) through a MIDI interface or the slave device's MIDI In port.

There's another dimension to MIDI connections, and that's a neat little connection called *MIDI Thru*. This cool little plug takes data coming into the MIDI In port and passes it on to other devices in a MIDI chain. What that means is that you can have more than one MIDI device connected to one MIDI output from your computer. Here's how it would work (see Figure A.7).

Figure A.7

Using multiple devices.

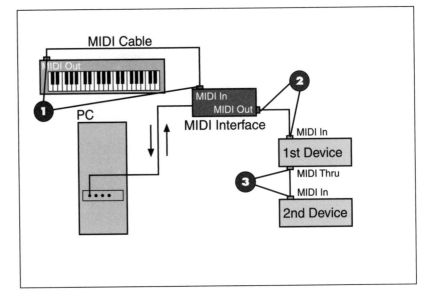

1. MIDI Out of the keyboard controller goes to the MIDI In port of the MIDI interface. This is how data can get recorded into your DAW.

2. MIDI data is sent out of the MIDI interface to the MIDI In port of a first MIDI device. (This could also be your MIDI controller if it has built-in sounds.) This way your DAW can trigger any sounds that may be available in that first device.

3. MIDI Thru from the first MIDI device goes to the MIDI In port of a second MIDI device. This is how your DAW can also trigger sounds on this second device. In fact, you can connect the MIDI Thru port of the second device and go even further to the MIDI In of a third device.

❋ NOTE

This kind of configuration, where the MIDI Thru of one device goes to another device, and so on, is commonly called a *daisy chain setup.*

B MIDI Notes, Names, and Numbers

Okay, you press a key on a keyboard, or look at a note on a staff, and you associate a pitch with that action. To a computer, however, it's not so much the note name, but the note *number* that's important. Sometimes, it's hard to know what number is associated with what note, and that confusion can lead to frustration. Not to worry, that's what this appendix is designed to help.

This section is a series of charts designed to let you know the numbers that go with the notes. As you get deeper into the world of MIDI, you'll find that these charts are a real advantage, especially when editing your MIDI data. Enjoy!

Keyboard Note Assignments

This chart is based upon a traditional 88-key keyboard. Your keyboard might not have as many keys, but the logic behind this diagram remains the same. Just find middle "C" (MIDI note number 60) on your keyboard (it will be marked) and work your way from there (see Figure B.1).

 NOTE

Note names are notated with the note letter, followed by the octave, and then by the MIDI note number (in parentheses). For example, middle C is notated as C4 (#60). Sharped notes are shown with a # sign, and flatted notes are marked with what looks like a lower-case b.

✳ **NOTE**

Although MIDI note numbers are fully standardized, the naming of middle "C" is not. While most applications will give you the option of choosing to call middle C "C4," others will call it "C5" and some will even name it "C3." Don't worry, the MIDI note numbers won't change—only the numbering of the octaves.

To configure Cakewalk Home Studio to match this chart, go to the Options menu and choose the General menu item. In the Global Options window, choose the General tab and set Base Octave for Pitches to –1.

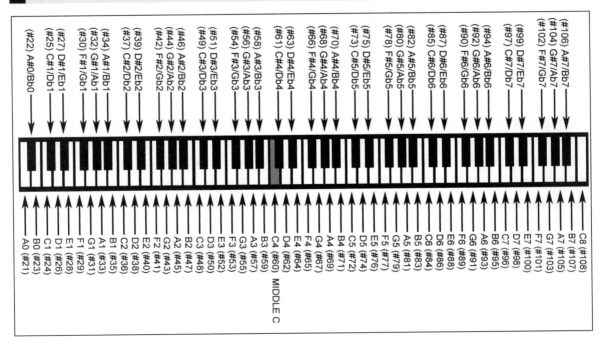

Figure B.1

Note names and MIDI note numbers as they relate to a musical keyboard.

Keyboard General MIDI Drum Assignments

The General MIDI specification has some specific rules about drums. First, drums are reserved for MIDI channel 10. Secondly, different sounding drums are assigned to specific keys. The following diagram shows which drum sounds will be triggered by which keys (see Figure B.2).

✳ **NOTE**

As with the first diagram, MIDI note numbers are shown in parentheses.

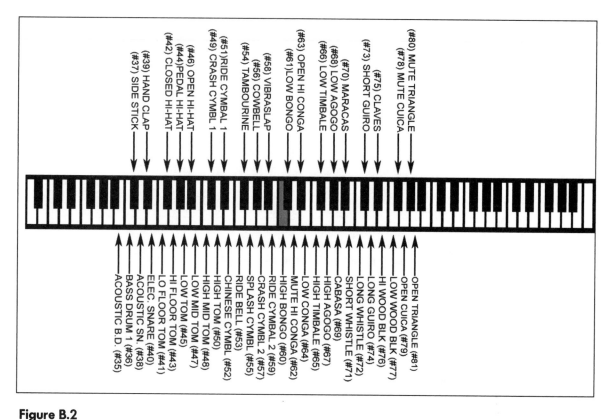

Figure B.2

General MIDI drum sounds as they relate to a musical keyboard.

Staff Note Assignments

Notes on the keyboard are one thing, but what about the notes on the staff? This next graphic shows the note names and MIDI note numbers associated with each note on the staff, starting with the bass clef (see Figure B.3)

> ❋ **NOTE**
>
> You'll notice that the first notes are actually written *below* the five-lined staff, with each note having short lines marking its distance from the staff. These small lines are called *ledger lines,* and they allow us to represent pitches that extend below or above the basic staff.

Figure B.3

Note names and MIDI note numbers as they relate to notes on a bass clef staff.

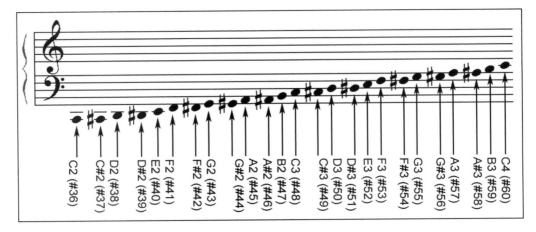

Now let's take a look at the notes of the treble clef (see Figure B.4).

NOTE

You'll notice that the first note in this series is C4 (MIDI note 60), more commonly known as "middle C." This note, one ledger line below the treble staff, is the same pitch as the last note you saw on the bass clef staff, one ledger line *above* the staff.

Figure B.4

Note names and MIDI note numbers as they relate to notes on a treble clef staff.

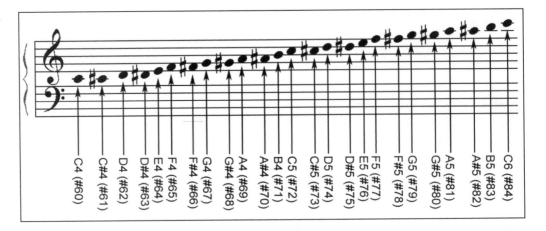

C The Basics of Digital Audio

There are more than a few myths and misconceptions about what exactly digital audio *is*, and the first order of business is to break down the ideas behind digital audio and dispel those wrong ideas.

Digital Audio versus MIDI

In our earlier discussion of MIDI, you learned that MIDI is most certainly *not* audio. Whereas, you will never be able to listen to MIDI on an audio CD, you will certainly be able to record the results of MIDI in the form of digital audio. Think of MIDI and digital audio as a symbiotic relationship with both MIDI and digital audio really shining when working together. MIDI makes music writing easier (in some cases, *possible*), and digital audio is the medium by which that audio is stored on an audio CD or distributed through the Internet.

There is a lot of sloppy language going around when it comes to MIDI and digital audio, mostly out of ignorance. Most of these phrases refer to the storage of MIDI's music on a digital audio track. You might hear the phrase "convert MIDI to audio," or the slightly hipper "bounce MIDI to audio," but these phrases, catchy as they are, are misleading. One might assume that MIDI was some form of audio, and by now you know that's simply not the case.

To clear up any possible misconceptions and to prevent miscommunication in the future, it's best to think of MIDI and digital audio as two isolated paths of information. The MIDI signal path you already know—it goes like this (see Figure C.1).

Figure C.1

The MIDI signal path.

1. A MIDI controller sends a MIDI note message out of its MIDI Out port.

2. The MIDI data is received at the MIDI In port of the system's MIDI interface.

3. Data is sent from the MIDI interface to the system computer.

4. Inside the computer, a MIDI application routes that data though a MIDI track.

5. MIDI data is sent from the computer to the MIDI interface

6. MIDI data leaves the MIDI interface through the selected MIDI Out port.

7. MIDI data is received by the MIDI slave device through its MIDI In port.

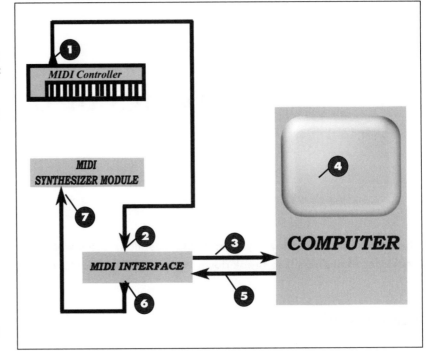

The MIDI device at the end of this chain of events responds by making *sound*. At that point, the MIDI has done its job, and now you can focus on getting the sound created by the MIDI module into your computer as digital audio. Here's the second half of the equation (see Figure C.2).

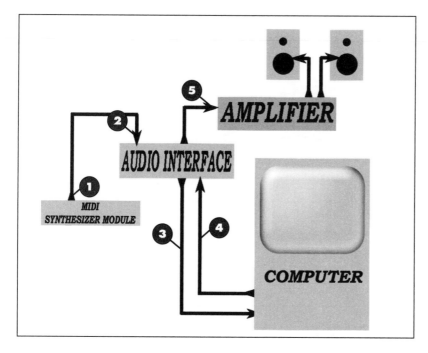

Figure C.2
The audio signal path.

1. Analog audio is sent from the MIDI module's audio outputs.

2. The audio is received by the line inputs of your audio interface (which in many cases is the computer's sound card), which converts the analog audio to digital audio.

3. The digitized audio is then sent to a digital audio application inside the computer, where it can be stored to the hard drive, edited, and mixed.

4. When it's time to play back (or monitor) that audio, the data is sent to the audio interface (or sound card), where it is converted from digital back to analog audio.

5. The analog audio is then sent to your speakers, and you hear the music.

MIDI and digital audio, though partners in the creative process, are hardly the same thing. So instead of thinking about "converting MIDI to audio," think rather of recording the audio output of your MIDI devices. So if digital audio isn't related to MIDI, what is it?

Sample Rates and Bit Depth

How exactly does digital audio work? Sometimes, it helps to think of digital audio being to analog audio what film is to vision. With film, individual pictures (frames) are played back at a specific speed to re-create a sense of motion. Each of these frames is a complete picture, representing a frozen moment in time, and can have a wide range of color depth, ranging from black and white to millions of colors, depending on the nature of the film. Digital audio doesn't work in *exactly* the same way as film, but the concept is very similar.

Instead of using frames like film does, digital audio uses *samples*. A sample is an audio "snapshot," recording the amplitude (or volume) of audio at a very specific time. If you take a look again at an analog audio wave, here is how it might be captured in Figure C.3.

Figure C.3

An analog wave with a single sample.

1. At this sample point, the amplitude of an analog audio waveform is captured (or digitized) and stored as a binary number.

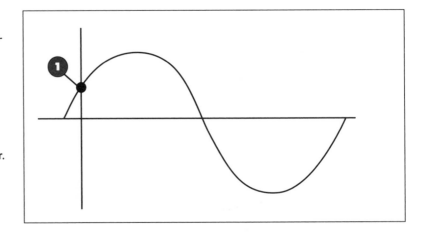

Notice that a single sample simply records the amplitude of a small fraction of a second, so you'll need to sample your audio many times per second to record the wave, like Figure C.4.

Figure C.4

Multiple samples record the wave.

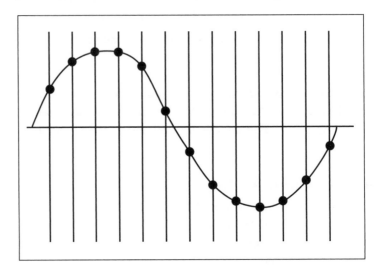

The number of samples per second is called a *sample rate*. There are a lot of samples per second. There must be, in order to capture the shape of high frequency waves. For example, there are 44,100 samples per second in an audio CD. DVD-video disks can have up to 96,000 samples per second, and DVD-audio disks can go up to 192,000. These numbers are so high that we usually refer to them in thousands (Kilohertz, represented by kHz, meaning one thousand per second)—values like 44.1kHz (CD audio), 96kHz, 192kHz, and so on.

There is a mathematical formula, called the *Nyquist Theorem*, which states that the sample rate of digital audio must be at least twice as high as the highest frequency you want to reproduce. For example, Figure C.5 shows a high frequency wave with two samples per waveform period, preserving the shape of the wave.

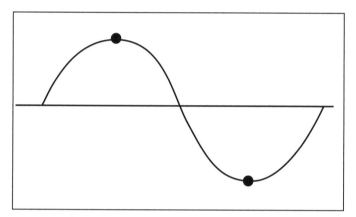

Figure C.5

A high frequency wave with two samples per waveform.

As long as there are at least two sample points per period, even if the sample points don't exactly match the highest and lowest points of the wave, the frequency is accurately recorded. If the sample points don't happen to fall on the highest and lowest points of the wave, the volume recorded will be a little lower, although the frequency of the wave will not change.

But what if there are *fewer* than two samples per period? Bad things. If you don't have enough samples, high frequencies can't be reproduced, and new frequencies of lower frequency, not present in the original wave, will be spontaneously created, like Figure C.6.

Figure C.6

Bad things happen when fewer than two samples are recorded.

1. Sample points—less than two per period, will result in a different frequency than the original analog wave.

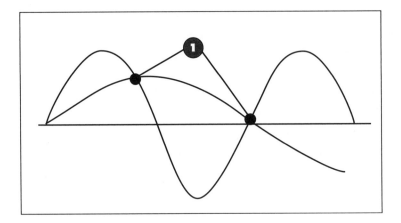

This nasty little effect is called *aliasing*. Don't fret about it too much at this stage, as your hardware and software automatically take measures to prevent aliasing when recording or processing audio.

It's important that you understand the importance of the Nyquist theorem, since much of digital audio is governed by this rule. For example, when you're talking about CDs, the sample rate is 44.1 kHz, right? Well, if the sample rate must be twice the highest frequency, then the highest frequency that CDs can reproduce (in an ideal system) works out to be 22.05 kHz (44,100 samples ÷ 2 = 22,050 Hz). This matches up nicely with the range of human hearing, which maxes out at 20 kHz. Reducing the sample rate below 44.1 kHz proportionately reduces the upper frequency content of audio, often with perceptible results. (It's pretty commonly done with Internet audio, which is part of the reason that it often sounds muffled.)

Each and every sample is composed of a number of digital 1s and 0s (called *bits*), which represents the sample's amplitude. *Bit depth* refers to the number of binary digits of each sample. Higher bit depth gives you the highest quality digital audio and yields many advantages. For example, higher bit depth provides a greater volume range (commonly called *dynamic range*), with each bit adding about 6 dB of range to your audio. Each sample of CD-quality audio, for example, has 16 ones and zeroes in each sample, so we say that CDs have 16-bit audio. Since each of the 16 bits adds 6 dB of dynamic range, CD-quality audio has a dynamic ranch of roughly 96 dB (16 × 6 = 96).

In addition to a greater dynamic range, higher bit depth will also provide a higher resolution sample. If you think of each sample as a "snapshot" of an instant of audio, more bits per sample will give a sharper picture. Remember how every sample is a representation of volume at a specific moment in time? The higher resolution that you get from greater bit depth will allow you to make that measurement with a higher degree of accuracy, ensuring that your audio will be as true to the original as possible. But how, exactly, do higher bits per sample translate into more accurate audio?

For a moment, put yourself in the mind of a computer. Instead of the normal ten digits that you use to count as a human being (decimal numbers), you only have *two* (binary numbers). These two digits are named *zero* and *one*. The decimal zero translates nicely to a binary zero, and the decimal one is a binary one, but what about the decimal number *two*? The problem is that there is no such thing as a binary two—the digit doesn't even exist! You'll have to add another digit and go to the next greatest value to express in binary form—one zero. It may look like the decimal number ten, but it's not. You can continue counting like Table C.1.

Table C.1 Counting in Decimal (base 10) and Binary (base 2)

Decimal	Binary
0	0
1	1
2	10
3	11
4	100
5	101
6	110
7	111
8	1000
9	1001
10	1010

So, if that's the way a computer brain counts, then what does each bit give you? Well, if you only had one digit, or bit, you could only count two numbers—zero or one. Add another bit, and all of a sudden you can count four numbers—00, 01, 10, and 11. So adding just one bit has doubled the numbers possible. Let's keep going and add a third digit. Now you can express 000, 001, 010, 011, 100, 101, 110, 111—again adding just one bit has doubled the possible numbers from four to eight. In fact, every digit you add will double the possible number combinations.

This is the real value of higher bit depths. Each bit added to a sample *doubles* the number of numeric possibilities, which allows for a much finer description of that sample's amplitude. For example, CD-quality audio is 16-bit, so a single CD sample has 65,536 (2 to the 16th power) different numeric possibilities! Compare that to lower bit-depth Internet audio with, say, 8 bits per sample—only

256 different numeric possibilities (2 to the 8ᵗʰ power). Bottom line: Greater bit-depths give you more accurate digital audio, and each additional bit *doubles* that accuracy.

❄ **NOTE**

The specs for CD audio are good ones to keep in the back of your mind. The sample rate for CD-quality audio is 44.1kHz, or 44,100 samples per second. The bit depth of CD-quality audio is 16 bits. CD-audio is always stereo (even if the left and right sides sound exactly the same and give a monophonic listening experience).

❄ **TIP**

When beginning new projects, you will often have to decide on a sample rate and a bit depth. It's a good general rule to choose the highest bit depth supported by your software. (Many applications support up to 24-bit audio.) The higher resolution will give you better final results, even if your final project will be in a lower bit depth (for example, CD audio at 16 bits). Higher sample rates are great, too, but higher sample rates can often put too much strain on a computer system.

Index

COURSE TECHNOLOGY

Professional ■ Trade ■ Reference

"A living underground legend, Michael Dean is one of the few integral rock 'n' roll spokesmen we have left of our generation."

—ERIC McFADDEN, Parliament-Funkadelic, EMT

"Making art your full-time job is a full-time job." If you're ready to take on this job, then you're ready to follow the advice that you'll find inside *$30 Music School*. Do-it-Yourself recording, distribution, and promotion have made it easier than ever to make a living making music. Learn how to thrive in this new business model. *$30 Music School* is for people who want to be musicians, not just look like musicians. It's all about cutting through the star-system garbage and getting to the heart of art, and making great music that can reach the world on no budget. No matter what type of music moves you—rock, Alternative, Metal, Punk, Hip Hop, Country, Jazz or Salsa—you can take this book and put it to work for you. Go one-on-one with musicians who have made music their life. Use their advice and learn from their experiences. Find out what it takes to create both realistic goals as well as a map to reach them.

$30 Music School
ISBN: 1-59200-171-8 ■ $30.00

THOMSON

COURSE TECHNOLOGY

Professional ■ Trade ■ Refere

You've Got a Great Imagination...

Game Art for Teens
ISBN: 1-59200-307-9 ■ $29.99

Game Programming for Teens
ISBN: 1-59200-068-1 ■ $29.99

Blogging for Teens
ISBN: 1-59200-476-8 ■ $19.99

Let it Out!

Web Design for Teens
ISBN: 1-59200-607-8 ■ $19.99

Digital Film Making for Teens
ISBN: 1-59200-603-5 ■ $24.99
December 2004

Game Design for Teens
ISBN: 1-59200-496-2 ■ $29.99

THOMSON

COURSE TECHNOLOGY

Professional ■ Trade ■ Reference

Call 1.800.354.9706 to order
Order online at www.courseptr.com

What's on the CD

This book includes an enhanced CD, which serves two roles. In an audio CD player, it will play back a single audio track, which you can use as a reference mix or even as a recording source in the exercises. In your computer's CD drive, the disc will also contain folders with all the materials you'll need for the tutorial exercises in this book. Each exercise chapter will direct you to the appropriate exercise. Once you've gone through the book, please feel free to experiment with the project files I've created and the audio files I've included to create your own music.

License Agreement/Notice of Limited Warranty

By opening the sealed disc container in this book, you agree to the following terms and conditions. If, upon reading the following license agreement and notice of limited warranty, you cannot agree to the terms and conditions set forth, return the unused book with unopened disc to the place where you purchased it for a refund.

License:
The enclosed software is copyrighted by the copyright holder(s) indicated on the software disc. You are licensed to copy the software onto a single computer for use by a single user and to a backup disc. You may not reproduce, make copies, or distribute copies or rent or lease the software in whole or in part, except with written permission of the copyright holder(s). You may transfer the enclosed disc only together with this license, and only if you destroy all other copies of the software and the transferee agrees to the terms of the license. You may not decompile, reverse assemble, or reverse engineer the software.

Notice of Limited Warranty:
The enclosed disc is warranted by Thomson Course Technology PTR to be free of physical defects in materials and workmanship for a period of sixty (60) days from end user's purchase of the book/disc combination. During the sixty-day term of the limited warranty, Thomson Course Technology PTR will provide a replacement disc upon the return of a defective disc.

Limited Liability:
THE SOLE REMEDY FOR BREACH OF THIS LIMITED WARRANTY SHALL CONSIST ENTIRELY OF REPLACEMENT OF THE DEFECTIVE DISC. IN NO EVENT SHALL THOMSON COURSE TECHNOLOGY PTR OR THE AUTHOR BE LIABLE FOR ANY OTHER DAMAGES, INCLUDING LOSS OR CORRUPTION OF DATA, CHANGES IN THE FUNCTIONAL CHARACTERISTICS OF THE HARDWARE OR OPERATING SYSTEM, DELETERIOUS INTERACTION WITH OTHER SOFTWARE, OR ANY OTHER SPECIAL, INCIDENTAL, OR CONSEQUENTIAL DAMAGES THAT MAY ARISE, EVEN IF THOMSON COURSE TECHNOLOGY PTR AND/OR THE AUTHOR HAS PREVIOUSLY BEEN NOTIFIED THAT THE POSSIBILITY OF SUCH DAMAGES EXISTS.

Disclaimer of Warranties:
THOMSON COURSE TECHNOLOGY PTR AND THE AUTHOR SPECIFICALLY DISCLAIM ANY AND ALL OTHER WARRANTIES, EITHER EXPRESS OR IMPLIED, INCLUDING WARRANTIES OF MERCHANTABILITY, SUITABILITY TO A PARTICULAR TASK OR PURPOSE, OR FREEDOM FROM ERRORS. SOME STATES DO NOT ALLOW FOR EXCLUSION OF IMPLIED WARRANTIES OR LIMITATION OF INCIDENTAL OR CONSEQUENTIAL DAMAGES, SO THESE LIMITATIONS MIGHT NOT APPLY TO YOU.

Other:
This Agreement is governed by the laws of the State of Massachusetts without regard to choice of law principles. The United Convention of Contracts for the International Sale of Goods is specifically disclaimed. This Agreement constitutes the entire agreement between you and Thomson Course Technology PTR regarding use of the software.